Relational Trauma i

This book presents an interdisciplinary discussion between researchers and clinicians about trauma in the relationship between infants and their parents. It makes an innovative contribution to the field of infant mental health in bringing together previously separated paradigms of relational trauma from psychoanalysis, attachment and the neurosciences.

With contributions from a range of experts, areas of discussion include:

- intergenerational transmission of relational trauma and earliest intervention
- the nature of the traumatising encounter between parent and infant
- the therapeutic possibilities of parent–infant psychotherapy in changing the trajectory of transmitted trauma
- training and supporting professionals working with traumatised parents and infants.

Relational Trauma in Infancy will be of particular interest to trainee and qualified child and adult psychotherapists, clinical psychologists, child and adult psychiatrists, psychoanalysts, health care professionals and social workers.

Tessa Baradon developed and manages the Parent–Infant Project at The Anna Freud Centre. She is a practising child psychotherapist and supervisor and writes and lectures on applied psychoanalysis and parent–infant psychotherapy.

Relational Trauma in Infancy

Psychoanalytic, attachment and neuropsychological contributions to parent–infant psychotherapy

Edited by Tessa Baradon

LONDON AND NEW YORK

First published 2010
by Routledge
27 Church Road, Hove, East Sussex BN3 2FA

Simultaneously published in the USA and Canada
by Routledge
711 Third Avenue, New York, NY 10017

*Routledge is an imprint of the Taylor & Francis Group,
an Informa business*

© 2010 selection and editorial matter, Tessa Baradon;
individual chapters, the Contributors

Typeset in Times by
RefineCatch Limited, Bungay, Suffolk
Paperback cover design by Lisa Dynan
Cover illustration: *Alone*, Mary Kuper

British Library Cataloguing in Publication Data
A catalogue record for this book is available from the British Library

Library of Congress Cataloging-in-Publication Data
    Relational trauma in infancy : psychoanalytic, attachment, and
neuropsychological contributions to parent–infant psychotherapy /
edited by Tessa Baradon.
      p. ; cm.
    Includes bibliographical references.
    ISBN 978–0–415–47374–3 (hbk) — ISBN 978–0–415–47375–0
(pbk.) 1. Parent–infant psychotherapy. 2. Infants—Mental health.
3. Family psychotherapy. I. Baradon, Tessa.
    [DNLM: 1. Family Therapy. 2. Parent–Child Relations. 3. Infant.
4. Parenting—psychology. 5. Stress Disorders, Post-Traumatic—
therapy. WM 430.5.F2 R3815 2010]
    RJ502.5.R45 2010
    618.92'8914—dc22
                                            2009023075

ISBN: 978–0–415–47374–3 (hbk)
ISBN: 978–0–415–47375–0 (pbk)

This book is dedicated to HJB

Contents

Contributors

Tessa Baradon came from the field of Public Health to child psychoanalysis and psychotherapy. She has been responsible for the planning and provision of services for parents and infants in the National Health Service, and initiated and developed the Parent–Infant Project at The Anna Freud Centre. She is a practising child therapist and supervisor and writes and lectures on child psychoanalysis and parent–infant psychotherapy. She is a member of the Association of Child Psychotherapists and the Association of Child Psychoanalysis.

Elisa Bronfman received her PhD from Boston College and has been a staff psychologist at Children's Hospital since 1998 and affiliated with Harvard Medical School since 1991. She wrote the AMBIANCE scale with colleagues Elizabeth Parsons and Karlen Lyons-Ruth. Elisa has trained many research groups with regard to the AMBIANCE measure with Dr Lyons-Ruth and has published scholarly articles in the field of attachment.

Carol Broughton is a child and adolescent psychotherapist trained at The Anna Freud Centre and working in the NHS. She works as a parent–infant psychotherapist in the Parent–Infant Project at The Anna Freud Centre, where she also runs the Parent–Infant Mental Health Module and is currently engaged in research into the measurement of risk in the early parent–infant relationship.

Anita Chakraborty is a child and adolescent psychotherapist trained at The Anna Freud Centre. She works there as a parent–infant psychotherapist in the Parent–Infant Project, co-faciliating the postnatal analytic group for mothers and babies at The Anna Freud Centre, and the New Beginnings groups within mother–baby units in prisons. Prior to her psychoanalytic training, she worked with groups of adolescent offenders in community-based projects.

Tessa Dalley is a member of the Parent–Infant Project at The Anna Freud Centre. She is a child and adolescent psychotherapist and also works in an inpatient adolescent unit and has a small private practice. She has published a number of books and articles.

Peter Fonagy is Freud Memorial Professor of Psychoanalysis and Director of the Sub-Department of Clinical Health Psychology at University College London; chief executive of The Anna Freud Centre, London; and consultant to the Child and Family Program at the Menninger Department of Psychiatry and Behavioral Sciences at the Baylor College of Medicine, Houston, Texas. He is chair of the Postgraduate Education Committee of the International Psychoanalytic Association and a Fellow of the British Academy. He is a clinical psychologist and a training and supervising analyst in the British Psycho-Analytical Society in child and adult analysis. His work integrates empirical research with psychoanalytic theory, and his clinical interests centre around borderline psychopathology, violence, and early attachment relationships.

Jessica James is a group analyst who works with parents and babies in different group contexts. She has been involved with the PIP project since its inception, and runs groups independently for families preparing for childbearing and analytic groups at the Women's Therapy Centre. Jessica has written about her work in journals and chapters in books, as well as teaching in this field.

Amanda Jones is head of the National Health Service specialist Parent–Infant Mental Health Service. She trained as a family therapist and has a long-standing commitment to psychoanalytic and systemic understandings. Her doctoral research at the Tavistock Centre looked at the process of change in psychodynamic parent–infant psychotherapy.

Angela Joyce is a training analyst and Fellow of the Institute of Psychoanalysis in London, and trained as a child analyst at the British Psycho-Analytical Society and The Anna Freud Centre. She works in the Parent–Infant Project and is an honorary lecturer at UCL. She teaches child and adult psychoanalysts in the UK and abroad. Angela is an editor with the Winnicott Trust and is Deputy Director of the Squiggle Foundation.

Linda C. Mayes is the Arnold Gesell Professor of Child Psychiatry, Psychology, and Psychiatry at the Yale Child Study Centre in New Haven, Connecticut. She trained as a developmental paediatrician and an adult and child psychoanalyst. Her research focuses on the long-term impact of early stressful events during pregnancy and early pre-school years on children's neurocognitive and emotional development.

Anne Murphy is a clinical psychologist at the Center for Babies, Toddlers and Families at the Albert Einstein College of Medicine, where she is an Assistant Professor of Clinical Paediatrics. She helped develop the Infant Mental Health Project, a parent–child programme, serving infants and pre-school age children who have been exposed to trauma. She is collaborating with Miriam and Howard Steele on study of maternal and child representations of attachment. Anne has been invited to become a committee member for the New York City Mayor's Task Force on Domestic Violence and Abuse.

Julia Newbury is a research psychologist at The Anna Freud Centre. She has a background in health psychology, and is currently working on the evaluation of psychotherapeutic group interventions in outreach settings focusing on parent–infant relationships and interactions, infant development and maternal representations in hard-to-reach and high-risk populations.

Inge-Martine Pretorius is a child and adolescent psychotherapist and parent–toddler group leader at The Anna Freud Centre in London. She is a clinical tutor for psychoanalytic developmental psychology at University College London and The Anna Freud Centre, where she organizes and teaches the MSc Child Development course. She has published articles and book chapters in the field of molecular genetics and psychoanalysis.

Allan N. Schore is on the clinical faculty of the Department of Psychiatry and Biobehavioral Sciences, UCLA David Geffen School of Medicine, and at the UCLA Center for Culture, Brain, and Development. He is author of three seminal volumes, *Affect Regulation and the Origin of the Self*, *Affect Dysregulation and Disorders of the Self*, and *Affect Regulation and the Repair of the Self*, as well as numerous articles and chapters. He is editor of the Norton Series on Interpersonal Neurobiology, and a reviewer or on the editorial staff of 30 journals. His ground-breaking contributions have impacted the fields of affective neuroscience, neuropsychiatry, trauma theory, developmental psychology, attachment theory, paediatrics, infant mental health, psychotherapy, behavioural biology, clinical social work and psychoanalysis.

Michelle Sleed is a senior research psychologist at The Anna Freud Centre. She has worked on a number of projects in the field of early intervention and family support. She is currently working on studies of parent–infant relationships and interaction, maternal representations, maternal mental health, infant development, and outcomes of psychotherapeutic interventions for parents and infants.

Howard Steele is Professor of Psychology at the New School for Social Research, New York. He is founding and senior editor of *Attachment & Human Development*. He has published widely on attachment across the life cycle and across generations, including the effects of loss and trauma in low-risk normative and high-risk clinical populations.

Miriam Steele trained at the Anna Freud Centre and received her PhD from

University College London. Her research began with the study of inter-generational patterns of attachment, providing empirical data to demonstrate the importance of parental states of mind in the social and emotional development of children. More recently, Miriam has become interested in the field of adoption and foster care with a view to understanding the impact of attachment representations from both the adopters' and the children's point of view. She is Associate Professor and Associate Director of Clinical Psychology at the New School for Social Research.

Ju Tomas-Merrills worked in education before undertaking an MSc in the Psychodynamics of Human Development and then training at the BAP in psychoanalytic psychotherapy. Within the Parent–Infant Project at The Anna Freud Centre, she is a group facilitator for the *New Beginnings* Programme working with mothers and babies in prison. She works as a psychotherapist and supervisor at a multi-ethnic counselling service in London and has a private practice. She is a member of the British Psychoanalytic Council.

Judith Woodhead is a Jungian analyst (Society of Analytical Psychology), a parent–infant psychotherapist at The Anna Freud Centre, an infant observation seminar leader at the British Association of Psychotherapists, and a supervisor and consultant in adult and infancy work. She has published papers on diverse themes from parent–infant psychotherapy.

Preface

> She remembers almost nothing, but she is repeating the past in the present, and the repetition – dreadful to watch – has caught a baby in its morbid path.
> (Fraiberg, 1980: 55)

Traumatisation of the infant intuitively confounds the primate instinct to protect the young and propagate the species. Furthermore, ordinarily the suffering of a baby is shocking to the adult and calls his/her own attachment system into action. Relational trauma in the primary love and caretaking relationship, thus, preoccupies researchers and clinicians alike with questions such as the interplay between genetics and environment in the transmission of trauma down the generations, how current parental trauma is titrated into the relationship with the baby, how to identify infants at risk, and how to change what seem like inevitable trajectories.

This book has grown out of the passion for our work in The Anna Freud Centre Parent–Infant Project (PIP). A significant element of our clinical work is with the severe end of trauma: parents with grave mental health problems, histories of abuse, violence and social care, refugees from genocide in their countries of origin. The minds of these parents are often suffused and saturated with unprocessed feelings, with little capacity for primary preoccupation with their baby. Furthermore, and contrary to conscious intention, the very essence of infancy – vulnerable, dependent, needy – may evoke a driven need in the parent to stifle these features, which so resonate with their own helplessness.

Another aspect of the work in the PIP that has given rise to this book is the accumulating evidence of the efficacy of our interventions. Outcomes, in terms of reflective functioning in the parent and of infant development, suggest that this psychodynamic- and attachment-based model (Baradon et al., 2005; Woodhead & James, 2007) is helpful even for very high-risk populations (Fonagy et al., 2002; Baradon et al., 2008; James et al., 2009).

Finally, a network of professionals around the world is sharing in the work with this model. Our colleagues constantly augment our knowledge through the challenge of their specific national histories and circumstances. We are inspired by their pioneering work in their own countries and enriched by the transcultural dialogues. This book has thus also been nourished by our experiences in working with and in different social conditions.

The individual chapters reflect the singular contribution of each therapist within the PIP team, and the collaborations with expert colleagues in interfacing fields of research who have influenced our clinical work.

Linda Mayes offers a scholarly introduction to interdisciplinary partnership in the study and treatment of early trauma. Mayes also highlights the bidirectionality of influence in addressing a central concern of this book: 'how parental care gets into the body, brain and mind' of their infant offspring, and the shapes it can take.

Inge-Martine Pretorius and *Allan N. Schore* introduce us to current scientific thinking in genetics and the neurosciences regarding the interface with psychoanalytic ideas and therapy.

Inge-Martine Pretorius argues for the integration of findings from genetic and psychoanalytic study to clarify the roles played by the psyche, genes and environment in the impact and consequences of traumatic experiences. Summarising current knowledge regarding salient mediators and moderators of gene–environment interaction, her focus is on the individual's subjective perception of the event or trauma as a potentially significant factor influencing the path from gene to behaviour. In this way, Pretorius posits, intrapsychic representational processes – the individual's understanding and processing of the traumatic event/relationships – may be critical moderators of consequences of environmental and genetic effects. Allan Schore develops his work on regulation theory, which integrates interdisciplinary data to study the mechanisms by which attachment trauma negatively impacts the developmental trajectory of the right brain/mind/body system. He presents data for an 'interpersonal neurobiological model' that embeds attachment mechanism in the facial, tactile and auditory right- to right-hemisphere parent–infant interactions. Schore also discusses the aetiology and neurobiology of dissociation, which he describes as 'the bottom-line defence' against overwhelming, severely disregulating states. He argues that the impact of relational trauma in infancy is a critical risk factor to later psychiatric disorders, through impairment of right-brain capacity for emotional processing and regulation and the creation of a predisposition to use pathological dissociation. This theoretical perspective has direct clinical implications for models of both treatment and prevention.

The primarily scientific chapters are followed by case studies. These highlight the parent's traumatised state of mind and baby's unconscious ways of defending against the disorganising effects of terror and psychic pain, such that trauma becomes embedded in their relationship. The chapters reveal the idiosyncratic stamp of each therapeutic encounter, as the therapist joins with parent(s) and infant to create a singular, distinctive experience.

Judith Woodhead and *Angela Joyce* address babies' subjective experience in attempts to adapt to intrusion of the parental state of mind. Woodhead studies bodily response and communication, and discusses the embodiment of trauma in the 'melodic shape of the words, the pitch of the sounds, the speed of delivery, facial and bodily expressions . . . of [emotion]'. Presenting sequences of clinical material, Woodhead illustrates the triadic relationship that evolved between mother, infant and herself. The therapy provided a new embodied relational experience for both mother and baby, thus impacting on the formation of different implicit knowledge of relating. Joyce describes how in the earliest period after birth the baby's ways of managing impingements of her mother's traumatised state of mind are often observable at the bodily level. She describes *petit mal* seizures in the infant with whom she was working as fissures of her developing psychosomatic integrity which, Joyce suggests, expressed her predicament in the face of rupture of her mother's parental capacities through the multifaceted trauma. From a somewhat different angle, *Amanda Jones* considers the questions of the defensive organisation of the parent and the influence of their psychopathology on the possibility of engaging in a therapeutic process that can lead to change. Jones also considers the link between parental projection and their ability to enter into the realm of 'as if' thinking, which is critical for the mother to recognise the impact of her own powerful projections rather traumatically 'saturating' the baby through the process of projective identification.

Three further clinical chapters consider working with relational trauma in community settings. Outreach in the community takes place primarily in order to make access possible for populations who would not normally attend a mental health centre. Conducting therapy in a setting that is used for other purposes raises particular issues; for example, creating a safe space for the therapeutic work to take place, interfacing with other networks and facets of the organisation. It also involves applying the model flexibly to the specific population group, without losing the core elements that make for the efficacy of the intervention.

Jessica James works with families and their babies in temporary accommodation. She suggests that hostel babies have increased vulnerability to relational trauma since risk factors, such as family breakdown and adult mental health problems, combine with characteristics of living conditions of a hostel to place greater psychological pressure on families during pregnancy, birth and the postnatal period. *James* and *Newbury* describe a new model of baby clinic, provided on hostel premises, which integrates health visiting services and a drop-in parent infant group and where creating a 'group rhythm that is responsive to infants' is privileged. They emphasise that a collaborative team approach is essential (see also Chapter 8) for the families to feel safe and for the babies to be prioritised in the clinic. In parallel, integrating the research component in the clinical framework makes for a coherent, fulfilling experience for the families. *Ju Tomas-Merrills* and *Anita Chakraborty* discuss therapeutic challenges and countertransference issues in working with mothers and babies in HMP Mother Baby Units. The prison population is high risk in terms of histories associated with trauma, and the context of the units offers a paradoxical experience in providing both holding and destabilising elements for the mothers and their babies. The AFC *New Beginnings* programme that the authors facilitate on the units also holds this paradox of containment and challenge. Intergenerational patterns of relational trauma interplay with dynamics on the unit, and are replicated in the *New Beginnings* group. The facilitators try to model predictability, transparency and empathy in the group, informed also by their own experiences in the prison environment and the strong countertransference this provokes. *Tessa Dalley* considers parent–infant and staff consultation work in a community with high levels of social and economic deprivation and population transience. Practitioners working closely with traumatised families often take in much of their emotions of trauma and loss. Their responses may, unconsciously, be influenced by their own experiences of trauma and loss and may contribute to a state of mind being re-enacted in the relationship with their clients. Parallels are drawn with the need for containment of practitioners and attending to the relationship between traumatised mothers and their babies in parent–infant psychotherapy in a community based setting.

The clinical chapters conclude with a brief discussion of the father–infant relationship in relation to trauma, by *Tessa Baradon*. Questions are addressed such as the roles a father who is present in the family may play when the trauma lies in the mother–infant relationship, whether trauma in the father–infant relationship differs from trauma in the mother–infant relationship, and whether the absence of the father constitutes a trauma. Elucidation of these issues suggests that trauma in the crucible of the father–infant relationship is multifaceted and often shaped by the representation of father and father-in-relation-to-baby in the mother's mind. In our experience, the process of parent–infant psychotherapy with fathers is as with mothers, although the therapist may hold a different psychic position in the therapeutic encounter.

At the interface of research and clinical work is a discussion of current salient tools of measurement, their theoretical underpinnings and contributions to understanding of early relational trauma, and how they relate to clinical process.

Michelle Sleed and *Peter Fonagy* argue that given the association between trauma and disorganised attachments in infancy, it is essential to delineate aspects of the parent–child relationship that are traumatogenic to the infant. The authors review some of the salient behavioural (interactive) and representational methods used for assessing the quality of the parent–infant relationship and delineate features of parental behaviour and representation that mark out traumatic relationships. They suggest that it is the disruption of the baby's expectation of a contingent responsiveness on the part of the parent, aligned to reduced parental mentalising capacity, that creates an overwhelming, dysregulated self state in the infant. *Tessa Baradon* and *Elisa Bronfman* present material from the treatment of a borderline mother to consider the contribution of the research lens to clinical practice, and how clinical practice can inform research in this field. Their dialogue is conducted through analysis of two brief segments of sessional material and of the mother's AAI. The clinician's dynamic formulations and the research coding of the AMBIANCE – Atypical Maternal Behaviour Instrument for Assessment and Classification (see also Chapter 9) – are discussed in terms of maternal representations of her attachment history and of her baby, taken from the AAI as well as the clinical process. The authors consider the translation of clinical hunches and unconscious processes into standardised language through these research tools, which are highly sensitive to trauma. In tandem, material from the clinical encounter enhances the accuracy of description of the individually nuanced, psychological process the researchers are trying to study. *Miriam Steele, Howard Steele* and *Anne Murphy* discuss the application of attachment theory and research to trauma, specifically within the family, mainly through the lens of the Adult Attachment Interview (AAI). They argue that for those working with relational trauma it is important to have reliable information about the meaning of past trauma in the mind of the parent, given the link between unresolved trauma and disorganisation in the attachment of the baby/child. The authors demonstrate the use of the AAI in helping to facilitate the clinical process and in demonstrating the efficacy of the intervention in a parent–infant programme with a population with very high indices of trauma.

The research tools discussed so far do not incorporate the baby as key co-constructor of the research/evaluative process. This is addressed by *Carol Broughton*, who illustrates the use of an observational risk-assessment tool, developed in the AFC Parent–Infant Project, in the study of trauma in the relationship between a mother and her baby. The Parent–Infant Relational Assessment Tool (PIRAT) was developed and manualised to facilitate early identification of difficulties by the broader professional milieu working with babies and their families, and Broughton conducted a reliability study with a group of health professionals. In this chapter she elucidates the process by which the study participants came to understand what was happening in a mother–infant dyad. The usefulness of PIRAT in clarifying the nature of concern is borne out by the discourse of the participants in relation to the codings and the codings themselves.

The final chapter, by *Tessa Baradon*, considers factors that work for transformation of relational trauma and those forces that work against change. 'Ghosts' (Fraiberg, 1980) and 'Angels' (Leiberman et al., 2005) in the nursery refer to the parent's own earliest experiences with primary love objects as embodied in implicit ways of relating to intimate others, and in the individual's transactions with his/her children. In the therapeutic encounter, working through of 'ghosts' and reinforcing access to benevolent memories and

representations – the 'angels' – is made possible through the therapist's interest, compassion, reflectiveness, which provide for new experiences of safety.
Thereby, the therapist herself may become an 'angel' in the present experience.
The tenacity of the developmental pull in infancy and the direct therapeutic
work done with the infant, which keep his attachment pathways open, are a
further buttress for change. While some traumatised mothers and fathers
seem to be endowed with a capacity to take in and make good with very little,
there remain a minority of cases where there seems an unyielding split
between the 'good' and 'bad', 'loving' and 'hating', 'safe' and 'dangerous'. Unfortunately, the therapeutic work with the relational trauma in these cases is
not always successful, and concerns for the baby and his parent(s) will remain.

While each essay in the book can stand alone in its input to the topic, there
is also an intention in the collection to lead the reader to some of the influential contributors to the interdisciplinary dialogue about the development,
measurement and treatment of trauma in infancy. Often the discussion is held
within the discipline – scientist with scientists, researcher with researchers and
therapist with therapists. Moreover, often the discussions that are taking
place are held within a range of disparate learned journals not easily available
to a practitioner who is not attached to an academic organisation. This
book, we hope, offers a modest but satisfying roam through this critical,
ever-expanding field.

Tessa Baradon
July 2009

References

Baradon, T. with Broughton, C., Gibbs, I., James, J., Joyce, A. & Woodhead, J. (2005)
The practice of psycho-analytic parent–infant psychotherapy: Claiming the baby.
London: Routledge.

Baradon, T., Fonagy, P., Bland, K., Lenard, K. & Sleed, M. (2008) New Beginnings –
an experience-based programme addressing the attachment relationship between
mothers and their babies in prisons. *Journal of Child Psychotherapy*, 34(2):
240–258.

Fonagy, P., Sadie, C. & Allison, L. (2002) *The Parent–Infant Project (PIP) outcome
study.* London: The Anna Freud Centre (unpublished manuscript).

Fraiberg, S. (1980) *Clinical studies in infant mental health: The first year of life.*
New York: Basic Books.

James, J., Ibison, L. & Newbury, J. (2009) A collaborative project between health
visiting and parent infant psychotherapy at a hostel for homeless families: Practice
and evaluation. *Community Practitioner* (in press).

Lieberman, A.F., Padron, E., Van Horn, P. & Harris, W.W. (2005) Angels in the
nursery: Intergenerational transmission of benevolent parental influences. *Infant
Mental Health Journal*, 26(6): 504–520.

Woodhead, J. & James, J. (2007) Transformational process in parent infant psychotherapy: Provision in community drop-in groups. In M. Pozzi & B. Tydeman
(Eds.), *Innovations in Parent–Infant Psychotherapy.* London: Karnac.

Acknowledgements

Many have contributed directly or indirectly to this book. Incisive discourse about infants and their families is deeply embedded at The Anna Freud Centre, where innovative clinical work and research in this field have grown to cohabit easily with each other. The Directors and Board of Trustees at the Centre have supported the Parent–Infant Project (PIP) and the ambience of our work and aspirations.

For my fellow clinicians and myself in the Project, this is the second collaborative book. It is yet another celebration of our 'teamness'. The contributions of valued colleagues who have truly broadened our thinking are also reflected. Many of them have interfaced the psychoanalytic foundations of our practice with their respective disciplines' investigation into infancy and development.

The details of getting the book ready for print were assisted by PIP administration staff, particularly Cressida Stevens.

Finally, and centrally, it is our patients that invariably show us a way to learn and to assist.

Introduction

Linda C. Mayes

For over a century, clinicians and scholars have been concerned about the enduring impact of early trauma in infancy and early childhood. That early hardship shaped an adult's fortune and place in family and community was surely accepted well before Freud's considerations of infantile trauma based on the reconstructed narratives of his adult patients. But it was not until the late nineteenth and early twentieth century, especially with the emergence of attachment theory, that a more considered awareness emerged on how the quality of an infant's early care and parental attachment left an indelible mark on an individual child's psychology, capacity for love, and ability to care for others as an adult. Anna Freud's compassionate care of children and families trapped in the terror of war, René Spitz's careful detailing of anaclitic depression and physical decline among orphaned children, Henry Kempe's startling reports on battered children and the impact of maltreatment by parents, and Selma Fraiberg's understanding of how neglectful parenting echoed well into adulthood as a new parent struggled to care for their infant – each called our attention to the potentially devastating effects of trauma and neglect in the infant's early attachment relationships. Based on these ground-breaking clinical studies, many services and intervention approaches were developed to protect and/or rescue children from potentially devastating failures in early parenting.

Today, there has been a productive and exciting marriage between clinicians devoted to helping children who are growing up in adverse circumstances and developmental scientists trying to understand how early adversity has such an enduring impact on a child's psychic and physical health. Accumulating evidence from both preclinical and clinical developmental psychology and neuroscience laboratories indicates that early failures in parental care have a compromising and enduring impact on the stress regulatory capacities of offspring and on the parenting abilities of those offspring as adults (Plotsky & Meaney, 1993; Francis et al., 1999). Such early adversities also make adults more vulnerable to stress and stress-related conditions such as cardiovascular disease and substance abuse (Garmezy et al., 1984; Nemeroff et al., 2006). Further, it is becoming clearer how early trauma and/or deprivation greatly increases the likelihood of later depression in adolescence and adulthood, and also how early adversity may increase the risk for later post-traumatic conditions subsequent to trauma in adulthood (Friedman et al., 1995; Southwick et al., 2005). Bringing behavioral and molecular genetic perspectives to studies of early trauma has revealed how particular genetic variations may render individuals more or less vulnerable to the detrimental effects of current and past adversity in childhood (Caspi et al., 2003), and how poor social support dramatically increases vulnerability to the negative consequences of early adversity if the individual carries an 'at-risk' genetic profile (Kaufman et al., 2004). (Conversely, more and more evidence is accumulating for how adequate early care may diminish genetically conveyed risks for later maladaptive behavior; Suomi et al., 1983; Suomi, 2004, 2005a, 2005b.) Considerable progress has also been made in understanding the neural and gene regulatory mechanisms of how adversity resets the neural threshold for responding to stress later in life and at the same time how it changes the ways in which regions of the brain – including the amygdala, hippocampus, and prefrontal cortex – process information, appraise consequences, and influence decisions. Also becoming clearer in the accumulating research is how these changes in brain function increase the risk for maladaptation and serious psychiatric disturbances.

Paralleling the extensive work on the psychological and biological impact of early childhood trauma are more recent studies of the neural circuitry of parenting and on how individual differences in parental care get into both the child's mind and brain (Meaney, 2001). Recent work in both preclinical and clinical settings is delineating a specific neural circuitry that is key to early parenting and attachment to offspring. The initiation and maintenance of maternal behavior appears to involve a specific neural circuit based in reward and stress response systems (e.g., amygdala, hippocampus, striatum) (Fleming et al., 1999). Further, at least ten genes have been identified in animal models that are necessary for the expression of one or more aspects of maternal behavior in the initial contact with offspring (Leckman & Herman, 2002). With pregnancy or with repeated exposure to offspring, structural and molecular changes occur, most of which are not yet completely understood, in specific limbic, hypothalamic, and midbrain regions. Functional imaging studies with new parents suggest that experience with infants may consolidate neural circuitry, and that for first-time parents there are key changes in attachment-related circuitry in the first months postpartum (Leckman et al., 2004).

This attachment-related neural circuitry appears to regulate how adults respond to their infants' salient attachment-related cues such as cries or visual emotional cues, and there has been considerable work characterizing key aspects of maternal behavior in animal models and linking normal individual variation in these behaviors to offspring development. Findings suggest that maternal behavior in the days following birth serves to 'program' the subsequent maternal behavior of the adult offspring as well as establishing the offspring's level of hypothalamic–pituitary–adrenal responsiveness to stress (Francis et al., 1999). This complex programming also appears to influence aspects of learning and memory. Furthermore, it seems clear now that the influence of maternal care on the development of stress-regulatory capacities is mediated by changes in gene expression in regions of the brain that regulate stress responses. The biochemical structure of the promoter or regulatory region of the gene regulating glucocorticoid or stress hormone production is altered by differing levels of maternal care. It appears that this biochemical alteration, termed 'methylation', may be an enduring change that is then passed on to offspring and, in this way, may be one of the mechanisms for the intergenerational transmission of parenting behavior – or the clinical truism that 'we parent as we were parented' (Meaney, 2001).

In sum, the nature of early caregiving experiences has enduring consequences on individual differences in subsequent maternal behavior, patterns of stress response, learning and memory through specific neurobiological and neurogenetic mechanisms. Much work remains to increase the specificity of understanding those mechanisms and also for understanding how parental psychopathology such as depression, addiction, or personality disorder modifies the attachment-related neural circuitry. It is also not clear what it is exactly about adequate maternal care that 'gets into the body, brain, and genes', as it were. Is it the amount of maternal touch that stimulates key neurochemical cascades relating to upregulation of dopaminergic reward systems and downregulation of stress? Is it a more complex combination of touch, language, and sensitivity to infants' states of arousal that leads to a similar neurochemical, neurogenetic cascade?

Clearly, far more translational work is needed and it is here that the partnership between clinicians, clinical investigators, and developmental neuroscientists is so crucial. For example, how do individual differences in maternal sensitivity, a central construct in so many studies of parent–infant interaction and the focus of so many clinical interventions, relate to individual differences in the activation of attachment-related neural circuits in response to infant cues? Similarly, as described in several chapters in this book, a key aspect of much of parent–infant psychotherapeutic work is to enhance a parent's ability to reflect on her infant's emotional needs and to understand how her needs, feelings, wishes, and behaviors as a parent directly impact her infant's feelings and needs. What are the neural correlates of individual differences in maternal reflectiveness, and is a change in maternal reflective ability correlated with a change in attachment-related neural circuitry? Elucidating these neural mechanisms underlying human attachment, the range of individual differences in these mechanisms, and their behavioral correlates has implications for understanding, first, how early childhood experience impacts an adult's ability to be a caring and empathic parent – a failure of which may be perpetuated across generations – and, second, how these failures in early parental care increase the intergenerational risk for depression, disorders of attachment, and addiction. Understanding basic neural mechanisms for failure in early parenting may also facilitate more refined and presumably earlier interventions during pregnancy and in the immediate postpartum period to help parents at risk invest in and provide sufficient and necessary care for their infant despite the earlier compromises they may bring to their parenting role. It is this latter point that brings us to the importance of this book.

The central questions preoccupying the clinicians contributing to this volume are how best to prevent and/or interrupt the later impact and inter-generational cycle of early attachment difficulties, disruptions, and traumas. The lessons already possible from developmental neuroscience perspectives on attachment point to the necessity of working directly with parents and focusing on how they are able or not to make room in their minds for their infant. The accumulated evidence also underscores the importance of inter-vening early, even in pregnancy but certainly in the first months after birth. And attending carefully to how parents understand and regulate their own feelings in an effort to both understand and help their infants is likely a crucial part of that complex mechanism alluded to earlier that may be the conduit for how maternal care has such a profound impact on stress modulation, memory, and learning at the level of mind, brain chemistry, brain structure, and gene regulation. Each of the chapters in this book addresses the question of how clinicians working directly with parents and infants in many different contexts may get the dyadic system back on track.

What is especially key to this book is the careful assessment of how parents' own trauma in infancy and early childhood as outlined in chapters by Baradon and Bronfman, Broughton, and Sleed and Fonagy. These assessments move beyond a simple narrative accounting of early adversity to how the mental and emotional residues of early trauma are re-enacted in caring interactions with infants. These 'ghosts', as Baradon discusses, require careful attention from the therapist working with both parent and infant, for the parent's own fragility may make it difficult for her to respond to her infant's distress. Indeed, her infant's distress may be so stressful for the parent that she is simply unable to reflect on her infant's needs – the clinical hallmarks of stress-regulatory difficulties and the link to basic science. Careful clinical accountings as presented in this volume offer critical material for social neuroscientists working on the clinically relevant issues of how parental care gets into body, brain, and mind.

References

Caspi, A., Sugden, K., Moffitt, T.E., Taylor A., Craig, I.W., Harrington, H. et al. (2003). Influence of life stress on depression: Moderation by a polymorphism in the 5-htt gene. *Science*, 301: 386–389.

Fleming, A.S., O'Day, D.H. & Kraemer, G.W. (1999) Neurobiology of mother–infant interactions: Experience and central nervous system plasticity across development and generations. *Neuroscience & Biobehavioral Reviews*, 23: 673–685.

Francis, D., Diorio, J., Liu, D. & Meaney, M. (1999) Non-genomic transmission across generations of maternal behavior and stress responses in the rat. *Science*, 286: 1155–1158.

Friedman, M.J., Charney, D.S. & Deutch, A.Y. (Eds.) (1995) *Neurobiological consequences of stress: From normal adaptation to post-traumatic stress disorder*. New York: Raven Press.

Garmezy, N., Masten, A.S. & Tellegen, A. (1984) The study of stress and competence in children: A building block for developmental psychopathology. *Child Development*, 55: 97–111.

Kaufman, J., Yang, B.Z., Douglas-Palumberi, H., Houshyar, S., Lipschitz, D., Krystal, J.H. et al. (2004) Social supports and serotonin transporter gene moderate depression in maltreated children. *Proceedings of the National Academy of Sciences of the United States of America*, 101: 17315–17321.

Leckman, J.F., Feldman, R., Swain, J.E., Eicher, V., Thompson, N. & Mayes, L.C. (2004) Primary parental preoccupation: Circuits, genes, and the crucial role of the environment. *Journal of Neural Transmission*, 111(7): 753–771.

Leckman, J.F. & Herman, A. (2002) Maternal behavior and developmental psychopathology. *Biological Psychiatry*, 51: 27–43.

Meaney, M.J. (2001) Maternal care, gene expression, and the transmission of individual differences in stress reactivity across generations. *Annual Review of Neuroscience*, 24: 1161–1192.

Nemeroff, C.B., Bremner, J.D., Foa, E.B., Mayberg, H.S., North, C.S. & Stein, M.B. (2006) Posttraumatic stress disorder: A state-of-the-science review. *Journal of Psychiatric Research*, 40: 1–21.

Plotsky, P.M. & Meaney, M.J. (1993) Early, postnatal experience alters hypothalamic corticotropin-releasing factor (CRF) mRNA, median eminence CRF content and stress-induced release in adult rats. *Brain Research. Molecular Brain Research*, 18: 195–200.

Southwick, S.M., Vythilingam, M. & Charney, D.S. (2005). The psychobiology of depression and resilience to stress: Implications for prevention and treatment. *Annual Reviews of Clinical Psychology*, 1: 255–291.

Suomi, S.J. (2004) How gene–environment interactions influence emotional development in rhesus monkeys. In C.G. Coll, E.L. Bearer & R.M. Lerner (Eds.), *Nature and nurture: The complex interplay of genetic and environmental influences on human behavior and development* (pp. 35–51). Mahwah, NJ: Lawrence Erlbaum Associates.

Suomi, S.J. (2005a) Genetic and environmental factors influencing the expression of impulsive aggression and serotonergic functioning in rhesus monkeys. In R.E. Tremblay, W.W. Hartup & J. Archer (Eds.), *Developmental origins of aggression* (pp. 63–82). New York: Guilford Press.

Suomi, S.J. (2005b) How gene–environment interactions shape the development of impulsive aggression in rhesus monkeys. In D.M. Stoff & E.J. Susman (Eds.), *Developmental psychobiology of aggression* (pp. 252–268). New York: Cambridge University Press.

Suomi, S.J., Mineka, S. & DeLizio, R.D. (1983) Short- and long-term effects of repetitive mother–infant separations on social development in rhesus monkeys. *Developmental Psychology*, 19: 770–786.

Chapter 1

Genetic and environmental contributors to the intergenerational transmission of trauma and disorganized attachment relationships

Inge-Martine Pretorius

Genes and environment are inextricably intertwined. Old notions of the nature–nurture and brain–mind dichotomy have been supplanted by a rich web of synergistic relations between nature and nurture, soma and psyche. In attempting to address the nature–nurture debate, the two dominant psychological approaches of the last century – learning theory and psychoanalysis – agreed that experience with parents was pivotal in shaping the individual's characteristics, values and dysfunctions in adaptation. Of the two approaches, psychoanalysis continued to emphasise that biologically inherited traits limited the changes that could be effected by socialisation and environmental influences (Freud, 1920). During the last decades of the twentieth century, quantitative behavioural genetic research[1] eroded classical socialisation theories that emphasised the role of parenting and early family experiences (Scarr, 1992). The role of the environment was further eclipsed by the excitement of the human genome project and the promise that molecular genetics would uncover single mutated genes that caused specific behaviours and psychiatric disorders. Instead, epigenetics revealed that the environment can lead to heritable changes in gene expression in an organism, thus focusing anew on the important role played by the social environment in the final phenotype. Furthermore, molecular genetic methods uncovered even more complex and subtle mediators and moderators of gene–environment interaction in the pathways from genotype to phenotype. The individual's subjective perception of the event or trauma has emerged as a potentially significant additional factor influencing the path from gene to behaviour. Thus, intrapsychic representational processes are not merely the consequences of environmental and genetic effects, but may be the critical moderators of these effects.

---

1 Qualitative behavioural genetics research uses quasi-experimental designs such as family, twin and adoption studies and combinations of these to attempt to decompose phenotypic (measured) variance in behaviour into genetic and environmental components of variance.

This chapter reviews the nature–nurture debate and the advances brought by molecular genetics to the current understanding of gene–environment interaction. It argues for the need to integrate the findings of genetics with the insights of psychoanalytic theory, in order to enhance our understanding of the role played by the psyche, genes and environment in the impact and consequences of traumatic experiences.

Gene–environment interaction

The modern history of the nature–nurture debate began with two cousins: Darwin, the father of the modern theory of evolution, and Galton, the father of human behavioural genetics. While Darwin (1864) investigated the genetic inheritance of characteristics,[2] Galton (1869, 1883, 1889) studied the inheritance of human behaviour.[3] Our understanding of human behaviour and mental life was revolutionised in the first half of the twentieth century by psychoanalysis (Kandel, 1999). Freud and his followers provided remarkable insights into unconscious mental processes, infantile sexuality and psychic determinism and about the irrationality of human motivation. Freud showed that powerful unconscious wishes motivate human behaviour and – to the extent that these motives remain unconscious – they determine behaviour. However, by analysing these unconscious wishes, phantasies, dreams and defence mechanisms, the individual can become more conscious of these powerful forces and no longer be subject to them, but have greater freedom of self-determination.

Although psychoanalytic thinking continued to progress in the second part of the twentieth century, there were fewer brilliant insights, with the exception of advances in the understanding of child development. Psychoanalysis still represents the most coherent and intellectually satisfying description of the mind. Its power derives from its ability to investigate mental processes from a subjective perspective, as experienced and constructed by the individual. This strength, however, is also a weakness as subjective processes do not easily lend themselves to empirical enquiry. Consequently, psychoanalysis did not progress like other areas of psychology and medicine in the latter half of the twentieth century.

Within the field of infant mental health, Anna Freud offered the first compelling evidence for the environment's important influence in early childhood. Working in the Hampstead War Nurseries in London, her study of the traumatic effects of family disruption during the Second World War revealed

---

2 Darwin studied the variance in life forms. He concluded that all species of life have evolved over time, from common ancestors through the process of natural selection. His theory of evolution provides a logical explanation for the diversity of life.

3 Galton studied variance in human behaviour. He attempted to decompose the variance in behaviour into genetic (nature) and environmental (nurture) components of variance.

the crucial importance of early relationships between parents and children (Freud & Burlingham, 1942, 1974). Her work was extended by Spitz (1945), and later by Bowlby (1951). Their work ushered in a period of environmentalism (from the 1950s to the early 1960s). Although important genetic research was conducted during that time (Slater & Cowie, 1971), its impact on mainstream psychiatry and psychology was minor.

As behavioural and psychiatric genetics gained momentum in the 1960s, 'environmentalism' waned (from the 1960s to the 1980s). Better twin designs and the greater availability of adoption data lead to convincing evidence for important genetic influences on most types of psychopathology. By the end of the 1980s, there was general acceptance of genetic influences on variations in the individual liability to mental disorders (Rutter et al., 1990a, 1990b, 2006). This acceptance, together with the development and application of molecular genetic strategies to psychiatric genetics, led to a decade in which environmental influences were denied (from the 1980s to the early 1990s). While quantitative genetics research determines the sum of heritable genetic influences on behaviour, it cannot identify which genes are responsible for genetic influence. Consequently, the new molecular genetic techniques initially brought great excitement and expectations that individual mutated genes would be discovered to be aetiological for specific behaviours and psychiatric disorders (Kidd, 1991). The initial claims of finding a gene 'for' specific behaviours and disorders were not replicated, leading to disillusionment about the possibility of understanding the role played by genes.

Five major changes in concept occurred in the early 1990s that ushered in the current era (from the early 1990s to the present) (Rutter et al., 2006). Firstly, the simplistic notion of single basic causes was abandoned in favour of accepting that genetic effects on normal and (most) pathological development reflect the actions of many genes, each with a small effect (Lykken, 2006). Secondly, there was growing criticism of empirical behavioural genetics and extreme biological determinism. Thirdly, research strategies testing environmental mediation re-established the importance of environmental influences. Fourthly, gene–environment interplay received renewed interest. Fifthly, epigenetic mechanisms[4] (described below) began to be elucidated. This led to the recognition that genetic effects are crucially dependent on gene expression (the functional activation of the gene) and that such expression is influenced by numerous factors including environmental features (Jaenisch & Bird, 2003).

The current understanding is that genes and environment are inextricably connected in shaping human behaviour. Numerous studies of twins, adoption and families that used quantitative genetic strategies have shown unequivocally the genetic influence on individual differences in the liability to

---

4 Epigenetics is the study of heritable changes in gene expression that occur without a change in DNA sequence.

show particular behaviours (Plomin, 1994; McGuffin et al., 2001). Despite the shortcomings and biases of quantitative genetic methods, there is no doubt that genes substantially influence all forms of human behaviour. However, according to Rutter (2002: 996), the genetic influences are 'strong and pervasive, but rarely determinative'.

Mounting evidence over the past two decades suggests that the social environment can moderate the expression of genetic influences on adaptive and pathological behaviour (for a review, see Reiss & Leve, 2007). The first evidence came from genetically informed twin and adoption studies that showed that psychopathology in birth parents predicts psychopathology in their adopted offspring only when the adoptive rearing environment is adverse (Cadoret & Cain, 1981). These studies do not reveal whether one or more genes are involved, nor identify the specific polymorphism (allele or form of the gene). Secondly, studies of specific alleles identified by molecular genetic techniques show that specific alleles manifest only if a child-rearing environment was adverse, or if the developing adult was exposed to stress. As in the case of genetic influences, 'empirical evidence shows that environmental influences are strong and pervasive, but rarely determinative' (Rutter, 2002: 997).

Studies of traumatic environmental effects have shown that there are large individual differences in responses: some individuals are severely affected, while others show few consequences. This has given rise to the concept of resilience: the relative resistance to the negative effects of psychosocial adversity (Luthar et al., 2000). Individual differences in response suggest that the individual's understanding and processing of the traumatic event may influence the pathway between gene and behaviour. Gabbard (quoted in Knowlton, 2005: 3) proposes that an individual's intrapsychic representational system forms an active filter between genotype and phenotype: 'whether or not environment factors trigger the expression of the gene may depend on the conscious or unconscious meaning attributed to these experiences'. Thus, intrapsychic representational processes are not merely the consequences of environmental and genetic effects; they may be the critical moderators of these effects.

Furthermore, parents and caretakers can contextualise events to enable the child to make sense of them in beneficial ways. Anna Freud documented that a child's response to wartime air raids was largely determined by their parent's reaction to the traumatic events. Children whose parents remained relatively calm were far less traumatised than children whose parents became distressed (Freud & Burlingham, 1974). Thus, the child's subjective experience of the early environment and the quality of parenting assume – once again – central roles in the pathway from genotype to phenotype. Psychoanalysis re-emerges to play a potentially crucial role in explaining these subjective experiences. One implication is that early intervention with parents or children might actually alter genetic expression in vulnerable children (Gabbard, 2000, 2005).

Explanations for intergenerational transmission of trauma and modes of relating

Genetic explanation

Traditional research on the combined effects of genetics and the environment on individual variation in behavioural and disease susceptibility has high-lighted the importance of the individual's genotype (the heritable genetic composition – genes and alleles). However, recent research implicates the role of epigenetics in addition to classical genetic mechanisms in gene–environment interactions. Epigenetics is the study of heritable changes in gene expression that occur without a change in the DNA sequence (Dolinoy et al., 2007).

The father of classical genetics, Mendel (1866), concluded that alternative forms of genes (alleles) were the units that were passed from generation to generation. Deoxyribonucleic acid (DNA) was shown to constitute the relevant genetic material; its double helix structure and sequence (order of base-pairs) were elucidated in 1953 (Franklin & Gosling, 1953; Watson & Crick, 1953). The causal chain from genotype (DNA) to phenotype (behaviour) can be simplified as follows. The DNA sequence specifies the synthesis (transcription) of messenger ribonucleic acid (mRNA), which in turn specifies the synthesis (translation) of polypeptides. These polypeptides ultimately form proteins (and enzymes) that bring about specific effects on phenotype (behavioural manifestations). The DNA content of all cells is very similar, but the actions of the DNA are crucially dependent on their func-tional activation (expression) in particular cells and at particular phases of development. The activation involves transcription, translation and epi-genetic mechanisms. These epigenetic mechanisms include DNA methylation, post-translational modification of histone tails and DNA packaging around histones (Watson et al., 2008). Both chromatin condensation (DNA packaging around histones) and DNA methylation are associated with gene silencing (the functional deactivation of a gene) (Dolinoy et al., 2007).

Thus, what Mendel conceptualised as simple deterministic inheritance of alleles has proved to be an immensely more complex, multidimensional causal chain that brings together the actions of genes *and* the actions of the environment (hormones, diet, chemical substances and rearing experience), through the effects on gene expression (Alberts et al., 2008; Watson et al., 2008). Traditionally, it was assumed that environmental factors might influence psychological development and functioning, but that they could not alter the genes. While it is true that the DNA sequence is not altered, the discovery of epigenetic mechanisms shows that environmental factors could alter the *expression* of genes. In that sense environments can, and do, have effects on genes.[5]

Thus, epigenetic changes allow the organism to respond to the environment through changes in gene expression. Epigenetic modifications are inherited during mitosis and, in some cases, during meiosis[6] (the two forms of cell division) and can be transmitted from generation to generation (Abdolmaleky et al., 2003). This intergenerational transmission can persist into the fourth generation despite a lack of continued exposure to the environmental stimulus (Anway et al., 2005). This implies that traits or behaviours brought about by epigenetic changes due to exposure to a specific environmental stimulus could potentially persist and be seen in the third or fourth generation, despite the absence of the original environmental stimulus.

The publication of the human genome sequence (Venter et al., 2001) offers further opportunities to understand gene functioning and gene–environment interaction. The human genome consists of three billion base-pairs, forming approximately 25,000 genes, divided into 23 DNA molecules, the chromosomes. Individual variation is limited to an extremely small percentage of the overall genome. About 99.9% of the human DNA sequence is conserved relative to other great apes, leaving only 0.1% of the human genome to account for the entire diversity in the human species. DNA variation includes insertions and duplications, known as short tandem repeat polymorphisms (STRPs), deletions and single nucleotide polymorphisms (SNPs).

The discovery of SNPs enables investigators to identify candidate genes for specific behaviours and diseases. The candidate gene study design is appropriate when substantial evidence suggests that a particular gene contributes to heritable variation of risk – the extent to which the variation in a trait among members of a population is determined by inherited variation (Fossella & Casey, 2006). Candidate gene association studies focus on the individual SNPs that vary from person to person. The catechol-O-methyltransferase (COMT) and brain-derived neurotrophic factor (BDNF) genes are candidate genes for research into disorganised attachment relationships, because they are implicated in affective regulation, cognition and numerous psychiatric disorders (Bishop et al., 2006; Savitz et al., 2006; Hosak, 2007).

While behavioural genetics, heritability and candidate gene studies indicate the importance of genetic factors and provide evidence for the importance of

5 This is a somewhat misleading oversimplified description of the sub-cellular process of genotype to phenotype, as it ignores the important roles of factors like: transfer-RNA, transcription enhancers and silencers, the splicing of exons and introns during transcription, polypeptide folding during translation, and the interplay of different proteins.
6 Mitosis: cell division resulting in two daughter cells which each contains the same number of chromosomes as the original cell. Meiosis: cell reduction division resulting in two daughter cells which each contains half the number of chromosomes in the original cell. This occurs in sexual reproduction.

non-genetic influence, these methods cannot give definitive answers about the more complicated gene–environment interactions that give rise to specific cases of disorganised attachments. According to Jensen (2000), genetic studies are susceptible to an underestimation of the impact of common environmental contributors to the development of complex behaviour patterns. Similarly, Hosak (2007) notes that gene–environment interactions were neglected in most studies involving the COMT gene. It is likely that a number of factors, including the environmental triggering of a genetic vulnerability, underpin the development of attachment behaviours over the course of brain development *in utero*, in infancy and in early childhood. The COMT and BDNF genes are likely to have a pleiotropic[7] effect on human behaviour.

Psychoanalytic and attachment theory understanding

Freud (1920) recognised the influences of infancy and early childhood on adult personality and the tendency to repeat patterns of relationships. He described the child's relationship to the mother as, 'unique, without parallel, established unalterably for a whole lifetime as the first and strongest love-object and as the prototype of all later love relations' (Freud, 1940: 188).

Freud (1905) became aware that patterns of relating tend to be repeated during his analysis of Dora, whose feelings towards another man were acted out in relation to Freud. Freud (1914: 150) described the 'compulsion to repeat' and 'working through' (1914: 155). He linked the compulsion to repeat to transference, which 'is itself only a piece of repetition' (Freud 1914: 151), because it was in the relationship with the analyst that the patient's past was re-enacted in the present. He also linked the compulsion to repeat to the patient's resistance (defences), suggesting that the greater the resistance, the more extensively will acting out (repetition) replace remembering' (Freud, 1914: 395). The analytic setting became a space where the patient could 'work through' his resistance and become aware of repressed thoughts and feelings that constituted the unconscious motives of behaviour in the present.

Following Freud's notion of the compulsion to repeat and his conclusion that repressed material did not disappear, but 'inevitably reappears; like an unlaid ghost' (Freud, 1909: 122), Fraiberg et al. (1975) linked these two phenomena in their work with impaired mother–infant relationships. They showed that unresolved traumatic experiences of the past were compulsively repeated with disastrous consequences.

Parents caught up in pathological ways of relating with their infant tended to use two defence mechanisms: repression of affects and identification with the aggressor (Freud, 1936). These had developed during childhood to cope with overwhelming pain. On becoming a parent, these defence mechanisms

7 Pleiotropy occurs when a single gene influences multiple phenotypic traits.

were reactivated in relation to their own child. However, parents could break cycles of deprivation, abuse and developmental impairment if they were able to 'remember and re-experience' (Fraiberg et al., 1975: 420) affects that were repressed and defended against in their childhood. Many since Freud have emphasised the nurturing relationship between mother and child as the precursor for future relationship patterns and future development (Bowlby, 1973, 1979, 1988; Fonagy et al., 1991a). Parents tend to raise their children as they themselves were raised, and thus interaction and attachment patterns tend to be intergenerationally transmitted. Yet it is not the quality of childhood experiences that predicts the intergenerational transmission, but how parents talk and think (intrapsychic representation) about their experiences in the present (Stern, 1998; Fonagy et al., 1991b; Steele & Steele, 1994; see also Chapters 9 and 11 in the current volume). This accounts for both the stability and change in the intergenerational transmission of patterns of attachment (Bretherton & Munholland, 1999).

Epidemiologic studies also reveal the importance of family function in early life as a predictor of health in adulthood. Victims of childhood physical or sexual abuse are at considerably greater risk of developing mental illness, obesity, diabetes and heart disease as adults. Persistent emotional neglect and family conflict compromise growth and intellectual development, and increase the risk of depression, anxiety disorders and chronic illness in adulthood (for an overview, see Repetti et al., 2002).

Since the identification of disorganised/disoriented attachment behaviour, and subsequent reports of associations between disorganisation and later socio-emotional maladaptation, there has been much speculation about the environmental and genetic determinants of disorganised attachment behaviour (Lyons-Ruth & Jacobvitz, 1999). Various empirical and theoretical studies have considered different aetiological pathways to insecure and disorganised relationships, including contributions from the parents' behaviour (van den Boom, 1994; Seifer et al., 1996), as well as characteristics of the child's early temperament such as negative emotionality and reactivity (Spangler & Grossmann, 1993). However, the correlations reported are small to moderate, and the causal relationships between individual variations of temperament, parental behaviour and attachment quality await elucidation (Vaughn & Bost, 1999). A meta-analysis that combined results form nearly 80 studies concluded that within the normal, non-clinical range, insensitive parenting (i.e. environmental factors) *in itself* does not lead to disorganised attachment (van IJzendoorn et al., 1999).

Gene–environment interdependence

There is increasing evidence showing how genes interact with the environment to produce certain phenotypes and how the environment can change the expression of genes. Several experiments with rats have investigated the non-genomic influences on maternal behaviours such as licking, grooming and aggression towards an intruder. The findings suggest that the maternal behaviours in the days following birth serve to programme the pups' response to stress and the subsequent maternal behaviours of adult offspring (for an overview, see Mayes et al., 2005). Furthermore, the effects of early maternal deprivation in primates are difficult to reverse. Maternally deprived monkeys as adults are able to function normally under normal conditions, but cannot cope with stress (Suomi et al., 1976).

Human studies have demonstrated the interaction of specific alleles with adverse social environments. In a landmark longitudinal cohort study, Caspi and colleagues (2002) measured degree of maltreatment, monoamine oxidase-A (MAOA) gene activity and antisocial behaviour. Males with low MAOA activity (the allele with a functional deficit in the promoter region) who were maltreated in childhood had elevated antisocial scores. By contrast, males with high MAOA activity did not have elevated antisocial scores, even when they had experienced maltreatment in childhood. Thus a functional polymorphism of the MAOA gene moderates the impact of childhood mal-treatment on the development of antisocial behaviour. The study highlights the gene–environment interaction, because neither low activity MAOA alone nor maltreatment alone was sufficient to create antisocial behaviour. Thus, a gene and environment combination was necessary for the behaviour to manifest.

Another landmark study measured the impact of home visitation by a nurse on children's antisocial behaviour (Olds et al., 1998). The 15-year follow-up of the randomised controlled trial revealed that adolescents born to young, low-income women who received nurse visits had significantly lower rates of antisocial behaviour and substance abuse, and fewer lifetime sexual partners, than the controls. Thus, changing the child's environment through supporting the parents had a significant impact on the child's later behaviour. This study suggests that the nurse visit intervention may lower genetic vulnerability in the children of high-risk families.

Some studies suggest that developmental influences in response to risk – age differences – need to be considered in the pathway from genotype to phenotype. One study demonstrated that the effects of stress during early development seemed to be particularly affected by the genotype (Caspi et al., 2003). Researchers have highlighted the need to consider the child's gradual process of ontogenic[8] development as an important factor in the pathway from genotype to phenotype (Rutter, 2002). However, according to Reiss and Leve (2007), the early gene–environment studies do not yet show conclusive evidence that the timing of the adverse environmental exposure is crucial.

---

8 Ontogeny (or morphogeny) describes the origin and development of an organism from the fertilised egg to the mature form. Ontogeny is to be distinguished from phylogeny which describes the evolutionary (genetic) relatedness amongst various groups of organisms.

Efforts to search for gene–environment mechanisms have not yet fully addressed factors influencing an individual's active transformation of the social environment (called the evocative or active gene–environment correlation), except to rule them out as potential artefacts (Reiss & Leve, 2007). As described above, in infancy, heritable, temperamental features of children may evoke adverse responses from their parents. Later in development, characteristics of adolescents can influence their actively seeking out and being accepted by deviant or prosocial peer groups (Manke et al., 1995). These studies suggest that the individual's subjective perception of an event or of the environment plays a potentially crucial role in moderating the consequences of environmental and genetic effects. Freud's concept of the compulsion to repeat, and the psychoanalytic insights into the individual child, adolescent and parent's subjective experience, may further our understanding of this phenomenon. Thus, psychoanalytic insights have a potentially crucial role to play in understanding the contribution of the psyche, genes and environment. Furthermore, understanding these effects is crucial to developing effective therapeutic or preventative interventions.

References

Abdolmaleky, H.M., Smith, C.L., Faraone, S.V., Shafa, R., Stone, W., Glatt, S.J. et al. (2003) Methylomics in psychiatry: Modulation of gene–environment interactions may be through DNA methylation. *American Journal of Medical Genetics Part B: Neuropsychiatric Genetics*, 127B(1): 51–59.

Alberts, B., Johnson, A., Walter, P., Lewis, J., Raff, M. & Roberts, K. (2008) *Molecular biology of the cell* (5th ed.). New York: Garland Publishing.

Anway, M.D., Cupp, A.S., Uzumcu, M. and Skinner, M.K. (2005) Epigenetic trans-generational actions of endocrine disruptors and make fertility. *Science*, 308(5727): 1466–1469.

Bishop, S.J., Cohen, J.D., Fossella, J., Casey, B.J. & Farah, M.J. (2006) COMT genotype influences prefrontal response to emotional distraction. *Cognitive, Affective & Behavioral Neuroscience*, 6(1): 62–70.

Bowlby, J. (1951) *Maternal care and mental health*. Geneva, Switzerland: World Health Organisation.

Bowlby, J. (1973) *Attachment and Loss: Volume 2: Separation*. London: Hogarth Press.

Bowlby, J. (1979) *The making and breaking of affectional bonds*. London: Routledge.

Bowlby, J. (1988) *A secure base: Clinical application of attachment theory*. London: Routledge.

Bretherton, I. & Munholland, K.A. (1999) Internal working models in attachment relationships: A construct revisited. In J. Cassidy & P. Shaver (Eds.), *Handbook of attachment: Theory, research and clinical applications* (pp. 89–11). New York: Guilford Press.

Cadoret, R.J. & Cain, C.A. (1981) Genotype–environment interaction in antisocial behaviour. *Psychological Medicine*, 12: 235–239.

Caspi, A., McClay, J., Moffitt, T.E., Mill, J., Martin, J., Craig, I.W. et al. (2002) Role of genotype in the cycle of violence in maltreated children. *Science*, 297(5582): 851–854.

Caspi, A., Sugden, K., Moffitt, T.E., Taylor, A., Craig, I.W., Harrington, H. et al. (2003) Influence of life stress on depression: Moderation by the polymorphism in the 5-HTT gene. *Science*, 301: 386–389.

Darwin, C.R. (1864/2001) *On the origin of species by means of natural selection: Or the preservation of favoured races in the struggle of life*. Cambridge, MA: Harvard University Press.

Dolinoy, D.C., Weidman, J.R. & Jirtle, R.L. (2007) Epigenetic gene regulation: Linking early developmental environment to adult disease. *Reproductive Toxicology*, 23: 297–307.

Fonagy, P., Steele, M., Moran, M., Steele, H. & Higgitt, A. (1991a) Measuring the ghost in the nursery: A summary of the main findings of the Anna Freud Centre–University College London Parent–Child Study. *Bulletin of the Anna Freud Centre*, 14: 115–131.

Fonagy, P., Steele, H. & Steele, M. (1991b) Intergenerational patterns of attachment: Maternal representations during pregnancy and subsequent infant–mother attachments. *Child Development*, 62: 891–905.

Fossella, J.A. & Casey, B.J. (2006) Genes, brain and behaviour: Bridging disciplines. *Cognitive, Affective, & Behavioral Neuroscience*, 6(1): 1–8.

Fraiberg, S.H., Adelson, E. & Shapiro, V. (1975) Ghosts in the nursery. *Journal of the American Academy of Child Psychiatry*, 14: 387–421.

Franklin, R.E. & Gosling, R.G. (1953) Evidence for 2-chain helix in crystalline structure of sodium deoxyribonucleate. *Nature*, 172: 156–157.

Freud, A. (1936) *The ego and the mechanisms of defence*. London: Hogarth Press.

Freud, A. & Burlingham, D. (1942) *Young children in war-time: A year's work in a residential war nursery*. London: George Allen and Unwin.

Freud, A. & Burlingham, D. (1944–1945/1974) *Infants without families and reports on the Hampstead Nurseries 1939–1945*. London: Hogarth Press.

Freud, S. (1905) Fragment of an analysis of a case of hysteria. In J. Strachey (Ed.), *Standard edition of the complete works of Sigmund Freud* (Vol. XVII, pp. 1–124) London: Hogarth Press.

Freud, S. (1909) Analysis of a phobia in a five-year-old boy. In J. Strachey (Ed.), *Standard edition of the complete works of Sigmund Freud* (Vol. X, pp. 1–152). London: Hogarth Press.

Freud, S. (1914) Remembering, repeating and working-through. In J. Strachey (Ed.), *Standard edition of the complete works of Sigmund Freud* (Vol. XII, pp. 147–156). London: Hogarth Press.

Freud, S. (1920) Beyond the pleasure principle. In J. Strachey (Ed.) *Standard edition of the complete works of Sigmund Freud* (Vol. XVIII, pp. 1–64). London: Hogarth Press.

Freud, S. (1940) An outline of psychoanalysis. In J. Strachey (Ed.), *Standard edition of the complete works of Sigmund Freud* (Vol. XXIII, pp. 141–207). London: Hogarth Press.

Gabbard, G.O. (2000) A neurobiological informed perspective on psychotherapy. *British Journal of Psychiatry*, 177: 117–122.

Gabbard, G.O. (2005) Mind, brain and personality disorders. *American Journal of Psychiatry*, 162: 648–655.

Galton, F. (1869) *Hereditary genius*. London: Macmillan.
Galton, F. (1883) *Inquiries into human faculty and its development*. London: Macmillan.
Galton, F. (1889) *Natural inheritance*. London: Macmillan.
Hosak, L. (2007) Role of the COMT gene Val58Met polymorphism in mental disorders: A review. *European Psychiatry*, 20: 1–6.
Jaenisch, R. & Bird, A. (2003) Epigenetic regulation of gene expression: How the genome integrates intrinsic and environmental signals. *Nature Genetics Supplement*, 33: 245–254.
Jensen, P.S. (2000) ADHD: Current concepts on aetiology, pathophysiology and neurobiology. *Child and Adolescent Psychiatric Clinics of North America*, 9(3): 557–572.
Kandel, E.R. (1999) Biology and the future of psychoanalysis: A new intellectual framework for psychiatry revisited. *American Journal of Psychiatry*, 156(4): 505–524.
Kidd, K.K. (1991) Trials and tribulations in the search for gene causing neuropsychiatric disorders. *Social Biology*, 38: 163–196.
Knowlton, L. (2005) Nature versus nurture: How is child psychopathology developed? *Psychiatric Times*, 22(8): 1–5.
Luthar, S.S., Cicchetti, D. & Becker, B. (2000) The construct of resilience: A critical evaluation and guidelines for future work. *Child Development*, 71: 543–562.
Lykken, D. (2006) The mechanism of emergenesis. *Genes, Brain and Behaviour*, 5: 306–310.
Lyons-Ruth, K. & Jacobvitz, D. (1999) Attachment disorganization. In J. Cassidy & P.R. Shaver (Eds.), *Handbook of attachment: Theory, research and clinical applications* (pp. 520–554). New York: Guilford Press.
Manke, B., McGuire, S., Reiss, D., Hetherington, E.M. & Plomin, R. (1995) Genetic contributions to adolescents' extrafamilial social interactions: Teachers, best friends and peers. *Social Development*, 4: 238–256.
Mayes, L.C., Swain, J.E. & Leckman, J.F. (2005) Parental attachment systems: Neural circuits, genes, and experiential contributions to parental engagement. *Clinical Neuroscience Research*, 4(5–6): 301–313.
McGuffin, P., Riley, B. & Plomin, R. (2001) Towards behavioural genomics. *Science*, 291: 1232–1249.
Mendel, J.G. (1866) Versuche über Pflanzenhybriden. *Verhandlungen des naturforschenden Vereines in Brünn*, Bd für das Jahr, 1865: 3–47.
Olds, D., Henderson, C.R., Cole, R., Eckenrode, J., Kitzman, H., Luckey, D. et al. (1998) Long-term effects of nurse home visitation on children's criminal and antisocial behaviour: A 15-year follow-up of a randomized controlled trial. *Journal of the American Medical Association*, 280(14): 1238–1244.
Plomin, R. (1994) Genetic research and identification of environmental influences. *Journal of Child Psychology and Psychiatry*, 35: 817–834.
Reiss, D. & Leve, L.D. (2007) Genetic expression outside the skin: Clues to mechanisms of genotype × environment interaction. *Developmental Psychopathology*, 19(4): 1005–1027.
Repetti, R.L., Taylor, S.E. & Seeman, T.E. (2002) Risky families: Family social environments and the mental and physical health of offspring. *Psychological Bulletin*, 128(2): 330–366.

Rutter, M. (2002) The interplay of nature, nurture and developmental influences: The challenge ahead for mental health. *Archives of General Psychiatry*, 59: 996–1000.

Rutter, M., Bolton, P., Harrington, R., Le Couteur, A., Macdonald, H. & Simonoff, E. (1990a) Genetic factors in child psychiatric disorders – I. A review of research strategies. *Journal of Child Psychology and Psychiatry*, 31: 3–37.

Rutter, M., Macdonald, H., Le Couteur, A., Harrington, R., Bolton, P. & Bailey, A. (1990b) Genetic factors in child psychiatric disorders – II. Empirical findings. *Journal of Child Psychology and Psychiatry*, 31: 39–83.

Rutter, M., Moffit, T.E. & Caspi, A. (2006) Gene–environment interplay and psychoapathology: Multiple varieties but real effects. *Journal of Child Psychology and Psychiatry*, 47: 226–261.

Savitz, J., Solms, M. & Ramesar, R. (2006) The molecular genetics of cognition: Dopamine, COMT and BDNF. *Genes, Brain and Behavior*, 5: 311–328.

Scarr, S. (1992) Developmental theories for the 1990s: Development and individual differences. *Child Development*, 63: 1–19.

Seifer, R., Schiller, M., Sameroff, A.J., Resnick, S. & Riordan, K. (1996) Attachment, maternal sensitivity and infant temperament during the first year of life. *Developmental Psychology*, 32: 12–25.

Slater, E. & Cowie, V. (1971) *The genetics of mental disorders*. London: Oxford University Press.

Spangler, G. & Grossmann, K. (1993) Biobehavioural organisation in securely and insecurely attached infants. *Child Development*, 64: 1439–1450.

Spitz, R. (1945) Hospitalism: An enquiry into the genesis of psychiatric conditions in early childhood. *Psychoanalytic Study of the Child*, 1: 53–73.

Steele, H. & Steele, M. (1994) Intergenerational patterns of attachment. In K. Bartholomew & P. Perlman (Eds.), *Advances in personal relationships* (Vol. 5, pp. 93–120). New York: Jessica Kingsley Publishers.

Stern, D.N. (1998) *The motherhood constellation*. London: Karnac Books.

Suomi, S.J., Delizio, R. & Harlow, H.F. (1976) Social rehabilitation of separation-induced depressive disorders in monkeys. *American Journal of Psychiatry*, 133: 1279–1285.

van den Boom, D. (1994) The influence of temperament and mothering on attachment and exploration: An experimental manipulation of sensitive responsiveness among lower-class mothers and irritable infants. *Child Development*, 65: 1457–1477.

van IJzendoorn, M.H., Schuengel, C. & Bakermans-Kranenburg, M.J. (1999) Disorganized attachment in early childhood: A meta-analysis of precursors, concomitants and sequelae. *Developmental Psychopathology*, 11: 225–249.

Vaughn, B.E. & Bost, K.K. (1999) Attachment and temperament. In J. Cassidy & P.R. Shaver (Eds.), *Handbook of attachment: Theory, research and clinical applications* (pp. 198–225). New York: Guilford Press.

Venter, J.C., Adams, M.A., Myers, E.W., Li, P.W., Mural, R.J., Sutton, G.G. et al. (2001) The sequence of the human genome. *Science*, 291(5507): 1304–1351.

Watson, J.D., Baker, T.A., Bell, S.P., Gann, A., Levine, M. & Losick, R. (2008) *Molecular biology of the gene* (6th ed). Menlo Park, CA: Benjamin Cummings.

Watson, J.D. & Crick, F.H.C. (1953) Molecular structure of nucleic acids. *Nature*, 4356: 737–747.

Chapter 2

Relational trauma and the developing right brain

The neurobiology of broken attachment bonds

Allan N. Schore

Over the past two decades I have integrated ongoing scientific studies and clinical data in order to construct regulation theory, a neuropsychoanalytic model of the development, psychopathogenesis, and treatment of the implicit self. Towards that end, in 2001 I edited an issue of the *Infant Mental Health Journal*, and in it I offered an article, 'The effects of early relational trauma on right brain development, affect regulation, and infant mental health'. In this chapter I build on that work and provide very recent interdisciplinary developmental data that allow for a deeper understanding of the psychological *and* biological effects of early relational trauma. A particular focus will be on current studies of the early developing right brain, the biological substrate of the human unconscious and the site of the highest cortical–subcortical regulatory centers. This interpersonal neurobiological model explicates the mechanisms by which attachment trauma negatively impacts the developmental trajectory of the right brain/mind/body system over the course of the lifespan. Also discussed is the etiology of pathological dissociation, the bottom-line defense of all early-forming severe developmental psychopathologies. Pierre Janet (1889) defined pathological dissociation as a phobia of memories, expressed as excessive or inappropriate physical responses to thought or memories of 'old traumas'. It is now clear that these 'old traumas' specifically refer not just to childhood traumas but also to relational trauma occurring in infancy, the critical period of attachment. This theoretical perspective has direct clinical applications for models of both treatment and prevention.

Developmental interpersonal neurobiology of secure attachment

The essential task of the first year of human life is the creation of a secure attachment bond of emotional communication and interactive regulation between the infant and primary caregiver. There is now agreement that 'learning how to communicate represents perhaps the most important developmental process to take place during infancy' (Papousek & Papousek, 1997), and that 'In one sense we can consider the whole of child development to be the enhancement of self-regulation' (Fonagy & Target, 2002). In line with the essential attachment elements of affect communication and affect regulation, Schore and Schore (2008: 10) now suggest that:

> In line with Bowlby's fundamental goal of the integration of psychological and biological models of human development, the current clinical and experimental focus on how affective bodily-based processes are nonconsciously interactively regulated . . . has shifted attachment theory to a regulation theory.

Secure attachment depends not on the mother's psychobiological attunement with the infant's cognition or behavior, but rather on her regulation of the infant's internal states of arousal, the energetic dimension of the child's affective state. Through nonverbal visual–facial, tactile–gestural, and auditory–prosodic communication, the caregiver and infant learn the rhythmic structure of the other and modify their behavior to fit that structure, thereby co-creating a specifically fitted interaction. During the bodily based affective communications of mutual gaze, the attuned mother synchronizes the spatio-temporal patterning of her exogenous sensory stimulation with the infant's spontaneous expressions of endogenous organismic rhythms. Via this contingent responsivity, the mother appraises the nonverbal expressions of her infant's internal arousal and affective states, regulates them, and communicates them back to the infant. To accomplish this, the sensitive mother must successfully modulate nonoptimal high *or* nonoptimal low levels of stimulation that would induce supra-heightened or extremely low levels of arousal in the infant.

In order to enter into this communication, the mother must be psychobiologically attuned to the dynamic crescendos and decrescendos of the infant's bodily based internal states of autonomic nervous system (ANS) peripheral arousal. Indeed, the intersubjective dialogue between mother and infant consist of signals produced by the autonomic, involuntary nervous system in both parties. The attachment relationship mediates the dyadic regulation of emotion, wherein the mother co-regulates the infant's postnatally developing ANS, and thereby its internal homeostatic state. Also known as the vegetative nervous system (from the Latin *vegetare*, to animate or bring to life), it is responsible for the generation of what Stern (1985) calls vitality affects.

Research now clearly demonstrates that the primary caregiver is not always attuned and optimally mirroring, that there are frequent moments of mis-attunement in the dyad, ruptures of the attachment bond. The disruption of attachment transactions leads to a regulatory failure and an impaired autonomic homeostasis. In this pattern of 'interactive repair' following dyadic misattunement (Tronick, 1989) or 'disruption and repair' (Beebe & Lachmann, 1994), the 'good-enough' caregiver, who induces a stress response through misattunement, in a timely fashion reinvokes a reattunement, a regulation of the infant's negatively charged arousal.

If attachment is the regulation of interactive synchrony, then attachment stress is an asynchrony of psychobiological attunement. In optimal inter-personal contexts, following such stress, a period of re-established synchrony allows the child to recover his/her regulatory equilibrium. Resilience in the face of stress is an ultimate indicator of attachment security. In a secure attachment relationship the regulatory processes of affect synchrony that co-create positive arousal and interactive repair of negative arousal allow for the emergence of efficient self-regulation. These affectively synchronized experiences trigger homeostatic alterations of neuropeptides (oxytocin), neuromodulators (catecholamines), and neurosteroids (cortisol), which are critical to the establishment of social bonds and to brain development (Schore, 1994, 2005; Wismer Fries et al., 2005). Protective and growth-facilitating attachment experiences have long-term effects on the developing hypothalamic–pituitary–adrenocortical (HPA) axis, which plays a central role in the regulation of stress reactivity (Gunnar, 2000). Thus, the evolutionary mechanism of attachment represents the regulation of biological synchron-icity between and within organisms (Schore, 1994; Bradshaw & Schore, 2007).

A large body of studies now support the proposal that the long-enduring regulatory effects of attachment are due to its impact on brain development (Schore, 1994, 2003b, 2009b). Attachment transactions in the first year are occurring when total brain volume is increasing by 101%, and the volume of the subcortical areas by 130% (Knickmeyer et al., 2008). This growth, especially of white matter, is experience-dependent. Fonagy and Target (2005: 334) point out that:

> If the attachment relationship is indeed a major organizer of brain development, as many have accepted and suggested (e.g., Schore, 1994, 2003[a]), then the determinants of attachment relationships are import-ant far beyond the provision of a fundamental sense of safety or security (Bowlby, 1988).

Echoing this in the neuroscience literature, Ziabreva and colleagues (2003: 5334) conclude that:

> the mother functions as a regulator of the socio-emotional environment during early stages of postnatal development . . . subtle emotional regu-latory interactions, which obviously can transiently or permanently alter brain activity levels . . . may play a critical role during the establishment and maintenance of limbic system circuits.

Because the human limbic system myelinates in the first year and a half (Kinney et al., 1988) and the early-maturing right hemisphere (Geschwind

& Galaburda, 1987; Schore, 1994) – which is deeply connected into the limbic system (Tucker, 1992; Gainotti, 2000) – is undergoing a growth spurt at this time, attachment communications specifically impact limbic and cortical areas of the developing right cerebral brain (Cozolino, 2002; Henry, 1993; Schore, 1994, 2000, 2005; Siegel, 1999).

Indeed, in 1997 Chiron and her colleagues published a developmental neurobiological study entitled 'The right brain hemisphere is dominant in human infants'. In subsequent neuropsychological research on emotional lateralization in the second year of life, Schuetze and Reid (2005: 207) stated, 'Although the infant brain was historically reported to be undifferentiated in terms of cerebral lateralisation until 2 years of age, evidence has accumulated indicating that lateralised functions are present much earlier in development'. They further observe 'lateralisation of negative emotional production to the right hemisphere in infants as young as 12 months of age', and 'a developmental enhancement of right hemisphere control of negative emotional expression that is evident by 24 months'. More recently, Howard and Reggia (2007: 112) conclude, 'Earlier maturation of the right hemisphere is supported by both anatomical and imaging evidence'.

In my ongoing work I continue to offer data which indicate that the attachment mechanism is embedded in infant–caregiver right-hemisphere-to-right-hemisphere affective transactions, and that this interpersonal neuro-biological model is supported by a large body of recent developmental research (Schore, 1994, 2000, 2003b, in press). With respect to visual–facial attachment communications, it is now established that the development of the capacity to efficiently process information from faces requires visual input to the right (and not left) hemisphere during infancy (Le Grand et al., 2003). Developmental neuroscience documents that at two months of age, the onset of a critical period during which synaptic connections in the developing occipital cortex are modified by visual experience (Yamada et al., 2000), infants show right hemispheric activation when exposed to a woman's face (Tzourio-Mazoyer et al., 2002). Recent near-infrared spectroscopy research (perhaps the most suitable of all neuroscience techniques applicable to human infants) reveals that specifically the five-month-olds' right hemisphere responds to images of adult female faces (Nakato et al., 2009; Otsuka et al., 2007).

Closer to an interpersonal face-to-face perspective, an electroencephalography (EEG) study by Grossmann et al. (2007) reports that four-month-old infants presented with images of a female face gazing directly ahead show enhanced gamma electrical activity over right prefrontal areas. These authors conclude that the brain mechanisms underlying eye gaze perception show a high degree of specialization early in ontogeny, recruiting areas in the right hemisphere. Other researchers have established that mutual gaze activates face-processing areas of the right hemisphere (Pelphrey et al., 2004).

In terms of tactile–gestural attachment communications, Nagy (2006: 227) demonstrates 'lateralized system for neonatal imitation' and concludes, 'The early advantage of the right hemisphere (Chiron et al., 1997; Schore, 2000; Trevarthen, 2001) in the first few months of life may affect the lateralized appearance of the first imitative gestures'. Sieratzki and Woll (1996) describe the effects of touch on the developing right hemisphere, and assert that the emotional impact of touch is more direct and immediate if an infant is held to the left side of the body. Studies also demonstrate that spontaneous gestures that express feeling states communicated within a dyad activate right hemispheric structures (Gallagher & Frith, 2004). And mirror neuron researchers now contend that developing children rely on a 'right hemisphere-mirroring mechanism – interfacing with the limbic system that processes the meaning of observed or imitated emotion' (Dapretto et al., 2006).

As for auditory–prosodic attachment communications, prosodic processing in three-month-old infants activates the right temporoparietal region (Homae et al., 2006). At 11 months the voice of a woman's child-directed speech (i.e. with somewhat exaggerated prosody) elicits a right-lateralized event-related potential (ERP) (Thierry et al., 2003). According to Bogolepova and Malofeeva (2001: 353):

> The right hemisphere of the neonate is actively involved in the perception of speech melody and the intonations of the voices of mother and surrounding people. The pre-speech stage of child development is characterized by interactions of the descriptive and emotional components due mainly to mechanisms operating within the hemispheres on the principle of non-verbal communication.

And on the other side of the attachment dyad, researchers now describe the mother's processing capacities: 'A number of functions located within the right hemisphere work together to aid monitoring of a baby. As well as emotion and face processing the right hemisphere is also specialized in auditory perception, the perception of intonation, attention, and tactile information' (Bourne & Todd, 2004: 22–23).

This right lateralized system stores a vocabulary of nonverbal affective facial expressions, gestures, and prosody, right brain signals used in implicit attachment communications (see Schore's model of affect regulation and right brain development in Table 2.1). The output of the right hemisphere, 'the emotional brain', is a conscious affect. The highest centers of this hemisphere, especially the orbitofrontal (ventromedial) cortex, the locus of Bowlby's attachment system, act as the brain's most complex affect and stress regulatory system (Schore, 1994, 2003a, 2003b; Sullivan & Gratton, 2002). The organization of dendritic and synaptic networks in the orbitofrontal (and anterior cingulate) cortex, including its connections into the limbic system, are thus dramatically shaped by early relational emotional experience (Schore, 1994; Bock et al., 2008).

Table 2.1 Schore's model of affect regulation and right-brain development

	Infant context	Mother context	Interactive right brain to right brain
RIGHT BRAIN COMMUNICATION PROCESSES			
Visual/Facial			
Regulated response	• Orients, explores, gazes at face of mother and others, seeks eye contact. • Displays bright, wide-eyed facial expressions. • Uses a wide range of affective expressions. • Resting quiet–alert state of pleasant facial expressions.	• Responds (attunes) to infant's cues with variety of affectively expressive facial expressions (eye contact, smiling, pleasant facial expressions).	• Dyadic visual–affective arousal regulation. • Each member of dyad focuses gaze upon the other, engaging in mutual eye contact, smiling, bright facial expressions. • Interpersonal resonance amplifies positive states in both.
Stress response	• During relational stress, transiently avoids orienting, exploring, or gazing at mother's face or engaging in eye contact.	• Flat, absent, fear-inducing, or incongruent facial expressions (laughing when infant is distressed).	• One breaks off mutual gaze and/or eye contact. • Dyad transiently out of sync (misattuned): acute dyadic stress. • Absence or avoidance of eye contact by either mother or infant may be a significant indicator requiring further investigation.
Vocal tone and rhythm			
Regulated response	• Turns towards mother's voice. • Uses inviting/playful tone in response (cooing, babbling).	• Vocalizes soothing responses with varied tones and rhythms. • Modulates tones and rhythms of voice to infant's psychobiological state.	• Dyadic auditory–affective arousal regulation. • Matches or imitates each other's vocal tones and rhythms.

Stress response	• During relational stress, transiently turns away from mother's voice. • Uses distressed tone (crying) in response or is nonresponsive.	• Uses discordant, harsh, loud, or unmodulated tone and rhythm of voice or does not use vocalizations in response to infant's emotional communication. • Does not vocalize or mirror (match) infant's vocalizations.	• One uses discordant tone while the other is silent or both are using distressed or discordant tones. • *Nonresponsivity or turning away from mother's voice may be a significant indicator requiring further investigation.*
Gestural/Postural Regulated response	• Moves limbs and body evenly and fluidly, relaxed posture, reaches and turns toward other or novel social stimulus.	• Approaches to soothe, manipulate, or manoeuver infant gently and cautiously. • Responds to and interprets social bodily based gestures.	• In intimate physical context, dyad's rhythmic matching allows bodies to cradle/mold into other. • In social referencing late in first year, gestures become purposeful and synchronized, promoting intersubjective engagement.
Stress response	• In socially stressed contexts, moves limbs unevenly and/or frantically. • Fails to reach out, averts head, turns body away, stiffens or arches body to mother's touch.	• Approaches infant too quickly or responds to infant in threatening or fearful manner. • Handles awkwardly or roughly. • Misinterprets infant's gestures or does not attempt to soothe, respond, or interpret gestures and body movements.	• Infant continues or increases distressed gestures and postures and is unresponsive to mother's efforts. • Mother increases rough/awkward gestures/postures. • Mother continues to misinterpret infant's gestures/body movements. • Dyad becomes frustrated or ceases/fails to attempt to soothe and comfort interactively.

(Continued overleaf)

Table 2.1 Continued

	Infant context	Mother context	Interactive right brain to right brain
RIGHT BRAIN AFFECT PROCESSING			
Positive affect processing			
Regulated response	• High, positive arousal. • Enjoyment–joy, interest–excitement. • Vitality expressed freely.	• Happy demeanor; responsive to, supportive of, and matching of infant's affect and positive arousal.	• Mutual delight. • Mother or infant leads affective interaction while other follows. • Non-overwhelming and turn-taking behaviors. • Dyadic amplification of positive arousal in relational play.
Stress response	• Hyperaroused/overstimulated or hypoaroused/understimulated.	• Incongruent happy demeanor to infant's distressed cues or sad demeanor to infant's positive cues. • Continues to fail to create regulated, positive arousal stimuli for infant. • Low frequency of play behavior.	• Mismatched (misattuned) arousal states. • One or both hyperaroused/ overstimulated or one is in positive arousal state while the other is hypoaroused/understimulated or hyperaroused/overstimulated. • Overwhelmed dyad.
Negative affect processing			
Regulated response	• Fussy, moody affect expressed freely. • Resilience.	• Able to tolerate and express sadness, anger, fear in self and infant while seeking to interact appropriately. • Participates in interactive repair.	• Mutual attuning to disquieting stimuli or condition.
Stress response	• Withdraws or is nonresponsive or becomes agitated, frustrated, or fearful when experiencing sensations of distress (dysregulated states). • Increasing intensity and duration of either state precludes infant's quick response to soothing attempts and return to regulated state.	• Unable to tolerate own negative feelings and responds inappropriately (expresses anger, irritation, or frustration or withdraws and is nonresponsive toward infant). • Poor capacity for interactive repair.	• Mutual frustration. • Mother cannot or does not soothe infant and repair negative affect: dyad remains in distressed state.

RIGHT BRAIN REGULATION

Interactive regulation	• Expresses and recognizes affective facial expressions, vocalizations, and gestures. • Infant seeks out mother to co-regulate inner state of being.	• Responds with arousal/regulating facial expressions, vocalizations, and gestures. • Mother seeks to affect infant's inner state of being.	• Each member of dyad contingently responds to other's facial expressions, vocalizations, and gestures (right brain to right brain) • Mother and infant interactively seek attunement. • Frequent episodes of interactive play.
Autoregulation	• Self-soothing behaviors (sucks finger/pacifier, rocks body, holds soft object). • Self-created solutions for regulating inner state of being.	• Self-calming behaviors (deep breaths, self-talk). • Mother lets infant struggle with distress briefly and then regulates (assists in autoregulation).	• Each member of dyad remains calm in presence of other. • Each regulates own state of being autonomously.

RIGHT BRAIN DYSREGULATION

Interactive dysregulation	• Averts gaze, becomes agitated by sounds and gestures. • Startles to parent. • Habitually disconnects from mother's attempts to coregulate while inner state escalates. • Sense of safety threatened by interaction.	• Frequent angry, hostile facial expressions, harsh tone and uneven rhythms, threatening gestures. • Does not look at the infant or unresponsive 'dead face.' • Repeatedly fails to respond to infant's affective struggle despite infant's escalating inner distress.	• Mutual arousal dysregulation. • Individually or dyadically ignores cues of other: dyad fails to collaborate in regulating infant's inner need state. • Inconsolable infant may lead to mother's negative feelings toward him/her and diminish mother's confidence in her being a 'good enough' mother.
Autodysregulation	• Crying, arching, flailing, and vomiting; or blank stare, limp, motionless. • Infant repeatedly fails to self-regulate inner state, becoming overwhelmed, eventually exhausted and withdrawn. • Dissociates to maternal stimuli. • Chronic sense of threat or lack of sense of safety.	• Irritable, threatening, intrusive, and rough or flat affect, unresponsive. • Disregards infant's ability to autoregulate by quieting or stimulating self. • Dissociates to infant's stimuli.	• Agitated or withdrawn in presence of other. • Both fail to allow infant to enlarge his/her capacity to self-regulate affect. • No relational or intersubjective context.

Confirming this right-brain-to-right-brain interpersonal neurobiological model, in very recent functional magnetic resonance imaging studies of mother–infant emotional communication Lenzi et al. (2009) offer data 'supporting the theory that the right hemisphere is more involved than the left hemisphere in emotional processing and thus, mothering', and Noriuchi et al. (2008) show activation of the mother's right orbitofrontal cortex during moments of maternal love triggered by viewing a video of her own infant. A near-infrared spectroscopy study of infant–mother attachment at 12 months concludes, 'our results are in agreement with that of Schore (2000) who addressed the importance of the right hemisphere in the attachment system' (Minagawa-Kawai et al., 2009: 289).

At the end of the first year, right cortical–subcortical circuits imprint in implicit–procedural memory, an internal working model of attachment which encodes strategies of affect regulation that nonconsciously guide the individual through interpersonal contexts. This working model generates unconscious 'procedural expectations' of the emotional availability of others during stress (Cortina & Liotti, 2007). Although these expectations are not experienced as left-brain conscious thoughts, they are consciously experienced as subjective right-brain affectively charged, embodied cognitions ('gut feelings'). At all points of the lifespan attachment communications are expressed not in left-brain secondary process but in right-brain primary process cognitions (Dorpat, 2001; Schore & Schore, 2008; Schore, in press).

Attachment neurobiology of relational trauma

Optimal attachment communications directly affect the maturation of the central nervous system (CNS) limbic system that processes and regulates social–emotional stimuli and the autonomic nervous system (ANS) that generates the somatic aspects of emotion. It is important to stress that a growth-facilitating emotional environment is required for a child to develop an internal system that can adaptively regulate arousal and an array of psychobiological states (and thereby affect, cognition, and behavior). The good-enough mother offers her securely-attached infant access to her after a separation; she tends to respond appropriately and promptly to his/her emotional expressions. She also allows high levels of positive affect to be generated during co-shared play states. Such events scaffold and support an expansion of the child's right-brain regulatory coping capacities and underlie the developmental principle that secure attachment is the primary defense against trauma-induced psychopathology.

In contrast to caregivers who foster secure attachment, an abusive or neglectful caregiver not only plays less but also induces enduring negative affect in the child. Such caregivers provide little protection against other environmental impingements, including that of an abusive father. In contexts of relational trauma this caregiver is emotionally inaccessible, given to inappropriate and/or rejecting responses to her infant's expressions of emotions and stress, and provides minimal or unpredictable regulation of the infant's states of over-arousal. Instead, she induces extreme levels of stimulation and arousal (i.e., the very high stimulation of abuse and/or the very low stimulation of neglect). And finally, because she provides no interactive repair, she leaves the infant to endure extremely stressful intense negative states for long periods of time.

There is now extensive evidence that stress is a critical factor that affects social interactions, especially the mother–child interaction (Suter et al., 2007). Overviewing the literature, these researchers report that during stressful life episodes mothers were less sensitive, more irritable, critical and punitive, and showed less warmth and flexibility in interactions with their children. They conclude, 'Overall, stress seems to be a factor that has the power to disrupt parenting practices seriously and results in a lower quality of the mother–child interaction' (Suter et al., 2007: 46). In a review of parenting issues for mothers who manifest chronic stress dysregulation and are diagnosed with borderline personality disorders, Newman and Stevenson (2005: 392) conclude, 'Clearly, this group of women are very fragile and experience high levels of inner turmoil. This distress, often a product of their own experiences of early abuse and attachment disruption in abusive relationships, can be re-enacted with their own infants.'

This re-enactment occurs in episodes of relational trauma (Schore, 2001, 2002, 2009a, 2009b, in press). Interdisciplinary evidence indicates that the infant's psychobiological reaction to severe interpersonal stressors comprises two separate response patterns, hyperarousal and dissociation. Beebe (2000: 436) describes the initial state of 'mutually escalating overarousal' of a disorganized attachment pair:

> Each one escalates the ante, as the infant builds to a frantic distress, may scream, and, in this example, finally throws up. In an escalating over-arousal pattern, even after extreme distress signals from the infant, such as ninety-degree head aversion, arching away . . . or screaming, the mother keeps going.

In the earliest stage of threat, the child's sudden alarm or startle reaction indicates activation of the infant's right hemisphere (Bradley et al., 1996). This, in turn, evokes a sudden increase of the sympathetic branch of the ANS, resulting in significantly elevated heart rate (cardiac acceleration), blood pressure, and respiration. Distress is expressed in crying and then screaming.

The infant's state of 'frantic distress', or fear–terror, is mediated by sympathetic hyperarousal that is expressed in increased secretion of corticotropin releasing factor (CRF) – the brain's major stress hormone. CRF regulates sympathetic catecholamine activity (Brown et al., 1982). Thus, brain adrenaline, noradrenaline, and dopamine levels are significantly ele-vated, creating a hypermetabolic state within the developing brain. In add-ition, there is increased secretion of vasopressin, a hypothalamic neuropeptide that is released when the environment is perceived to be unsafe and chal-lenging (Kvetnansky et al., 1990).

But a second, later forming reaction to relational trauma is dissociation, in which the child disengages from stimuli in the external world – traumatized infants are observed to be 'staring off into space with a glazed look'. Tronick and Weinberg (1997: 66) note that:

> when infants' attempts fail to repair the interaction infants often lose postural control, withdraw, and self-comfort. The disengagement is pro-found even with this short disruption of the mutual regulatory process and break in intersubjectivity. The infant's reaction is reminiscent of the withdrawal of Harlow's isolated monkey or of the infants in institutions observed by Bowlby and Spitz.

Winnicott (1958) holds that a particular failure of the maternal holding environment causes a discontinuity in the baby's need for 'going-on-being'. Kestenberg (1985) refers to dead spots in the infant's subjective experience, an operational definition of dissociation's restriction of consciousness.

The child's dissociation in the midst of terror involves numbing, avoidance, compliance and restricted affect. This parasympathetic-dominant state of conservation–withdrawal occurs in helpless and hopeless stressful situations in which the individual becomes inhibited and strives to avoid attention in order to become 'unseen' (Schore, 1994, 2003a, 2003b). In writings on psy-chic trauma and 'emotional surrender', Anna Freud (1951/1968, 1964/1969) also referred to helplessness, defined as a state of 'disorientation and power-lessness' that the organism experiences in the traumatic moment. This state of metabolic shutdown and cardiac deceleration is a primary regulatory pro-cess that is used throughout the lifespan. In conservation–withdrawal, the stressed individual passively disengages in order 'to conserve energies . . . to foster survival by the risky posture of feigning death, to allow healing of wounds and restitution of depleted resources by immobility' (Powles, 1992: 213). This parasympathetic mechanism mediates the 'profound detachment' (Barach, 1991) of dissociation. If early trauma is experienced as 'psychic catastrophe' (Bion, 1962), then dissociation is a 'detachment from an unbear-able situation' (Mollon, 1996), 'the escape when there is no escape' (Putnam, 1997), 'a last resort defensive strategy' (Dixon, 1998).

The neurobiology of dissociative hypoarousal is different from than of hyperarousal. In this passive state of pain-numbing and pain-blunting, endogenous opiates are elevated. The dorsal vagal complex in the brainstem medulla is activated, which decreases blood pressure, metabolic activity, and heart rate – despite increases in circulating adrenaline. This elevated parasympathetic arousal is a survival strategy that allows the infant to maintain homeostasis in the face of the internal state of sympathetic hyperarousal. It is seldom acknowledged that sympathetic energy-expending hyperarousal *and* parasympathetic energy-conserving hypoarousal are both states of 'extreme emotional arousal'.

Although vagal tone is defined as 'the amount of inhibitory influence on the heart by the parasympathetic nervous system' (Field et al., 1995), it is now known that there are two parasympathetic vagal systems. The late-developing 'mammalian' or 'smart' ventral vagal system in the nucleus ambiguus enables contingent social interactions and secure attachment transactions via the ability to communicate with facial expressions, vocalizations, and gestures. On the other hand, the early developing 'reptilian' or 'vegetative' system in the dorsal motor nucleus of the vagus shuts down metabolic activity during intense social stress, generating immobilization, death feigning, and hiding behaviors (Porges, 1997). As opposed to the mammalian ventral vagal complex that can rapidly regulate cardiac output to foster engagement and disengagement with the social environment, the dorsal vagal complex 'contributes to severe emotional states and may be related to emotional states of "immobilization" such as extreme terror' (Porges, 1997: 75).

There is now agreement that sympathetic nervous system activity manifests in tight engagement with the external environment and a high level of energy mobilization and utilization, while the parasympathetic component drives disengagement from the external environment and utilizes low levels of internal energy (Recordati, 2003). The traumatized infant's sudden switch from high-energy sympathetic hyperarousal to low-energy parasympathetic dissociation is reflected in Porges' (1997: 75) characterization of:

> the sudden and rapid transition from an unsuccessful strategy of struggling requiring massive sympathetic activation to the metabolically conservative immobilized state mimicking death associated with the dorsal vagal complex.

Similarly, Krystal (1988: 114–115) describes the switch from sympathetic hyperaroused terror to parasympathetic hypoaroused hopelessness and helplessness:

> The switch from anxiety to the catatonoid response is the subjective evaluation of the impending danger as one that cannot be avoided or modified. With the perception of fatal helplessness in the face of destructive danger, one surrenders to it.

Whereas the nucleus ambiguus exhibits rapid and transitory patterns (associated with perceptive pain and unpleasantness), the dorsal vagal nucleus exhibits an involuntary and prolonged pattern of vagal outflow. This prolonged dorsal vagal parasympathetic activation explains the lengthy 'void' states that are associated with pathological dissociative detachment (Allen et al., 1999).

Developmental neuropsychology of dissociation

How are the trauma-induced alterations of the developing right brain expressed in the socioemotional behavior of a traumatized toddler? Main and Solomon's (1986) classic study of attachment in traumatized infants revealed a new attachment category, Type D, an insecure–disorganized/disoriented pattern that occurs in 80% of maltreated infants (Carlson et al., 1989) and is associated with prenatal and/or postnatal maternal alcohol or cocaine use (Espinosa et al., 2001). Hesse and Main (1999) note that Type D disorganization and disorientation is phenotypically similar to dissociative states. Main and Solomon (1986) conclude that Type D infants have low stress tolerance and that their disorganization and disorientation indicate that the infant is alarmed by the parent. Because infants inevitably seek the parent when alarmed, these authors assert that frightening parents places infants in an irresolvable bind wherein they cannot approach the mother, shift their attention, or flee. These infants are utterly unable to generate a coherent strategy to actively cope with their frightening parents.

Main and Solomon detail the uniquely bizarre behaviors of 12-month-old Type D infants in the Strange Situation procedure. These infants displayed brief (frequently only 10–30 s) but significant interruptions of organized behavior. At such times, Type D infants may exhibit a contradictory behavior pattern such as 'backing' towards the parent rather than approaching face to face. Main and Solomon (1986: 117) note that:

> The impression in each case was that approach movements were continually being inhibited and held back through simultaneous activation of avoidant tendencies. In most cases, however, proximity-seeking sufficiently 'over-rode' avoidance to permit the increase in physical proximity. Thus, contradictory patterns were activated but were not mutually inhibited.

Maltreated infants exhibit apprehension, confusion, and very rapid shifts of state during the Strange Situation. Main and Solomon (1986: 119) describe the child's entrance into a dissociated state:

> One infant hunched her upper body and shoulders at hearing her mother's call, then broke into extravagant laugh-like screeches with an excited forward movement. Her braying laughter became a cry and distress-face without a new intake of breath as the infant hunched forward. Then suddenly she became silent, blank and dazed.

These behaviors are not restricted to the infant's interactions with the mother. Indeed, the intensity of the baby's dysregulated affective state is often heightened when the infant is exposed to the added stress of an unfamiliar person. At a stranger's entrance, two infants moved away from both mother and stranger to face the wall; another 'leaned forehead against the wall for several seconds, looking back in apparent terror'. These infants exhibit 'behavioral stilling' – that is, 'dazed' behavior and depressed affect, behavioral manifestations of dissociation. One infant 'became for a moment excessively still, staring into space as though completely out of contact with self, environment, and parent'. Another showed 'a dazed facial appearance . . . accompanied by a stilling of all body movement, and sometimes a freezing of limbs which had been in motion'. Yet another 'fell face-down on the floor in a depressed posture prior to separation, stilling all body movements' Guedeney and Fermanian (2001) offer an alarm distress scale that assesses the sustained withdrawal that is associated with disorganized attachment. This withdrawal state is expressed in frozen, absent facial expression, total avoidance of eye contact, immobility, absence of vocalization, absence of relating to others, and the impression that the child is beyond reach.

Dissociation in infants has also been studied with the Still-Face procedure, an experimental paradigm of traumatic neglect. In this procedure, the infant is exposed to a severe relational stressor: the mother maintains eye contact with the infant, but she suddenly inhibits all vocalization and suspends all emotionally expressive facial expressions and gestures. This severe inhibition of nonverbal communication and interactive affect regulation triggers an initial increase of interactive behavior and arousal in the infant. According to Tronick (2004), the infant's confusion and fearfulness at the break in connection is accompanied by the idea that 'this is threatening'. This arousal intensification is ultimately followed by bodily collapse, loss of postural control, withdrawal, gaze aversion, sad facial expression, and self-comforting behavior.

Furthermore, this behavior is accompanied by a 'dissipation of the infant's state of consciousness' and a diminishment of self-organizing abilities that reflect 'disorganization of many of the lower level psychobiological states, such as metabolic systems'. Recall that dissociation, a hypometabolic state, has been defined in the American Psychiatric Association's *Diagnostic and Statistical Manual* as 'a disruption in the usually integrated functions of consciousness' and described as 'a protective activation of altered states of consciousness in reaction to overwhelming psychological trauma' (Loewenstein, 1996). Tronick (2004) suggests that infants who have a history of chronic breaks of connections exhibit an 'extremely pathological state' of emotional apathy. He equates this state with Spitz's concept of hospitalism and Romanian orphans who fail to grow and develop. Such infants ultimately adopt a communication style of 'stay away, don't connect'. This defensive stance is a very early-forming, yet already chronic, pathological dissociation that is associated with loss of ventral vagal activation and dominance of dorsal vagal parasympathetic states.

The Strange Situation and Still-Face biphasic induction of arousal and affect dysregulation occurs in face-to-face communications with the mother. The mother's face is the most potent visual stimulus in the child's world, but it is well known that direct gaze can mediate not only loving but also aggressive messages. Hesse and Main (1999: 511) describe the mother's frightening behavior: 'in non-play contexts, stiff-legged "stalking" of infant on all fours in a hunting posture; exposure of canine tooth accompanied by hissing; deep growls directed at infant'. Thus, during the trauma, the infant is presented with an aggressive expression on the mother's face. The image of this aggressive face and the associated alterations in the infant's bodily state are indelibly imprinted into limbic circuits.

Main and Solomon (1986) document that Type D infants often encounter a second kind of disturbing maternal behavior: a maternal expression of fear–terror. This occurs when the mother withdraws from the infant as though the *infant* were frightening. Indeed, studies show that the caregiver of Type D infants exhibits dissociated, trancelike, and fearful behavior. Current research underscores a link between frightening maternal behavior, dissociation, and disorganized infant attachment (Schuengel et al., 1999). In recent work, Hesse and Main (2006: 320) observe that when the mother enters a dissociative state, a fear alarm state is triggered in the infant. The caregiver's entrance into the dissociative state is expressed as 'parent suddenly completely "freezes" with eyes unmoving, half-lidded, despite nearby movement; parent addresses infant in an "altered" tone with simultaneous voicing and devoicing'. In describing the mother as she submits to the freeze state, they note (321):

> Here the parent appears to have become completely unresponsive to, or even [un]aware of, the external surround, including the physical and verbal behavior of their infant ... we observed one mother who remained seated in an immobilized and uncomfortable position with her hand in the air, blankly staring into space for 50 sec.

In an early history of traumatic attachment the developing infant/toddler is too frequently exposed to a massively misattuning primary caregiver who triggers and does not repair long-lasting intensely dysregulated states. The growth-inhibiting environment of relational trauma generates dense and prolonged levels of negative affect associated with extremely stressful states of hyperarousal and hypoarousal. And so for self-protective purposes it severely restricts its overt expressions of an attachment need for dyadic regulation. The child thus significantly reduces the output of its right-lateralized emotion-processing, limbic–autonomic attachment system. When one is stressed, defensive functions are rapidly initiated that quickly shift the brain from interactive regulatory modes into long-enduring, less complex autoregulatory modes. These patterns are primitive strategies for survival that remain online for long intervals of time, periods in which the developing brain is in a hypometabolic state, detrimental to the substantial amounts of energy required for critical period biosynthetic processes.

During these episodes, the infant is matching the rhythmic structures of the mother's dysregulated states, and this synchronization is registered in the firing patterns of the stress-sensitive cortical and limbic regions of the infant's brain, especially in the right brain which is in a critical period of growth. Infants designated as 'very fearful' at seven months show larger ERPs over the right hemisphere when viewing fearful facial expressions (De Haan et al., 2004). An EEG study of five-month-old infants observes increased theta activity over the right posterior temporal area while they are looking at a blank face (Bazhenova et al., 2007).

It is now established that maternal care influences both the infant's reactivity (Menard et al., 2004) and the infant's defensive responses to threat (Parent et al., 2005). These dyadic processes 'serve as the basis for the transmission of individual differences in stress responses from mother to offspring' (Weaver et al., 2004: 847). Because many mothers suffer from unresolved trauma, their chaotic and dysregulated alterations of state become imprinted into the developing brain and self-system of the child. This intersubjective psychopathogenetic mechanism thus mediates the psychobiological intergenerational transmission of both relational trauma and the dissociative defense against overwhelming and dysregulating affective states. In accord with this model, research now indicates that severe early maternal dysfunction is associated with high dissociation in psychiatric patients (Draijer & Langeland, 1999), and that physical abuse and parental dysfunction on the part of the mother – not the father – is associated with somatoform dissociative symptoms (Roelofs et al., 2002).

From a developmental psychology viewpoint, the profound negative psychological effect of relational trauma (early abuse and neglect) is the generation of a disorganized–disoriented attachment that endures over the later stages of childhood, adolescence and adulthood, and acts as a risk factor for later psychiatric disorders (Schore, 2001, 2002, 2003a). From a developmental neuroscience perspective, the immediate detrimental impact is on the altered metabolic processes that poorly sustain critical period growth of the developing right brain, and the lasting impairment is an immature and functionally limited right-brain capacity to regulate later life stressors that generate intense affect states. Relational traumatic experiences are stored in imagistic procedural memory of the visuospatial right hemisphere (Schiffer et al., 1995), the locus of implicit (Hugdahl, 1995) and autobiographical (Markowitsch et al., 2000) memory. These psychological and biological perspectives converge on a basic developmental principle of regulation theory – that early traumatic sundering of attachment bonds is critical to the genesis

of an enduring predisposition to a variety of early forming severe psychopathologies that characterologically access the auto-regulating, affect-
deadening defense of pathological dissociation.

Enduring effect of relational trauma on right brain development: Impaired emotion processing and pathological dissociation

Neuropsychoanalytic authors now contend that 'If children grow up with
dominant experiences of separation, distress, fear and rage, then they will
go down a bad pathogenic developmental pathway, and it's not just a bad
psychological pathway but a bad neurological pathway' (Watt, 2003: 109).
Current workers in the field of developmental traumatology now agree that
the overwhelming stress of maltreatment in childhood is associated with
adverse influences on not just behavior, but also brain development (de Bellis
et al., 1999), especially the right brain which is dominant for coping with
negative affects (Davidson et al., 1990) and for 'regulating stress- and
emotion-related processes' (Sullivan & Dufresne, 2006). Describing the essential survival functions of this lateralized system, Schutz (2005: 15) notes:

> The right hemisphere operates a distributed network for rapid respond-
> ing to danger and other urgent problems. It preferentially processes
> environmental challenge, stress and pain and manages self-protective
> responses such as avoidance and escape. Emotionality is thus the right
> brain's 'red phone,' compelling the mind to handle urgent matters
> without delay.

In states of pathological dissociation the right brain's 'red phone line' is dead.
The right brain is fundamentally involved in an avoidant defensive mechanism for coping with emotional stress, including the passive survival strategy
of dissociation. These adaptive right brain functions are impaired in histories
of early relational trauma. A large body of psychiatric, psychological,
and neurological studies supports the link between childhood trauma and
pathological dissociation (e.g., Dikel et al., 2003; Diseth, 2005; Liotti, 2004;
Merckelbach & Muris, 2001; Macfie et al., 2001).

Recent neurobiological data can also be utilized to create models of the
psychopathogenetic mechanism by which attachment trauma negatively
impacts right brain development. Adamec and colleagues (2003) report
experimental data that 'implicate neuroplasticity in right hemispheric limbic
circuitry in mediating long-lasting changes in negative affect following brief
but severe stress'. According to Gadea et al. (2005), mild to moderate
negative affective experiences activate the right hemisphere, but an intense
experience 'might interfere with right hemisphere processing, with eventual
damage if some critical point is reached'. This damage is specifically

hyperarousal-induced apoptotic cell death in the hypermetabolic right brain. Thus, via a switch into a hypoarousal, a hypometabolic state allows for cell survival at times of intense excitotoxic stress (Schore, 2001, 2002).

Recall that right cortical areas and their connections with right subcortical structures are in a critical period of growth during early human development. The massive psychobiological stress associated with attachment trauma impairs the development of this system, and sets the stage for the charactero-logical use of right-brain pathological dissociation when encountering later stressors. Converging evidence indicates that early abuse negatively impacts limbic system maturation, producing enduring neurobiological alterations that underlie affective instability, inefficient stress tolerance, memory impairment, and dissociative disturbances. In this manner, traumatic stress in childhood leads to self-modulation of painful affect by directing attention away from internal emotional states (Lane et al., 1997). The right brain, dominant for attention (Raz, 2004) and pain processing (Symonds et al., 2006) thus generates dissociation, a defense by which intense negative affects associated with emotional pain are blocked from consciousness.

Congruent with this developmental model, Spitzer et al. report a trans-cranial magnetic stimulation study of adults and conclude, 'In dissociation-prone individuals, a trauma that is perceived and processed by the right hemisphere will lead to a 'disruption in the usually integrated functions of consciousness' (2004: 168). In functional magnetic resonance imaging research, Lanius et al. (2005) show predominantly right hemispheric acti-vation in psychiatric patients while they are dissociating, and conclude that dissociation, an escape from the overwhelming emotions associated with the traumatic memory, can be interpreted as representing a nonverbal response to the traumatic memory. In the clinical literature, Bromberg (2006) links right-brain trauma to autonomic hyperarousal, 'a chaotic and terrifying flooding of affect that can threaten to overwhelm sanity and imperil psycho-logical survival'. Dissociation is then automatically and immediately triggered as the fundamental defense to the arousal dysregulation of overwhelming affective states.

Both researchers and clinicians are now exploring the evolution of a devel-opmentally impaired regulatory system and provide evidence that prefrontal cortical and limbic areas of the right hemisphere are centrally involved in the deficits in mind and body associated with a pathological dissociative response (Schore, 2002, 2009a, 2009b, in press). This hemisphere, more than the left, is densely reciprocally interconnected with emotion-processing limbic regions, as well as with subcortical areas that generate both the arousal and auto-nomic bodily-based aspects of emotions. Recall, SNS activity is manifest in tight engagement with the external environment and a high level of energy mobilization, while the parasympathetic component drives disengagement from the external environment and utilizes low levels of internal energy. These ANS components are uncoupled for long periods of time in stressful interpersonal experiences in infants, children, adolescents and adults who have histories of attachment trauma, and thus they are expressed in bodily based visceral–somatic disturbances.

Pathological dissociative detachment represents a bottom-line defensive state driven by fear–terror, in which the stressed individual copes by pervasively and diffusely disengaging attention 'from both the *outer and inner* worlds' (Allen et al., 1999: 164, emphasis added). I have suggested that the 'inner world' is more than cognitions, the realm of bodily processes, central components of emotional states (Schore, 1994). Kalsched (2005) describes operations of defensive dissociative processes used by the child during traumatic experience by which 'Affect in the body is severed from its corresponding images in the mind and thereby an unbearably painful meaning is obliterated'. Nijenhuis (2000) asserts that 'somatoform dissociation' is an outcome of early onset traumatization expressed as a lack of integration of sensorimotor experiences, reactions, and functions of the individual's self-representation. Dissociatively detached individuals are not only detached from the environment, but also from the self – their body, their actions, and their sense of identity (Allen et al., 1999). This is expressed as a deficit in the right hemispheric 'corporeal self' (Devinsky, 2000). Crucian et al. (2000) describe 'a dissociation between the emotional evaluation of an event and the physiological reaction to that event, with the process being dependent on intact right hemisphere function'.

In a number of works I have offered interdisciplinary evidence that the implicit self, equated with Freud's system *Ucs*, is located in the right brain (Schore, 1994, 2003a, 2007). The lower subcortical levels of the right brain (the deep unconscious) contain all the major motivational systems (including attachment, fear, sexuality, aggression, etc.) and generate the somatic autonomic expressions and arousal intensities of all emotional states. On the other hand, higher orbitofrontal–limbic levels of the right hemisphere generate a conscious emotional state that expresses the affective output of these motivational systems. In an optimal attachment scenario, this right lateralized hierarchical prefrontal system, the system *Pcs* performs an essential adaptive motivational function – the relatively fluid switching of internal bodily based states in response to changes in the external environment that are nonconsciously appraised to be personally meaningful.

In contrast, relational trauma elicits more than a disruption of conscious cognition and a disorganization of overt behavior; it negatively impacts the early organization of right brain survival mechanisms that operate beneath levels of conscious awareness. Pathological dissociation is manifest in a maladaptive highly defensive rigid, closed self system, one that responds to even low levels of intersubjective stress with parasympathetic dorsal vagal parasympathetic hypoarousal, heart rate deceleration, and passive disengagement. This fragile unconscious system is susceptible to relational stress-induced mind–body metabolic collapse and thereby a loss of energy-dependent synaptic connectivity within the right brain, expressed in a sudden implosion of the implicit self and a rupture of self-continuity. This collapse of the implicit self is signaled by the amplification of the parasympathetic affects of shame and disgust, and by the cognitions of hopelessness and helplessness. Because the right hemisphere mediates the communication and regulation of emotional states, the rupture of intersubjectivity is accompanied by an instant dissipation of safety and trust.

Dissociation thus reflects the inability of the right brain cortical–subcortical implicit self system to adaptively recognize and process external stimuli (exteroceptive information coming from the relational environment) and on a moment-to-moment basis integrate them with internal stimuli (interoceptive information from the body, somatic markers, the 'felt experience'). This failure of integration of the higher right hemisphere with the lower right brain induces an instant collapse of both subjectivity and intersubjectivity. Stressful affects, especially those associated with emotional pain, are thus not experienced in consciousness. Dissociated affect is thus unconscious affect, described by Freud: 'Unconscious ideas continue to exist after repression as actual structures in the system *Ucs*, whereas all that corresponds in that system to unconscious affects is a potential beginning which is prevented from developing' (1915: 178).

At all points of the lifespan, although dissociation represents an effective short-term strategy, it is detrimental to long-term functioning, specifically by preventing exposure to potential right-brain socioemotional attachment object learning experiences embedded in intimate intersubjective contexts that are necessary for emotional growth. The endpoint of chronically experiencing catastrophic states of relational trauma in early life is a progressive impairment of the ability to adjust, take defensive action, or act on one's own behalf, and a blocking of the capacity to register affect and pain, all critical to survival. Clinical research shows pathological dissociation, a primitive defense against overwhelming affects, is a key feature of not only reactive attachment disorder of infants and pediatric maltreatment disorder, but also dissociative identity disorder, posttraumatic stress disorder, psychotic disorders, eating disorders, substance abuse and alcoholism, somatoform disorders and sociopathic and borderline personality disorders.

Psychotherapy with such patients needs to attend to more than the significant dysregulation of affect that characterizes these severe self pathologies. It must also address the early forming defense that blocks these overwhelming affects from reaching consciousness, thereby denying the possibility of interactive regulation and the organization of more complex right-brain stress regulation. Bromberg (2006) observes that in the clinical encounter pathological dissociation acts as an 'early warning system' that anticipates potential affect dysregulation before the trauma arrives. The current paradigm shift from cognition to affect also includes a shift from repression to the survival strategy of dissociation as the major mechanism of psychopathogenesis. It thus represents a major obstacle to the intersubjective change process in all affectively focused psychotherapies (Schore, 2007, in press), and to the effectiveness of early intervention programs, a major theme of this book.

References

Adamec, R.E., Blundell, J. & Burton, P. (2003) Phosphorylated cyclic AMP response element bonding protein expression induced in the periaqueductal gray by predator stress: Its relationship to the stress experience, behaviour, and limbic neural plasticity. *Progress in Neuro-Psychopharmacology & Biological Psychiatry*, 27: 1243–1267.

Allen, J.G., Console, D.A. & Lewis, L. (1999) Dissociative detachment and memory impairment: Reversible amnesia or encoding failure? *Comprehensive Psychiatry*, 40: 160–171.

Barach, P.M.M. (1991) Multiple personality disorder as an attachment disorder. *Dissociation*, 4: 117–123.

Bazhenova, O.V., Stroganova, T.A., Doussard-Roosevelt, J.A., Posikera, I.A. & Porges, S.W. (2007) Physiological responses of 5-month-old infants to smiling and blank faces. *International Journal of Psychophysiology*, 63: 64–76.

Beebe, B. (2000) Coconstructing mother–infant distress: The microsychrony of maternal impingement and infant avoidance in the face-to-face encounter. *Psychoanalytic Inquiry*, 20: 412–440.

Beebe, B. & Lachmann, F.M. (1994) Representations and internalization in infancy: Three principles of salience. *Psychoanalytic Psychology*, 11: 127–165.

Bion, W.R. (1962) *Learning from experience*. London: Heinemann.

Bock, J., Murmu, R.P., Fredman, N., Leshem, M., & Braun, K. (2008) Refinement of dendritic and synaptic networks in the rodent anterior cingulate and orbitofrontal cortex: Critical impact of early and late social experience. *Developmental Neurobiology*, 68: 685–695.

Bogolepova, I.N. & Malofeeva, L.I. (2001) Characteristics of the development of speech motor areas 44 and 45 in the left and right hemispheres of the human brain in early post-natal ontogenesis, *Neuroscience and Behavioural Physiology*, 31: 349–354.

Bourne, V.J. & Todd, B.K. (2004) When left means right: An explanation of the left cradling bias in terms of right hemisphere specializations. *Developmental Science*, 7: 19–24.

Bowlby, J. (1988) *A secure base: Parent–child attachment and healthy human development*. New York: Basic Books.

Bradley, M., Cuthbert, B. N. & Lang, P. J. (1996) Lateralized startle probes in the study of emotion. *Psychophysiology*, 33: 156–161.

Bradshaw, G.A. & Schore, A.N. (2007) How elephants are opening doors: developmental neuroethology, attachment and social context. *Ethology*, 113: 426–436.

Bromberg, P.M. (2006) *Awakening the dreamer: Clinical journeys*. Mahwah, NJ: Analytic Press.

Brown, M.R., Fisher, L.A., Spiess, J., Rivier, C., Rivier, J. & Vale, W. (1982) Corticotropin-releasing factor: Actions on the sympathetic nervous system and metabolism. *Endocrinology*, 111: 928–931.

Carlson, V., Cicchetti, D., Barnett, D. & Braunwald, K. (1989) Disorganized/disoriented attachment relationships in maltreated infants. *Developmental Psychology*, 25: 525–531.

Chiron C., Jambaque, I., Nabbout, R., Lounes, R., Syrota, A. & Dulac, O. (1997) The right brain hemisphere is dominant in human infants. *Brain*, 120: 1057–1065.

Cortina, M. & Liotti, G. (2007) New approaches to understanding unconscious processes: Implicit and explicit memory systems. *International Forum of Psychoanalysis*, 16: 204–212.

Cozolino, L. (2002) *The neuroscience of psychotherapy*. New York: Norton.

Crucian, G.P., Hughes, J.D., Barrett, A.M., Williamson, D.J.G., Bauer, R.M., Bowres, D. et al. (2000) Emotional and physiological responses to false feedback. *Cortex*, 36: 623–647.

Dapretto, M., Davies, M.S., Pfeifer, J.H., Scott, A.A., Sigman, M., Bookheimer, S.Y. et al. (2006) Understanding emotions in others: Mirror neuron dysfunction in children with autism spectrum disorders. *Nature Neuroscience*, 9: 28–31.

Davidson, R.J., Ekman, P., Saron, C., Senulis, J. & Friesen, W.V. (1990) Approach/withdrawal and cerebral asymmetry: 1. Emotional expression and brain physiology. *Journal of Personality and Social Psychology*, 58: 330–341.

de Bellis, M.D., Baum, A.S., Birmaher, B., Keshavan, M.S., Eccard, C.H., Boring, A.M. et al. (1999) Developmental traumatology Part I: Biological stress systems. *Biological Psychiatry*, 45: 1259–1270.

De Haan, M., Belsky, J., Reid, V., Volein, A. & Johnson, M.H. (2004) Maternal personality and infants' neural and visual responsivity to facial expressions of emotion. *Journal of Child Psychology and Psychiatry*, 45: 1209–1218.

Devinsky, O. (2000) Right cerebral hemisphere dominance for a sense of corporeal and emotional self. *Epilepsy & Behaviour*, 1: 60–73.

Dikel, T.N., Fennell, E. & Gilmore, R.L. (2003) Post traumatic stress disorder, dissociation, and sexual abuse history in epileptic nonepileptic seizure patients. *Epilepsy and Behaviour*, 4: 644–650.

Diseth, T.H. (2005) Dissociation in children and adolescents as reaction to trauma – an overview of conceptual issues and neurobiological factors. *Nordic Journal of Psychiatry*, 59: 79–91.

Dixon, A. K. (1998) Ethological strategies for defense in animals and humans: Their role in some psychiatric disorders. *British Journal of Medical Psychology*, 71: 417–445.

Dorpat, T.L. (2001) Primary process communication. *Psychoanalytic Inquiry*, 3: 448–463.

Draijer, N. & Langeland, W. (1999) Childhood trauma and perceived parental dysfunction in the etiology of dissociative symptoms in psychiatric inpatients. *American Journal of Psychiatry*, 156: 379–385.

Espinosa, M., Beckwith, L., Howard, J., Tyler, R. & Swanson, K. (2001) Maternal psychopathology and attachment in toddlers of heavy cocaine-using mothers. *Infant Mental Health Journal*, 22: 316–333.

Field, T., Pickens, J., Fox, N.A., Nawrocki, T. & Gonzalez, J. (1995) Vagal tone in infants of depressed mothers. *Development and Psychopathology*, 7: 227–231.

Fonagy, P. & Target, M. (1997) Attachment and reflective function: Their role in self-organization. *Development and Psychopathology*, 9: 679–700.

Fonagy, P. & Target, M. (2002) Early intervention and the development of self-regulation. *Psychoanalytic Inquiry*, 22: 307–335.

Fonagy, P. & Target, M. (2005) Bridging the transmission gap: An end to an important mystery of attachment research? *Attachment & Human Development*, 7: 333–343.

Freud, A. (1951/1968) Notes on the connection between the states of negativism and psychic surrender. In *The writings of Anna Freud* (Vol. 4, pp. 256–259). New York: International Universities Press.

Freud, A. (1964/1969) Comments on psychic trauma. In *The writings of Anna Freud*, (Vol. 4, pp. 221–241). New York: International Universiites Press.

Freud, S. (1915) The unconscious. *Standard Edition* (Vol. 14, pp. 159–205). London: Hogarth Press, 1957.

Gadea, M., Gomez, C., Gonzalez-Bono, R.E. & Salvador, A. (2005) Increased cortisol and decreased right ear advantage (REA) in dichotic listening following a negative mood induction. *Psychoneuroendocrinology*, 30: 129–138.

Gainotti, G. (2000) Neuropsychological theories of emotion. In J. Borod (Ed.), *The neuropsychology of emotion*. New York: Oxford University Press.

Gallagher, H.L. & Frith, C.D. (2004) Dissociable neural pathways for the perception and recognition of expressive and instrumental gestures. *Neuropsychologia*, 42: 1725–1736.

Geschwind, N. & Galaburda, A. M. (1987) *Cerebral lateralization: Biological mechanisms, associations, and pathology*. Boston: MIT Press.

Grossman, T., Johnson, M.H., Farroni, T. & Csibra, G. (2007) Social perception in the infant brain: Gamma oscillatory activity in response to eye gaze. *Social Cognitive and Affective Neuroscience*, 2: 284–291.

Guedeney, A. & Fermanian, J. (2001) A validity and reliability study of assessment and screening for sustained withdrawal in infancy: The alarm distress scale. *Infant Mental Health Journal*, 22: 559–575.

Gunnar, M.R. (2000) Early adversity and the development of stress reactivity and regulation. In C.A. Nelson (Ed.), *The Minnesota Symposium on Child Psychology: Vol. 31, The effects of early adversity on neurobehavioural development* (pp. 163–200). Mahwah, NJ: Lawrence Erlbaum Associates, Inc.

Henry, J.P. (1993) Psychological and physiological responses to stress: The right hemisphere and the hypothalamo–pituitary–adrenal axis, an inquiry into problems of human bonding. *Integrative Physiological & Behavioural Science*, 28: 369–387.

Hesse, E. & Main, M.M. (1999) Second-generation effects of unresolved trauma in nonmaltreating parents: dissociated, frightened, and threatening parental behaviour. *Psychoanalytic Inquiry*, 19: 481–540.

Hesse, E. & Main, M. (2006) Frightened, threatening, and dissociative parental behavior in low-risk samples: Description, discussion, and interpretations. *Development and Psychopathology*, 18(2): 309–343.

Homae, F., Watanabe, H., Nakano, T., Asakawa, K. & Taga, G. (2006) The right hemisphere of sleeping infants perceives sentential prosody. *Neuroscience Research*, 54: 276–280.

Howard, M.F. & Reggia, J.A. (2007) A theory of the visual system biology underlying development of spatial frequency lateralization. *Brain and Cognition*, 64: 111–123.

Hugdahl, K. (1995) Classical conditioning and implicit learning: The right hemisphere hypothesis. In R. J. Davidson & K. Hugdahl (Eds.), *Brain asymmetry* (pp. 235–267). Cambridge, MA: MIT Press.

Janet, P. (1889) *L'automatisme psychologique*. Paris: Alcan.

Kalsched, D. (2005) Hope versus hopelessness in the psychoanalytic situation and Dante's *Divine Comedy. Spring*, 72: 167–187.

Kestenberg, J. (1985) The flow of empathy and trust between mother and child. In E.J. Anthony & G.H. Pollack (Eds.), *Parental influences in health and disease* (pp. 137–163). Boston: Little, Brown.

Kinney, H.C., Brody, B.A., Kloman, A.S. & Gilles, F.H. (1988) Sequence of central nervous system myelination in human infancy. II. Patterns of myelination in autopsied infants. *Journal of Neuropathology and Experimental Neurology*, 47: 217–234.

Knickmeyer, R.C., Gouttard, S., Kang, C., Evans, D., Wilber, K., Smith, J.K., et al. (2008) A structural MRI study of human brain development from birth to 2 years. *Journal of Neuroscience*, 28: 12176–12182.

Krystal, H. (1988) *Integration and self-healing: Affect–trauma–alexithymia*. Hillsdale, NJ: Analytic Press.

Kvetnansky, R., Jezova, D., Oprsalova, Z., Foldes, O., Michjlovskij, N., Dobrakovova, M. et al. (1990) Regulation of the sympathetic nervous system by circulating vasopressin. In J.C. Porter & D. Jezova (Eds.), *Circulating regulatory factors and neuroendocrine function* (pp. 113–134). New York: Plenum Press.

Lane, R.D., Ahern, G.L., Schwartz, G.E. & Kaszniak, A.W. (1997) Is alexithymia the emotional equivalent of blindsight? *Biological Psychiatry*, 42: 834–844.

Lanius, R.A., Williamson, P.C., Bluhm, R.L., Densmore, M., Boksman, K., Neufeld, R.W.J. et al. (2005) Functional connectivity of dissociative responses in post-traumatic stress disorder: A functional magnetic resonance imaging investigation. *Biological Psychiatry*, 57: 873–884.

Le Grand, R., Mondloch, C., Maurer, D. & Brent, H. P. (2003) Expert face processing requires visual input to the right hemisphere during infancy. *Nature Neuroscience*, 6: 1108–1112.

Lenzi, D., Trentini, C., Pantano, P., Macaluso, E., Iacaboni, M., Lenzi, G.I. et al. (2009) Neural basis of maternal communication and emotional expression processing during infant preverbal stage. *Cerebral Cortex*, 19(5): 1124–1133.

Liotti, G. (2004) Trauma, dissociation, and disorganized attachment: Three strands of a single braid. *Psychotherapy: Theory, Research, Training*, 41: 472–486.

Loewenstein, R.J. (1996) Dissociative amnesia and dissociative fugue. In L.K. Michaelson & W.J. Ray (Eds.), *Handbook of dissociation: Theoretical, empirical, and clinical perspectives* (pp. 307–336) New York: Plenum.

Macfie, J., Cicchetti, D. & Toth, S.L. (2001) Dissociation in maltreated versus nonmaltreated preschool-age children. *Child Abuse & Neglect*, 25: 1253–1267.

Main, M. & Solomon, J. (1986) Discovery of an insecure–disorganized/disoriented attachment pattern: Procedures, findings and implications for the classification of behaviour. In T.B. Brazelton & M.W. Yogman (Eds.), *Affective development in infancy* (pp. 95–124). Norwood, NJ: Ablex.

Markowitsch, H.J., Reinkemeier, A., Kessler, J., Koyuncu, A. & Heiss, W.-D. (2000) Right amygdalar and temperofrontal activation during autobiographical, but not fictitious memory retrieval. *Behavioural Neurology*, 12: 181–190.

Menard, J.L., Champagne, D.L. & Meaney, M.J.P. (2004) Variations of maternal care differentially influence 'fear' reactivity in response to the shock-probe burying test. *Neuroscience*, 129: 297–308.

Merckelbach, H. & Muris, P. (2001) The causal link between self-reported trauma and dissociation: A critical review. *Behaviour Research and Therapy*, 39: 245–254.

Minagawa-Kawai, Y., Matsuoka, S., Dan, I., Naoi, N., Nakamura, K. & Kojima, S. (2009) Prefrontal activation associated with social attachment: Facial–emotion recognition in mothers and infants. *Cerebral Cortex*, 19: 284–292.

Mollon, P. (1996) *Multiple selves, multiple voices: Working with trauma, violation and dissociation*. Chichester, UK: Wiley.

Nagy, E. (2006) From imitation to conversation: The first dialogues with human neonates. *Infant and Child Development*, 15: 223–232.

Nakato, E., Otsuka, Y., Kanazawa, S., Yamaguchi, M.K., Watanabe, S. & Kakiga, R. (2009) When do infants differentiate profile face from frontal face? A near-infrared spectroscopic study. *Human Brain Mapping*, 30: 462–472.

Newman, L. & Stevenson, C. (2005) Parenting and borderline personality disorder. *Clinical Child Psychology and Psychiatry*, 10: 385–394.

Nijenhuis, E.R.S. (2000) Somatoform dissociation: Major symptoms of dissociative disorders. *Journal of Trauma & Dissociation*, 1: 7–32.

Noriuchi, M., Kikuchi, Y. & Senoo, A. (2008) The functional neuroanatomy of maternal love: Mother's response to infant's attachment behaviours. *Biological Psychiatry*, 63: 415–423.

Otsuka, Y., Nakato, E., Kanazawa, S., Yamaguchi, M.K., Watanabe, S. & Kakigi, R. (2007) Neural activation to upright and inverted faces in infants measured by near infrared spectroscopy. *NeuroImage*, 34: 399–406.

Papousek, H. & Papousek, M. (1997) Fragile aspects of early social integration. In L. Murray & P.J. Cooper (Eds.), *Postpartum depression and child development* (pp. 35–53). New York: Guilford Press.

Parent, C., Zhang, T.-Y., Caldji, C., Bagot, R., Champagne, F.A., Pruessner, J. et al. (2005) Maternal care and individual differences in defensive responses. *Current Directions in Psychological Science*, 12: 229–233.

Pelphrey, K.A., Viola, R.J. & McCarthy, G. (2004) When strangers pass: Processing of mutual and averted social gaze in the superior temporal sulcus. *Psychological Science*, 15: 598–603.

Porges, S.W. (1997) Emotion: An evolutionary by-product of the neural regulation of the autonomic nervous system. *Annals of the New York Academy of Sciences*, 807: 62–77.

Powles, W.E. (1992) *Human development and homeostasis*. Madison, CT: International Universities Press.

Putnam, F. W. (1997) *Dissociation in children and adolescents: a developmental perspective*. New York: Guilford Press.

Raz, A. (2004) Anatomy of attentional networks. *Anatomical Record*, 281B: 21–36.

Recordati, G. (2003) A thermodynamic model of the sympathetic and parasympathetic nervous systems. *Autonomic Neuroscience: Basic and Clinical*, 103: 1–12.

Roelofs, K., Keijers, G.P.J., Hoogduin, K.A.L., Naring, G.W.B. & Moene, F.C. (2002) Childhood abuse in patients with conversion disorder. *American Journal of Psychiatry*, 159: 1908–1913.

Schiffer, F., Teicher, M. & Papanicolaou, A. (1995) Evoked potentials evidence for right brain activity during recall of traumatic memories. *Journal of Neuropsychiatry and Clinical Neuroscience*, 7: 169–175.

Schore, A.N. (1994) *Affect regulation and the origin of the self*. Mahwah, NJ: Lawrence Erlbaum Associates, Inc.

Schore, A.N. (2000) Attachment and the regulation of the right brain. *Attachment & Human Development*, 2: 23–47.

Schore, A.N. (2001) The effects of relational trauma on right brain development, affect regulation, and infant mental health. *Infant Mental Health Journal*, 22: 201–269.

Schore, A.N. (2002) Dysregulation of the right brain: A fundamental mechanism of traumatic attachment and the psychopathogenesis of posttraumatic stress disorder. *Australian & New Zealand Journal of Psychiatry*, 36: 9–30.

Schore, A.N. (2003a) *Affect regulation and the repair of the self*. New York: W.W. Norton.

Schore, A.N. (2003b) *Affect dysregulation and disorders of the self*. New York: W.W. Norton.

Schore, A.N. (2005) Attachment, affect regulation, and the developing right brain: Linking developmental neuroscience to pediatrics. *Pediatrics in Review*, 26: 204–211.

Schore, A.N. (2007) Review of *Awakening the dreamer: clinical journeys* by Philip M. Bromberg. *Psychoanalytic Dialogues*, 17: 753–767.

Schore, A.N. (2009a) Attachment trauma and the developing right brain: Origins of pathological dissociation. In P.F. Dell & J.A. O'Neil (Eds.), *Dissociation and the dissociative disorders: DSM-V and Beyond* (pp. 107–141). New York: Routledge.

Schore, A.N. (2009b) Relational trauma and the developing right brain: An interface of psychoanalytic self psychology and neuroscience. *Annals of the New York Academy of Sciences*, 1159: 189–203.

Schore, A.N. (in press) Right brain affect regulation: An essential mechanism of development, trauma, dissociation, and psychotherapy. In D. Fosha, D. Siegel & M. Solomon (Eds.), *The healing power of emotion: Affective neuroscience, development, and clinical practice*. New York: Norton.

Schore, J.R. & Schore, A.N. (2008) Modern attachment theory: The central role of affect regulation in development and treatment. *Clinical Social Work Journal*, 36: 9–20.

Schuengel, C., Bakersmans-Kranenburg, M.J. & Van IJzendoorn, M.H. (1999) Frightening maternal behaviour linking unresolved loss and disorganized infant attachment. *Journal of Consulting and Clinical Psychology*, 67: 54–63.

Schuetze, P. & Reid, H.M. (2005) Emotional lateralization in the second year of life: Evidence from oral asymmetries. *Laterality*, 10: 207–217.

Schutz, L.E. (2005) Broad-perspective perceptual disorder of the right hemisphere. *Neuropsychology Review*, 15: 11–27.

Siegel, A.M. (1996) *Heinz Kohut and the psychology of the self*. London and New York: Routledge.

Siegel, A.M. (1999) *The developing mind: Towards a neurobiology of interpersonal experience*. New York: Guilford Press.

Sieratzki, J.S. & Woll, B. (1996) Why do mothers cradle babies on the left? *The Lancet*, 347: 1746–1748.

Spitzer, C., Wilert, C., Grabe, H.-J., Rizos, T. & Freyberger, H. J. (2004) Dissociation, hemispheric asymmetry, and dysfunction of hemispheric interaction: A transcranial magnetic approach. *Journal of Neuropsychiatry and Clinical Neuroscience*, 16: 163–169.

Stern, D.N. (1985) *The interpersonal world of the infant*. New York: Basic Books.

Sullivan, R.M. & Gratton, A. (2002) Prefrontal cortical regulation of hypothalamic–pituitary–adrenal function in the rat and implications for psychopathology: Side matters. *Psychoneuroendocrinology*, 27: 99–114.

Sullivan, R.M. & Dufresne, M. M. (2006) Mesocortical dopamine and HPA axis regulation: Role of laterality and early environment. *Brain Research*, 1076: 49–59.

Suter, S.E., Huggenberger, H.J. & Schachinger, H. (2007) Cold pressor stress reduces left cradling preference in nulliparous human females. *Stress*, 10: 45–51.

Symonds, L.L., Gordon, N.S., Bixby, J.C. & Mande, M.M. (2006) Right-lateralized pain processing in the human cortex: An fMRI study. *Journal of Neurophysiology*, 95: 3823–3830.

Thierry, G., Vihman, M. & Roberts, M. (2003) Familiar words capture the attention of 11-month-olds in less than 250 ms. *NeuroReport*, 14: 2307–2310.

Trevarthen, C. (2001) The neurobiology of early communication: Intersubjective regulations in human brain development. In A.F. Kalverboer & A. Gramsbergen (Eds.), *Handbook on brain and behaviour in human development* (pp. 841–882). Dordrecht, The Netherlands: Kluwer.

Tronick, E.Z. (1989) Emotions and emotional communication in infants. *American Psychologist*, 44: 112–119.

Tronick, E.Z. (2004) Why is connection with others so critical? Dyadic meaning making, messiness and complexity governed selective processes which co-create and expand individuals' states of consciousness. In J. Nadel & D. Muir (Eds.), *Emotional development*. New York: Oxford University Press.

Tronick, E.Z. & Weinberg, M.K. (1997) Depressed mothers and infants: Failure to form dyadic states of consciousness. In L. Murray & P.J. Cooper (Eds.), *Postpartum depression in child development* (pp. 54–81). New York: Guilford Press.

Tucker, D.M. (1992) Developing emotions and cortical networks. In M.R. Gunnar & C.A. Nelson (Eds.), *Minnesota symposium on child psychology, Vol. 24, Developmental behavioural neuroscience* (pp. 75–128). Mahwah, NJ: Lawrence Erlbaum Associates, Inc.

Tzourio-Mazoyer, N., De Schonen, S., Crivello, F., Reutter, B., Aujard, Y. & Mazoyer, B. (2002) Neural correlates of woman face processing by 2-month-old infants. *NeuroImage*, 15: 454–461.

Watt, D.F. (2003) Psychotherapy in an age of neuroscience: Bridges to affective neuroscience. In J. Corrigall & H. Wilkinson (Eds.), *Revolutionary connections: Psychotherapy and neuroscience* (pp. 79–115). London: Karnac.

Weaver, I.C.G., Cervoni, N., Champagne, F.A., D'Alessio, A.C., Sharma, S., Seckl, J.R. et al. (2004) Epigenetic programming by maternal behaviour. *Nature Neuroscience*, 7: 847–854.

Winnicott, D.W. (1958) The capacity to be alone. *International Journal of Psycho-Analysis*, 39: 416–420.

Wismer Fries, A.B., Ziegler, T.E., Kurian, J.R., Jacoris, S. & Pollak, S.D. (2005) Early experience in humans is associated with changes in neuropeptides critical for regulating social behaviour. *Proceedings of the National Academy of Sciences of the United States of America*, 102: 17237–17240.

Yamada, H., Sadato, N., Konishi, Y., Muramoto, S., Kimura, K., Tanaka, M. et al.

(2000) A milestone for normal development of the infantile brain detected by functional MRI. *Neurology*, 55: 218–223.

Ziabreva, I., Poeggel, G., Schnabel, R. & Braun, K. (2003) Separation-induced receptor changes in the hippocampus and amygdala of *Octodon degus*: Influence of maternal vocalizations. *Journal of Neuroscience*, 23: 5329–5336.

Chapter 3

Trauma in the crucible of the parent–infant relationship

The baby's experience[1]

Judith Woodhead

Parent–infant psychotherapy creates a new relational system that works with the impact of trauma in the crucible of the parent–infant relationship, transforming the baby's intersubjective experience. This chapter portrays a baby's experience of a relational process that arose in parent–infant psychotherapy in the Parent–Infant Project at The Anna Freud Centre, London. The therapy was constructed between the baby, her mother and myself as therapist. The mother, Anna, in her twenties, and her first child – four-month old Nadia – were referred because of worry about their lack of smiling and of mutuality. I was the fifth professional to join their professional network. Later in the chapter I offer a detailed account of my work with Anna and Nadia. But first I offer a summary of some major theoretical ideas that informed my approach.

Relational processes and the development of self

When I first met Anna, she told me that she and her daughter 'were needing/wanting support for both of us in our relationship after really hard times'. I felt there was hope in this expression of need, for Anna was herself naming the relationship as in difficulty, in a context of traumatizing external and internal factors – political, historical, cultural, biological, and psychological. In asking for help with 'our' relationship Anna unknowingly highlighted a feature in this form of therapeutic work. Neither mother nor infant is viewed as the patient. The 'patient' is the relationship that exists between them. Infant and parent are viewed as a system. Winnicott (1957, 1965) was one of the first to view 'mother–infant' as a system – there is no such thing as a baby, only a mother and baby. His work prefigured that of future dynamic systems theorists (initially, Sander, 1962), whose work has current impact on psychoanalytic therapies, especially parent–infant psychotherapy (Schore, 1994; Tronick, 1989; Stolorow, 1997; Stern et al., 1998; Beebe & Lachmann, 2002).

---

1 This chapter is an edited version of a paper originally published as ' "Dialectical process" and "constructive method": Micro-analysis of relational process in an example from parent–infant psychotherapy', *Journal of Analytical Psychology*, 2004, 49: 143–160.

The Process of Change Study Group (Stern et al., 1998) have described in detail the ways in which an infant 'learns' about how to relate with others through the interaction between the mother's mind and the infant's mind – which creates a dyadic state of consciousness. As Tronick (1998: 292) put it:

> Each individual, in this case the infant and mother or the patient and therapist, is a self organizing system that creates his or her own states of consciousness (states of brain organization), which can be expanded into more coherent and complex states in collaboration with another self-organizing system.

I was alert from the beginning to the ways in which Anna and Nadia were co-creating a dyadic system. The therapy catalysed a triadic dimension which became the factor at the core of therapeutic change. The absence of the father in the therapy was a presence, and made my role as third the more important for the relational dynamics that Nadia needed to experience for her development. Therapeutic change in parent–infant psychotherapy depends on new relational experience within the parent–infant–therapist system, available to become structured in implicit memory as a blueprint for relationships throughout life.

Integrating this knowledge of separate memory systems with psychoanalysis and systems theory, The Process of Change Study Group added the concept of 'implicit relational knowing' (Lyons-Ruth, 1998: 284). They described this knowledge of how to be with others as pre-verbal, beyond conscious awareness, part of implicit memory, and thus not accessible by the undoing of repression (1998: 285). Their work described the constituents of relational experience that catalyse the formation of representations. Beebe and Lachmann (2002: 225) suggested that internalization occurs through the way mother and infant (and in this case, therapist):

> continuously construct, elaborate, and represent the emotional regulations, which are simultaneously interactive and self regulatory. The expectation and representation of the dyadic modes of regulation constitute the internal organization.

In other words, internalization takes place through the experience of the co-constructing of relationship; hence the need for my active involvement in this construction process. Applying this to my work with Anna and Nadia, the patterns they were forming with one another were being encoded within Nadia's implicit memory, likely to be played out, outside awareness, throughout her lifetime. Moreover, the urgency of intervening in relational difficulties was underpinned by the research evidence on the impact of traumatic experience on the infant's brain and on its capacity to regulate emotion (Teicher, 2002) and as written in Chapter 2 of this volume. As we shall see, in the early part of the therapy Anna begins to provide Nadia with the kind of support 'that permits the infant to achieve a more complex level of brain organization' (Tronick, 1998: 295).

Another key issue for parent–infant psychotherapy is about identifying what is the fundamental core component in relational process with others that can structure good and adverse relational memories. Winnicott (1949: 204) described the core component as the existence of the baby in the mother's mind, helping the developing infant achieve 'mutual interrelation' of psyche and soma. 'Mentalization' achieved through 'reflective function' and 'affect regulation' (Fonagy et al., 2002) illuminates this process. As we shall see, Anna and Nadia needed support to be able to build affective experience together so that Nadia could experience her self in her mother's mind, perceived through the nuances of affective meaning in Anna's responses to Nadia's vocal, facial and gestural expressions. Nadia needed to come to know over time that her mother has a mind, and that she herself has a mind that she can use and develop throughout her life as a basis for understanding both self and others. The relationship they were struggling with provided the substance for the representations Nadia could form and encode in implicit memory.

Within parent–infant psychotherapy, a new environment (the therapist) is introduced to help mother and infant towards a constructive way of being together, embodied in 'affective dialogue' (Baradon, 2002). Or, as Emde (1999: 317) put it, 'We are not just analysing, reducing, deconstructing and dying. We are integrating, accumulating, constructing and living.' In parent–infant work, the therapist engages with moment-to-moment lived experiences through the creation of 'real relationship', defined as the here-and-now part of the therapeutic relationship when 'the therapist feels a genuineness and immediacy' in the interaction with the patient (Morgan, 1998: 326). This demands that the therapist join in with the patients, fully participant in creating joint experience. The realness also contains the shared experience of each participant in the therapy, which forms a joint history that is unique to them.

These theoretical ideas are illustrated in the rest of this paper, through sequences of clinical material from my work with Anna and Nadia. They show the dyadic process of the mother–infant relationship, the triadic relationship that evolved between mother, infant and therapist, and the impact of the therapy on the construction of new relational experience – a foundation for the formation of different implicit relational representations. The case material is divided into sequences containing nodal points from the first and fourth sessions of the weekly therapy. After each sequence, one possible narrative on the therapeutic process is offered, while emphasizing other narratives that could be created.

Case material

First sequence: The trauma of war, loss and separation

In the extract below I summarize part of the first session where Anna had given permission for the sessions to be routinely video-recorded. This afforded the opportunity to analyse in detail sequences of therapeutic work and transcripts. To objectify the clinical work, in the transcripts that follow I refer to Anna as 'mother', Nadia as 'baby', and myself as 'the therapist'.

> Therapist and mother are seated on large cushions on the floor in the parent–infant therapy room. The baby, sixteen weeks old, is sitting near her mother in her car seat, which is turned away from her mother. In this first session, the baby looks at times towards this new person, the therapist, and glances fleetingly at her mother who speaks rapidly and with urgency. For the first twenty minutes of the session all three are immersed in the trauma expressed within the mother's narrative. Baby and therapist hear the mother's torrent of words, telling of her escape from war, of terrible experiences and their temporary status in England. The therapist asks supportive questions in order to clarify and explore the mother's experience, and makes empathic sounds in response. Traumatic affect fills the room. Mother, baby and therapist seem subsumed under the weight of the mother's suffering, disconnected from one another. The baby makes crying sounds. Next, the mother, speaking very fast, tells of becoming ill after her baby's birth, of emergency hospitalizations and separations from her infant during the first month of her life. She says the baby was said to have cried continuously (or become still and silent) during her first three months and could not be comforted, while her mother cried for her own loss of her family, country, language, and social and political status.

This first sequence set the scene for the therapy sessions that followed. Anna's overwhelmed state – experienced countertransferentially – warned me of her baby's likely mental state, filled with traumatic affect. The stream of affect was embedded in the melodic shape of the words, the pitch of the sounds, the speed of delivery and her mother's facial and bodily expressions of stress, including fast breathing. Nadia gained little maternal response and showed all the classic symptoms of avoidant attachment – pallor, withdrawal, squirmings, arching away, and self-comforting; having to regulate her own emotions, alone in her chair having to cope with being in 'an intensely disruptive psychobiological state that is beyond her immature coping strategies' (Schore, 2001: 209). The drawn expressions on Anna's face seemed to be reflected on Nadia's face. 'The precursor of the mirror is the mother's face. What does the infant see when he looks at his mother? He sees himself'

(Winnicott, 1957:131). This baby was likely to see her mother's preoccupied suffering rather than her (Nadia's) self. Beebe and Lachmann (2002: 37) describe how:

> the mere perception of emotion in the partner creates a resonant emotional state in the perceiver; what an infant perceived on the face of the partner altered his internal state, and the infant could not escape the face of the partner.

Traumatized by her own affects, Anna was not in a position to be able to provide affect mirroring of her baby's mental states. Her past memories and present trauma were, it seems, unwittingly becoming this baby's own present, depriving her of her own separate experience. Equation of Nadia's mental experience with her mother's (Fonagy et al., 2002: 9) suggests that Nadia is likely to experience her mother's traumatic affect as her own, a confusion between what belongs to the self (Nadia) and what belongs to the other (Anna).

In therapy, the baby was not alone with her mother's emotional narrative. She also experienced my presence and could see and hear my responses to her mother's story and their attachment predicament. I tended to speak quickly at first, mirroring the mother's speech, 'entering into the temporal world and feeling state of the other' (Beebe & Lachmann, 2002: 106). Later I spoke more slowly, echoing/affirming Anna's words and experience, at a speed that attempted to slow down the fast thinking, affording mother and baby a different model of communication and emotional regulation, embodied in prosody.

Affect-laden warmth, intensity, and reciprocity in the to-and-fro of face-to-face mother–infant–father affective communication are core aspects of an infant's requirements. It is not just what is said or done; it is how they are said and done. Referring to the lilting musical and emotional quality of motherese, Panksepp (2008: 47–48) states that 'musical affective prosody engages the communicative effort of infants more than any imaginable cognitive–propositional thought' and forms a musical prosodic bridge to the infant's right cerebral hemisphere language development. Meaning, constructed through phonic sounds, intonation and constituent (feet) rhythms, with degrees of intensity, speed, orderliness and shape (Charny, 1965), is formed in implicit memory (Mancia, 2006: 88).

While working with the affects arising within Anna's own personal experience, I aimed to understand and address the mother's verbal and non-verbal ways of relating and to provide and model 'reflective function' (Fonagy et al., 2002) for the mother's thoughts, emotional states, behaviours, attitudes towards her baby. All the evidence suggested that opportunities for new relational experiences needed to be provided urgently, due to the baby's developmental timetable, effect of trauma on brain structure, and impact of dissociative defences on the brain that can 'sever the link between memory systems' (Pally, 2000: 63–64). However, first the baby needed to be able to enter the session, the therapist's mind and the mother's mind. The next sequence from the first session portrays how this happened.

Second sequence: Naming the baby

> The mother looks towards her baby in the baby-chair and says one word, the baby's name, while reaching in her bag for a bottle of milk. The therapist also hears the name, looks at the infant and asks the mother about the name, its pronunciation, its abbreviation, and its cultural origins. The mother responds briefly and factually, affirming the name. She puts the teat of the bottle into the baby's mouth.

In the specific moment of hearing and asking about the name, I (although technically already knowing the baby's name) felt I did not know the name, as if the baby had no personal identity. In this moment, the flow of Anna's narrative was interrupted. The baby's self was named as separate from her mother's self. She was given her own place in the room, the therapy and my mind. A recognition process had taken place between the three (Sander, 2000: 14). Nadia could experience myself and her mother – two people speaking for a moment together, using their minds together, about herself. The interchange between Anna and myself allowed Nadia the possibility of an experience in which she came to know herself as being known by an other, a moment of awareness shared between the three of us. To return to the sequence:

> The baby then cries, struggles, and spits out the teat. The mother replaces the bottle of milk with one filled with water, and holds it at arm's length, and the baby sucks a little. The mother is looking away from the baby, disengaged from the feeding process, caught in the flow of her own thought and feelings. The therapist says softly to the baby, 'Some water – Is that what you might like? Haa? You didn't want to have milk – it's water that you would like?'

In this way, I entered into active engagement with the infant, demonstrating a mind that can think about the baby's experience. Through asking about the water, I signified that Nadia's own thoughts and feelings are different to mine; otherwise the question would be unnecessary. Softness of voice and facial demeanour were attuned to the baby's need for understanding. Witnessed by the mother, Nadia was shown that she can be talked to and related with in new ways, demonstrating that she has her own personal needs and wishes and these can be heard and seen, thought about, named, understood and attended to. Thus Nadia began to find her way into the session, initially into my mind. Later her cries and her gestures would slowly start to become part of her mother's mind as she became more able to give meaning to communications. This newly named baby was becoming, and was recognized as, an active participant in the session, with new agency. With Nadia named as separate, her mother progressed to tell of her anxiety at the possible impact of her thoughts on her baby's mind.

Third sequence: Murderous thoughts

The mother moves on to tell the therapist rapidly, with high anxiety, of thoughts that often come into her mind, thoughts she finds acutely disturbing. The thoughts seem to her to come from nowhere, and overwhelm her mind. The images are of picking up a knife and harming someone, of using the knife to kill her daughter. They are thoughts that to her felt as if they entered her mind with their own will and she can do nothing to keep them at bay except for trying to keep herself busy. Hence she had accessed the support of a psychiatrist and network. With both mother and infant in mind, the therapist explored aloud the murderous thoughts, seeking to clarify them so that she could think about them and their impact on this mother's relationship with her daughter.

In this part of the sequence Anna became less preoccupied with her past. Naming marked a 'moving along' (Stern et al., 1998: 903), a shift from immersion in her own pain to concern for its impact on her daughter who was becoming separately more present. Mother and baby were taking a first step towards the goal (expressed at the outset) of developing their relationship with one another. The theme of the sessions moved on to feeding experiences that implicitly mediate emotional interaction. It became clear that this baby could not accept a bottle of milk from her mother and struggled to accept water. By the fourth session the following sequences evolved.

Fourth sequence: From feeding on the floor to feeding in arms

The mother lays her baby on the mat, and tries to feed her lying down, alternating a bottle of milk with a bottle of water. She does so mechanically with little attempt to communicate. (This had occurred in the previous session and the therapist had felt anxious, unable to intervene, and had consulted with colleagues.) The mother tells the therapist of how often she tries to get milk into Nadia when she is asleep. The therapist feels confused, puzzled, surprised, shocked. She seeks to explore this with the mother and clarify her reasons for this kind of feeding. The mother explains that her baby only takes the bottle lying down, and does not like to be held. The therapist experiences the feeding on the floor as depriving, frustrating, and hopeless. Trusting her feeling that such a detached feeding mode is unhelpful to both, the therapist tentatively comments: 'because I think – if I was lying down, and I was trying to have – liquid – I would find that quite hard'. The mother picks up her baby, her head lagging, places her stiffly on her knee and gives her the bottle of water. The baby will not or cannot latch onto it. The therapist contributes: 'she looks as if she doesn't . . .' and the mother finishes off the sentence with 'yeah, like she doesn't like it'. The mother then tries again to give her the bottle of milk, and the struggles continue. Her mother's vocal tone, facial expression, and way of holding her baby suggest anger, despair and a giving up. The therapist feels that she herself cannot bear this situation. Unbearable affect fills the space. A little later their feeding history is described – how at three weeks the baby lost the breast she loved, due to her mother's hospitalization. During the story Nadia reaches up and places her hand on the side of her mother's breast. Her mother tells of how Nadia was so hungry at that time; the therapist asks if Nadia was crying then and is told she was 'crying, crying'.

Feeding experience became the central 'port of entry' (Stern, 1995) for exploring the relational difficulties. Fearing the mother might feel criticized and find it hard to take in my words, just as her baby found it hard to take in the milk, I placed myself in the baby's position through the words, 'if I was lying down . . .' etc., modelling a capacity for empathizing with and reflecting on Nadia's mental experience. My anxiety was due to concern that both mother and baby would find it difficult to move on from the defensive patterns developed in the feeding relationship which might become part of the baby's representational world.

At first, feeding in arms was indeed difficult. A change took place because instead of complete detachment from one another, the mother was now invited and encouraged to think about the difficulty and try to understand what was happening from the baby's point of view. She took my sentence and completed it, so that a joint thought was created, a cueing process that could develop between Nadia and Anna.

Addressing the past feeding experience evoked a mother–baby shared past that could be reconstructed in the present, the emotions experienced and relational difficulties named. The explanation of hunger ('she was crying, was she?') was expanded and reframed, differentiating somatic (hunger) and emotional responses. The hand to her mother's breast suggested Nadia's own experience of the loss of her mother's breast. Verbalization of their shared loss allowed new thought to come into being. This occurred in the next sequence from the same session.

Fifth sequence: She wants it and she doesn't want it

The baby reaches for the bottles in the bag.

Mother:	She wants it – and she doesn't want it – I don't know – it's just . . .
Therapist:	As we said so you must get upset sometimes – and you're in tears sometimes – and I should think sometimes you get quite angry – don't you?
Mother:	Yeah – I get angry – what's happening, you know, and . . . (*She laughs*)
Therapist:	I bet you do.
Mother:	(*addressing the baby*) And I say this is the milk you know – and I keep telling her – this is the one that you want. (*She brings the bottle out of the bag and holds it in front of her*) You want to, but . . .

She takes off the lid, her baby is making sounds, and at that moment looks back and up at her mother and seems for the first time to gain eye contact, her hand reaching up towards her mother's face. Her mother looks down at her, also with eye contact.

Therapist:	(*in the moment that the baby looks up*) Ahh, she's looking at you.
Mother:	(*to the baby*) It's the milk, yes (*putting the teat to her baby's mouth who pushes it away, pulls it towards her, then pushes it away with a look of disgust*)

The therapist is thinking about how the looking up at her has gone unnoticed – the maternal milk is not being given, and the literal milk is again put to her mouth.

Therapist:	(*to mother*) She really looked up at you just then, didn't she?

The baby is pushing the bottle away and her mother has her head lowered, silent.

Therapist:	And maybe, I am just wondering, and I may be wrong, whether perhaps in the early weeks and when you were so ill and having to go to hospital a lot, maybe you missed out a bit on having that time of her being able to look up at you, the very early baby–mummy time.
Mother:	Yes – my mother you know – my mother she was with her.
Therapist:	And was able to have some of that time with her.
Mother:	Yeah. (*looking sad*)
Therapist:	And it means you two missed out a bit, doesn't it – the two of you because it was a very hard . . .
Mother:	Time for both of us – yeah.
Therapist:	Ill time – hard emotional time.

In this sequence, it seemed that the baby was caught between wanting and not wanting the milk. My engagement with mother and baby was exploratory, inviting Anna to join in elaborating possible feelings between herself and her daughter. Her tone of voice after naming anger at Nadia was affirmatory and relieved. It was at this moment, with anger momentarily expressed and contained, that Nadia looked up at her mother and physically reached up to touch her face. Anna looked down at her but continued her train of thought about the milk, sounding exasperated, unable to respond to Nadia's invitation to look at her and emotionally engage with her. I needed to name the look twice, affirming to Nadia the motivational significance of her attachment-seeking and exploratory action. Still the mother hung her head, perhaps suggesting shame at her anger. Embedded in tentative language and acknowledging that I may be wrong (i.e., that the mother had the knowledge), naming all that they had missed out on in their earliest relationship led to expression of sadness. A new dimension of relational process could then arise – through a shift from wanting the milk to becoming able to want mother.

Sixth sequence: She wants you and she doesn't want you

Mother:	(*looking at her baby*) Say what's wrong?
Therapist:	(to mother) It's almost as though she kind of – and I don't know if this is the right kind of way of putting it at all – but kind of wants you – and doesn't want you, at the same time; would that be a right way of putting it? (*Mother lifts Nadia more in and against her, higher up crooked in her arm*)
Therapist:	I mean – she wants you lots, in playing and everything – she loves playing with you – but it is a little bit like she wants you and she doesn't want you, yeah? And that's a hard feeling isn't it, for both, for both of you. (*Nadia is struggling in her arms, not wanting the bottle – arching back with cries of protest*)
Mother:	(*to her baby*) Are you upset? (*She brings her face round to kiss her and kisses her twice*)

In the above moments, Anna directly asked her baby about what was wrong. I felt that Nadia was caught in her conflict between wanting and not wanting her mother. To speak, in affect-laden words, of how upsetting the conflict was for both of them enabled Anna to empathize with her daughter and ask her a direct question about her feelings – 'Are you upset?' I suggest this would not have been a possible question earlier in the work. A movement had taken place from expression of anger, to sadness, to mutual difficulty, and this allowed affection to enter with kisses. I could then ask in the following sequence, feeling less anxiety, about what would happen if 'we' put the bottle down – 'we' suggesting the mutual process occurring between the three of us.

Seventh sequence: From literal milk to emotional milk

Therapist: What happens without the milk, if we put the milk bottle down – what happens if you talk to her really closely? (*Mother holds her baby sideways*)

Therapist: (*feeling she is speaking to both of them*) Almost kind of looking at each other, holding her towards you a little bit – ah? – Is that a hard thing to do maybe? (*The mother is lifting her baby up and round towards her – and the baby's unhappy expression and struggle changes into growing pleasure*) Like in this sort of little bit of looking. (*Mother speaks to her baby softly and smilingly in her language*)

Therapist: (*addressing the mother*) She is listening to you, isn't she? (*Addressing the baby as she looks at the therapist*) Are you listening to your mum?

A little dialogue between them develops. Nadia again looks at her mother while her mother is looking to where the baby had been looking – also the baby looks directly at the therapist, who responds by speaking directly to her.

Therapist: Your mum is really trying to make contact with you, isn't she?

Mother: (*to her baby*) What are you looking at?

A few moments later the baby moves her face round and almost makes a kissing gesture, and her face continues round to face away and her mother follows her gaze. It seems that the mother is now feeling confident to try being with her baby in this new, supported, way. The sequence continues.

The baby soon makes many sounds and a 'ma' sound while turning more directly towards her mother's face. Her mother says softly, 'yeah', while the therapist also says, 'Yes, it's your mum you are looking at'. The baby's sounds increase in intensity as she brings her hands to hold the sides of her mother's face and their mouths come together and noses squash together – a real sensuous experience, then moving a little round their cheeks squash together. The baby moves away in her avoidant gesture of withdrawal – while her mother follows her with her gaze, lovingly. The baby appears to be expressing anxiety about this new closeness and its safety. She looks towards the therapist, as if to check that the process is safe, then round to her mother again, continuing right round to look the other way, while mother follows her intently, synchronized with her movement unlike earlier in the session. They nuzzle their mouths together. The baby takes a strand of her mother's hair and fingers it. She looks to the side of her mother and her mother looks that way too, and the baby places her hand on her mother's neck, daring to explore her mother physically. The mother then picks her baby up to be on a level with her, facing her. The baby adjusts to the position, initially looking distant, avoidant, and opening her mouth, perhaps a little yawn. The mother says (looking directly into her face), her own face lighting up, 'Whaaah, what a beautiful girl'. The baby now focuses on her mother and an intimate sequence unfolds of a few moments. She again says, 'What a beautiful girl', as she brings her face forward and touches the baby's nose with her nose – twice – and the mother is involved and smiling. The mother says, 'tzik, tzik' and her baby squeals pleasurably. The moment escalates until it becomes a little too much for the baby. She raises her hands above her head and does her circling away gesture. This time her mother follows her round to try to engage with her. Her baby circles back round, almost engaging with her mother's gaze, placing her hand over her mother's mouth – fingers almost in her mouth – making a sound. Her mother is responding with a little sound. The smiles diminish. The baby's body tone slackens, and her mother moves her round to sit on her lap, while continuing to look at her face. The baby is regulating the degree of arousal she can manage, and her mother follows her cue, neither forcing her to continue the sequence nor abandoning her.

An important 'now moment' (Stern et al., 1998) occurred as communicative states were synchronized between the three of us in 'heightened affective moments' (Beebe & Lachmann, 2002: 185). Anna spoke to Nadia in their own mother tongue. I spoke to Anna about Nadia listening to her, and to Nadia about listening to her mother – and the dialogue developed between them while Nadia looked at her mother and also at me. The intimate sequence unfolded with release of sensuous passion, activating the sensual sexual motivational system (Lichtenberg, 1983). Supported by my silent but affective presence, faces, noses, lips, cheeks, skin, hair, and gazing, nuzzling, touching, mouthing, tasting, voicing, evoked a new realm of their own unique intimacy, available for Nadia to construct in implicit memory, a foundation for new relational expectancies (Pally, 2007). Anna was freed to feel (at least for a few moments) that she had a beautiful daughter with whom she could be in love, while Nadia could in those moments find herself, a beautiful little person, in her mother's mind. Then, when Nadia had had sufficient arousal and needed to move on, Anna adjusted accordingly and helped her to resume a sitting position on her lap without withdrawing her own supportive attention. In this new relational situation, Nadia was able to communicate how much intimate exploration she wanted and was agent, supported by Anna, in moving to a more comfortable distance.

Conclusion

The above sequences have portrayed the sensitivity of an infant to the constituents of an intersubjective context. The infant's experience centred on a shift from the impact of overwhelming maternal trauma to an emergence of new patterns of relational responses within the whole system. These patterns emerged from verbalisation of affects but also from their embodiment in the implicit language of gesture, rhythm, tone and bodily experience. The baby made a move towards becoming more of an 'independent center for initiating, organizing and integrating his or her motivation and experience' (Lichtenberg, 1996: 56–57). The provision of a new relational system within therapeutic time and space transformed the impact of trauma and catalysed new relational experience within the crucible of the parent–infant relationship – an experience for the baby of becoming more of an individual self.

References

Baradon, T. (2002) Psychotherapeutic work with parents and infants – psychoanalytic and attachment perspectives. *Attachment and Human Development*, 4(1): 25–38.

Beebe, B. & Lachmann, F.M. (2002) *Infant research and adult treatment*. Hillsdale, NJ: Analytic Press.

Charny, E.J. (1965) *Soundmaking: The acoustic communication of emotion*, by Peter F. Otswald, M.D., Springfield, IL: Charles C. Thomas. *Psychoanalytic Quarterly*, 34: 128–130.

Emde, R. (1999) Moving ahead: Integrating influences of affective processes for development and for psychoanalysis. *International Journal of Psychoanalysis*, 80: 317–339.

Fonagy, P., Gergely, G.E., Jurist, E.L. & Target, M. (2002) *Affect Regulation, Mentalization, and the Development of the self*. New York: Other Press.

Lichtenberg, J.D. (1983) *Psychoanalysis and infant research*. Hillsdale, NJ: Analytic Press/Lawrence Erlbaum Associates, Inc.

Lichtenberg, J.D. (1996). Caregiver–infant, analyst–analysand exchanges: Models of interaction. *Psychoanalytic Inquiry*, 16: 54–66.

Lyons-Ruth, K. (1998) Implicit relational knowing: Its role in development and psychoanalytic treatment. *Infant Mental Health Journal*, 19: 282–291.

Mancia, M. (2006) Implicit memory and early unrepressed unconscious. *International Journal of Psychoanalysis*, 87: 83–103.

Morgan, A.C. (1998) Moving along to things left undone. *Infant Mental Health Journal*, 19: 324–332.

Pally, R. (2000) *The Mind–Brain Relationship*. London: Karnac.

Pally, R. (2007) The predicting brain: Unconscious repetition, conscious reflection and therapeutic change. *International Journal of Psychoanalysis*, 88(4): 861–881.

Panksepp, J. (2008) The power of the word may reside in the power of affect. *Integrative Psychological and Behavioral Science*, 42: 47–55.

Sander, L. (1962) Issues in early mother child interaction. *Journal of American Academy of Child Psychiatry*, 1: 141–166.

Sander, L. (2000) Where are we going in the field of infant mental health? *Infant Mental Health Journal*, 21: 5–20.

Schore, A.N. (1994) *Affect regulation and the origin of the self: The neurobiology of emotional development*. Hillsdale, NJ: Lawrence Erlbaum Associates, Inc.

Schore, A. N. (2001) The effects of early relational trauma on right brain development, affect regulation, and infant mental health. *Infant Mental Health Journal*, 22(1–2): 201–269.

Stern, D. (1994) One way to build a clinically relevant baby. *Infant Mental Health Journal*, 15: 36–54.

Stern, D. (1995) *The motherhood constellation*, London: Karnac.

Stern, D.N., Sander, L.W., Nahum, J.P., Harrison, A.M., Lyons-Ruth, K., Morgan, A.C. et al. (1998) Non-interpretive mechanisms in psychoanalytic therapy: The something more than interpretation. *International Journal of Psychoanalysis*, 79: 903–921.

Stolorow, R. (1997) Dynamic, dyadic, intersubjective systems: An evolving paradigm for psychoanalysis. *Psychoanalytic Psychology*, 14: 337–346.

Teicher, M. (2002) Scars that won't heal: The neurobiology of child abuse. *Scientific American*, March: 54–61.

Tronick, E. (1989) Emotions and emotional communication in infants. *American Psychologist*, 44: 112–119.

Tronick, E. (1998) Dyadically expanded states of consciousness and the process of therapeutic change. *Infant Mental Health Journal*, 19: 290–299.

Winnicott, D.W. (1949) Mind and its relation to the psyche–soma. *British Journal of Medicine and Psychology*, 27: 201–209.

Winnicott, D.W. (1957) *The child and the family*. London: Tavistock.

Winnicott, D.W. (1965) The theory of the parent infant relationship. In *The maturation process and the facilitating environment: Studies in the theory of emotional development*. London: Karnac.

Chapter 4

Infantile psychosomatic integrity and maternal trauma

Angela Joyce

Rozie is the only child of her refugee mother Nazneem. At five months she developed epilepsy. I first met her mother seven months previously. She had arrived in the UK an illegal immigrant, heavily pregnant. Her story was that in the early weeks of her pregnancy she had been arrested in her country of origin and raped. She was still overwhelmed, and in her account she repeatedly told me 'They raped me, they raped my baby'.

The purpose of this paper is to examine some of the possible consequences for the developing infant of traumatised maternal states of mind that interfere with the mother's capacity to adapt to her infant. Using my parent–infant psychotherapy work with this refugee mother and her baby, I will explore how this baby's developing psychosomatic integrity was disrupted by the coincidence of her own bodily vulnerability and her mother's traumatised and traumatising mental states.

Among the paediatrician and psychoanalyst Donald Winnicott's most profound explorations is his theorising about the earliest infantile mind. He emphasised the baby's absolute dependency on the presence of the adaptive mother in her state of primary maternal preoccupation (Winnicott, 1956). As a development of Winnicott's ideas we could say that in the earliest times the mother and baby exist in a paradoxical dyadic potential space where oneness and twoness coexist (Lee, 1997; Joyce, 2002). This dyadic potential space of separateness and merger is characterised by 'an absence of a sense of boundaries, a lack of real-world constraints and a potentially infinite, free flow of images and ideas' (Lee, 1997). It is of paramount importance that the paradox is held and not resolved. I propose that this paradox of duality and unity is essentially psychosomatic. From pregnancy and for some time afterwards the nursing couple are to all intents and purposes one, as well as also being separate. The very young baby, supported in the state of 'illusion', has created all s/he experiences, encompasses it and yet is separate; and from the mother's point of view, the baby who has been growing inside her for nine months is part of her in terms of her feeling, a part of her body image (James, 1962), and yet they are two bodies. This is the matrix out of which the baby's separate unique being emerges. If this paradox of separateness and merger is 'resolved' (Winnicott, 1971), for example when the infant is prematurely faced with his or her separateness (as when s/he falls out of the mother's mind) or indeed when the phantasy of oneness and merger is too real, then it collapses and with it, from this perspective, a crucial ingredient of what Winnicott called the infant/environment set-up that sustains ongoing psychic development.

Early psychosomatic processes

Freud's view was that first of all the ego was a body ego (Freud, 1923). He meant by this that at source the ego ultimately derives from bodily sensations, chiefly from those at the surface of the body (Freud, 1923: 26). The baby's bodily sensations are related to the sensitivity of care from the mother, and thus we can see that from a Freudian perspective the building blocks of the ego are from the outset connected to the nature of infant care. Winnicott took Freud's thinking to another level, that of the processes by which the infant comes to have a subjective sense of self, integrating body, psyche (by which he means the imaginative elaboration of the body), and mind (close to Freud's ego, the capacity for thought and adaptation) (Winnicott, 1947). Winnicott (1945) called these processes 'personalisation'. This complex picture involves the mother's adaptations, nearly absolute at the beginning, and her necessary but graduated 'failure' over time, employing her mind, body and psyche. The mother's holding and handling functions (Winnicott, 1956, 1960) are body-based but also contain her imaginative elaboration of her and her infant's experiences, and her capacity to think about and adapt to her baby's needs. From the baby's point of view this is all on loan, as it were, so that the baby has a strong ego . . . or not. We see here how linked are the mother and baby's body, psyche and mind.

This distinction between mind and psyche is crucial in Winnicott's thinking (Winnicott, 1947). If the baby has to take account of his mother and her mental states too early, that is if the mother's inevitable failures are too great and impinge too much and too early so that the baby has to adapt to her, then his mind part will be called into operation precociously (James, 1960). The baby's mind takes over the mother's functions of thinking and adaptation (one could say this is the origin of a child becoming 'parentified', reversing the looking-after role), threatening to rupture the unfolding of the psyche which in this sense is the elaboration of fantasy and imagination, rooted in bodily processes. We might ask then what the fate of the soma is when the psyche has been hijacked by the precocious mind. At this bodily level, I suggest, it is the emotional realm that is privileged. The baby registers and evaluates his perceptions in emotional terms: is something pleasurable or not; is something frightening or not? The baby also feels these emotions in the body in quantitative terms: surges of pleasure or unpleasure that require modulation. Young babies are unable to do this for themselves. They need an adapting, regulating other to help them manage these surges of emotion that otherwise threaten to overwhelm. If they do not have this other, or the other's capacities are impaired, at a bodily level babies show the consequences: they become distressed, scream, yell, thrash about, or if this does not work (either to bring this needed other or to calm themselves down), they still, quiet, immobilise, perhaps fall asleep for long periods or find other ways of being cut off or in dissociated states. There is much research evidence now for the long-term consequences of infants being left in prolonged states of unmitigated distress (Perry et al., 1995; Schore, 2001). My purpose in describing it here is to emphasise the predicament of the young infant whose parental other is unable to help them in these ways.

So what is this situation when the infant/environment set-up is undermined by disruptive disturbances in the parents? The human environment is of course idiosyncratic and is required to be so for the infant to become human with all its non-mechanical qualities. And infants come with their own strengths and vulnerabilities. But in circumstances where the parents are struggling with their own damaged histories or in current situations perhaps of disturbed states of mind for various reasons, their capacities to put the baby at the forefront of their concerns is often severely compromised.

Clinically and with the lens of developmental research (Beebe, 2004) we can observe how the baby co-creates with his mother (usually) the relational environment characterised by this paradox of oneness and twoness; merger and separateness. In those situations that are not 'good enough', likely where the parents' own functioning is disrupted, the baby has to contend with these impingements, elements of the relational environment that do not support his alive contribution. Winnicott (1986: 12) wrote that:

> Psychosomatic existence is an achievement and although its basis is an inherited growth tendency it cannot become a fact without the active participation of a human being who is holding and handling the baby. A breakdown in this area has to do with all the difficulties affecting bodily health which actually stem from uncertainty in personality structure.

Increasingly in our work we see how babies and parents are sometimes, wittingly or not, engaged in what amounts to relational trauma, perhaps similar to what Masud Khan (1963) called 'cumulative trauma'.

Clinical case

I will now turn to the clinical case that prompted me to think about these issues. Rozie's physical vulnerability emerged when she was five months old. The MRI scan revealed a lesion in her left temporal lobe which at first was thought to be an infection, then later a structural abnormality, but which when examined a year later with another MRI scan was no longer present.

Her consultant neurodevelopmental paediatrician said that Rozie's epilepsy was difficult to understand, that it was not a usual case and had not been clear from the start. Rozie's symptoms of epilepsy were described by her mother as being 'long moments of absence' in which she seemed to be not responsive and from which she would emerge and then sleep for a long time. I will argue that these *petit mal*-type seizures arose in the context of this mother's mental states being overwhelmed such that her growing capacity to provide the holding environment for her daughter was ruptured from time to time. In this space already compromised by trauma, Rozie was unable either to bear her mother's unpredictable states of mind or to continue her precocious adaptation to them. Instead her psychosomatic integrity was endangered and in *her* most overwhelmed states she fell into what amounted to dissociated states, a refuge from and expression of trauma. I will link this with my view that the paradoxical dyadic potential space variously collapsed in both directions: towards both separateness and merger, with potentially disastrous consequences for Rozie's ongoing development.

Nazneem had arrived in the UK heavily pregnant, an illegal immigrant. She was married in her country of origin to a political activist who had been arrested many times; he and then she were arrested. The week before they had discovered to their joy that she was pregnant with their first child; this was a planned, lovingly anticipated pregnancy. In the police station Nazneem was raped repeatedly. She managed to escape but her family was horrified and her mother was reported to have said that she wished Nazneem had died rather than having been raped. Nazneem was shunned as an object of shame and humiliation for this westernised family, who believed that the baby was not her husband's, but the outcome of the rape. She meanwhile knew nothing of her husband's fate. Several months later her father paid for her to be illegally transported to Europe, refusing to do anything to help her find her husband because of the rape. She arrived in the United Kingdom with just a phone number of a male friend whom she had known at home.

I saw Nazneem weekly for the last six weeks of her pregnancy. Initially all the aspects of the trauma – the rape, the disappearance of the husband, the rejection by the parents, the loss of her country of origin and her life and friends there – had been condensed into the fact of the rape. She felt overwhelmingly soiled by it and veered between feeling guilty but also helpless and psychically obliterated, as was any pleasure in her anticipation of her baby. She hated being pregnant and she had no feelings for her baby. She was deeply disturbed by this, afraid that she would not be able to connect with her baby. She dimly remembered having had a sense of a baby whom she looked forward to mothering, but that had been lost and she was overwhelmed by her family's sense of shame, recrimination and rejection. She thought that if her husband was to return he also might respond to her in that way, and want nothing to do with her because of the rape. She felt alone, cruelly abandoned and frighteningly persecuted by a recurring thought that in her rape, the baby was also raped. 'It has been the hardest time in my life, on my own, he not with me; I can't erase in my mind, they raped me, they raped my baby'. She was in a state of 'post-traumatic stress', constantly experiencing flashbacks, depressed and anxious, full of self-loathing, recrimination and blame for what had happened and barely defending against suicidal wishes. The earliest mother–infant psychosomatic unity was grossly distorted by the trauma, such that Nazneem believed there to be no difference between her and her daughter in her fantasy of them both being raped. Following Winnicott we could say that the paradox of unity and separateness was 'resolved' or collapsed, and that way lay the basis for the failure of integration that would manifest itself as the fragmentation of soma, psyche and mind.

When Rozie was born the impact of Nazneem's traumatised state of mind was immediately apparent, but also her capacity to find and use help. She didn't want to touch the baby, felt ashamed for her lack of loving feelings and guilty that this worsened her daughter's bad luck. She had however felt helped by one particular midwife who supported her in getting breastfeeding started. From this early beginning this mother was alert to her daughter's propensity to be affected by her own states. This was a persecution to her as when she believed there was no difference between them, but also an incentive to be a better mother for her daughter. Nazneem gave me the impression as her therapist that I was to be included from the beginning in this process of creating something better as she spoke softly to Rozie introducing me to her, telling her my name. This was a central feature of our work as I was promoted as a central figure for Rozie. It has many facets, not least having the function of my being the 'third' for both of them in the absence of Rozie's father; also a grandmother figure (Stern, 1995), representative of the lost past and extended family in her country of origin; but also sometimes a primary object in Nazneem's place when she was at her most crushed and vulnerable. This transference was multifaceted as the lost objects were imbued with various feelings; the judgemental, rejecting aspects for a long time were hidden behind an idealising sense for Nazneem of having been rescued by me. I have to say that countertransferentially I also struggled with hugely strong impulses to really rescue, take home with me, and provide a home for this baby and her mother.

In spite of Nazneem's poor self-care in pregnancy, Rozie weighed eight and a half pounds at birth and fed well from the beginning; she was able to take from her mother what she needed even in these inauspicious circumstances. But right from the beginning this mother saw her baby in complex and contradictory ways: she was unlucky to have Nazneem as a mother; Rozie's ordinary baby ways of being evoked the recent past and her cries were intolerable as they were woven into the continuing intrusion of flashbacks to the rape. It took Nazneem back to her own cries and the overwhelming reality of her helplessness, connected with Rozie, whom she believed to have experienced the same thing then. She understood that Rozie's cries were *her* own memories of what happened; that her daughter had really felt the same thing as she had done. Working with Nazneem's fear that what she had to give Rozie had been obliterated, I was the one who held in mind the fact that Rozie had nevertheless grown well inside her.

Nazneem struggled with Rozie's helplessness and her ordinary infantile dependency. Baby Rozie's vulnerability linked in too much to Nazneem's own, in relation to the experience of the actual traumatic events but also her ongoing feeling of helplessness. Just three weeks after Rozie's birth Nazneem announced that she was 'growing up'. She described how Rozie 'understands when I don't feel well, she sleeps more, doesn't make trouble, is quiet and doesn't make me tired . . . my breast makes her happy'. This indicated Nazneem's need for her baby to adapt to her prematurely. At the same time it was an expression of her satisfaction that her baby could be happy with what she got from her. However, the 'happy' was too mixed with Nazneem's relief that Rozie's need of her was assuaged and put to sleep.

A pattern emerged in the sessions of Rozie sleeping for much of the first part and of Nazneem, after placing her gently on the mat, withdrawing slightly. She would talk to me in an extremely soft voice about her preoccupations consequent on the trauma and her subsequent rejection by her family; but also the accruing small pleasures of being Rozie's mother as well as her pity for Rozie, not deserving to be born to someone in these awful circumstances. After about half an hour Rozie would wake and Nazneem's anxiety would palpably rise, expressed in the panicked tone of her voice, very anxious that Rozie would cry. Even whimpering seemed too much and the breast would be offered immediately. I would feel the immediate tension and its calming when Rozie took the breast and fed – almost but not quite as if the breast was being used as a dummy to quieten her. At the end of the feed Rozie would be returned to the floor, perhaps propelled by a sense that Nazneem's own contaminated body would contaminate her baby's. Identifying with the baby I would sometimes speak for her, voicing her need for closeness and longing to be in her mother's arms. Nazneem was very responsive and often would take Rozie back in her arms – suggesting that she needed my faith in her capacities, and in her goodness from which Rozie would benefit, before she could feel it in herself.

It was clear that the environmental set-up that held Rozie was severely impaired. Nazneem was both traumatised and isolated, lacking a husband/father to hold and protect her with Rozie, although her male friend did provide some important support. Despite her responsiveness to my interventions she often found it exceedingly difficult to sustain her emotional availability to her daughter when struggling with thoughts and feelings that erupted in her mind. In other ways Nazneem seemed to be finding herself as the good mother she had lost in the trauma. She was very soft and gentle with Rozie, speaking to her in a low voice with Rozie responsive, smiling and gazing but oddly quiet. The picture was mixed and I was concerned that

Rozie knew that her mother couldn't bear her cries and so was quiet. There seemed an injunction against crying because of its capacity to stir up unbearable associations and feelings in Nazneem. The silent baby is common in situations of trauma. Babies seem to learn very early that their cries cannot be tolerated, and we can misinterpret this as the baby being all right rather than silent and suffering.

At four months old I wrote in my process notes that Rozie

> drops from her mother's mind for a short while, although she is never so far away that Rozie becomes overtly distressed. Instead what happens is that Rozie stills and gazes at her mother, stopping the play with the rattle. She tentatively smiles or moves her limbs, seemingly to enliven the space with her mother. At other times Nazneem is much more interactive and Rozie is engaged playfully and smiling or not at her mother. She gurgles and makes other sounds. These are two quite distinct ways she has of being with her mother.

Later in that session I observed Rozie again looking at her solemnly as her mother told me of a telephone conversation with her husband's sister. I drew her attention to Rozie's gaze and Nazneem talked about how she felt so stirred up emotionally and in her body when she talked or thought of these things; she was afraid that Rozie picked up her feelings. She tried to distance herself in these circumstances here and at home, and we acknowledged then that Rozie sensed her absence. I talked directly to Rozie about her mummy seeming to go away and that she knew and was worried about this. After this Nazneem seemed to be more present and responsive in the session, albeit in a strained way.

Nazneem and Rozie were very responsive to these early interventions and the potential for a more benign circle seemed to be becoming established. Into this, however, came intrusions from the external environment that amounted to re-traumatisations, which put further pressure on this mother–infant couple, and repeatedly put their hard-won gains to the test. The first of these came as the news that her husband was dead, allegedly by suicide in prison but Nazneem thought murdered by the police. In the following sessions, when Rozie was just three months old, I noted that Rozie was awake and much livelier than I had previously seen her. It seemed she had made a developmental leap – reaching out and grasping a rattle and bringing it to her mouth. She moved her body more, kicking and moving, and I wondered to myself if this was in part a reaction to her mother's state of mind; in fact at one point Nazneem said that Rozie was now looking after her, but she felt worried about this. She was desolate and tearful but tried very hard to keep Rozie in mind, holding her and feeding her. However, she said she felt that she wasn't a good mother who played with her baby; Rozie had to do that for herself. This reinforced my sense of the precocity of Rozie's motor developmental move at this point, and the shift into becoming a 'parentified' baby – who looks after the adult – may help us understand something of the complicated, over-determined nature of Rozie's epilepsy.

The second re-traumatising event some weeks later was a further concrete rejection of Rozie and Nazneem, this time by a member of her husband's family; his sister told Nazneem that she held her responsible for the husband's death, and did not believe Rozie was her family. In a confused and confusing way Nazneem said to me: 'They believe you are not our baby'. She said 'Being raped made me nothing in their eyes', evidently connecting with her own sense that she was nothing. She was terrified and repeated many times her fear that Rozie would treat her in this way when she would eventually be told of the circumstances of her earliest pre-natal life. Nazneem was surrounded by people who voiced her own persecuting self-accusations.

This was the immediate context of Rozie's first symptoms of epilepsy. She had her first fits the week following the above events, when Nazneem was consumed by the resurgence of her post-traumatic symptoms. For the next five months Rozie had many fits which were like 'long moments of absence' and was hospitalised several times. They reached a climax during my summer break and then did not recur until the following spring, when her mother once again experienced further trauma related to her family's rejection. I never saw Rozie in these states; we can think about how the therapeutic function of 'holding' (Winnicott, 1960) the paradox of separateness and merger enabled this baby and her mother at least in the parent–infant sessions to be together in ways such that Rozie did not have to collapse into the dissociative defence of an epileptic state. It could be said that as therapist I became an auxiliary parental figure to both Rozie and her mother, which enabled this to be the case.

Discussion

In my clinical description I have concentrated on the unfolding infant–environment set-up (Winnicott, 1960) to contextualise the development of Rozie's 'unusual case' of epilepsy. It is significant to note that each occurrence of Rozie's symptoms took place in the times when her mother's mental states were most fragmented. At these times trauma led to the collapse of the integration of her mental processes so that Nazneem was unable to discern the difference between present and past reality, and the affective meaning of the trauma overwhelmed her. In these states, she could not emotionally attend to her daughter or be the holding, modulating, regulating other to help Rozie manage her own emotional states engendered by her mother's states: Rozie was lost from her mother's mind. From Rozie's point of view she had lost her mother through a premature and rupturing separateness at these times.

Using this case we can consider how the impingements on the baby consequent on the collapse of the paradox of dyadic potential space (including Nazneem's extreme fantasy of psychosomatic unity with Rozie, and its oscillating opposite of Rozie seemingly falling from her mother's mind) are likely to be observable in different ways, including at the bodily level. Some infants become apparently self-sufficient, privileging separateness, turning away from the mothering person, at its extreme cut off from the world of relating that may manifest itself as psychogenic autism (Tustin, 1981). In the direction of merger the baby may collapse into a state of undifferentiation and not be able to manage even the slightest separation, extremely clingy or unable to move from full dependency into relative independence. Others may precociously develop their minds and have quite fractured internal worlds with fundamental splits between their bodies, minds and psyches. Rozie was at risk of all these solutions. I worked actively with her oscillating attempts at managing the ongoing impingements, seeking to understand and verbalising the processes I observed happening in the room: she had adapted to her mother's fantasy of undifferentiation ('they raped me, they raped my baby', the sameness of her baby cries as her own) by becoming very quiet; she precociously scrutinised her mother's emotion-laden face and turned away. I observed the precocity of her motor development at twelve weeks following her mother's reaction to the news of the death of her husband.

It was in the aftermath of the news of the father's death and the rejection, again, by his family that this mother–infant pair was put under the strongest pressures that threatened breakdown. Although there was much to be concerned about previously, they had been responding and using the therapeutic set-up very well. Now in the re-traumatising context, the psychosomatic duality/unity of mother and baby collapsed in the direction of separateness (the dissociative core of the *petit mal* seizures). In this we can see that the 'accidental', as it were, presence of the lesion in Rozie's brain provided a conduit for the breakdown. As I have never seen Rozie in these states I can only imagine what has been described to me, but the long absences and sleep evoke a sense of this baby being so overwhelmed by her mother's states of psychosomatic distress that she gave herself over to the experience of psychic deadness. Thomas Ogden, discussing the ways in which mothers and babies together make the recognition of their separateness bearable, writes about them generating forms of sensory experience that are healing: 'When the mother infant dyad is unable to function in a way that provides the baby with a healing sensory experience, the holes in the fabric of the emergent self (Stern, 1985) become a source of unbearable "awareness of bodily separateness which results in an agony of consciousness" (Tustin, 1986: 43)' (Ogden 1989: 52). He goes on to cite Meltzer, who describes the psychological deadness that is thus induced as comparable to the absence in a *petit mal* seizure, in which there is a cessation or paralysis of the process of attributing meaning to experience. For Rozie her *petit mal* seizure expressed her predicament in the rupture of her mother's parental capacities.

It is of interest to consider why it was at this point that Nazneem became unable to attend to her baby well enough, when her failure (for a time) went beyond that which could be repaired and became a medical problem. Akhtar (1995) has described how the consequences of exile and immigration create a traumatic discontinuity. In addition to this Nazneem had experienced something near the extreme of trauma: her husband disappeared, her body violated, her family of origin disowning her and wishing her dead, and now with her young baby to care for. All this was more than enough for the strongest of us to bear, and indeed her mental state when I first met her was overwhelmed. But it was the rejection of herself and her baby by her husband's family that prompted this massive rupture.

This needs to be understood in a multifaceted way. We can see how the birth of a child is probably the most significant event in the life of a family and community. As Berg (2002: 270) has described, 'personal and collective fantasies, conscious and unconscious forces are activated with more power than in any other phase of life'. All mother–infant dyads are embedded in a particular culture, and for Nazneem and Rozie this was a Muslim culture where the paternal line is paramount and the woman's sexuality a matter of family honour. In times of social breakdown rape is used often to attack the family through the woman, but perhaps especially to attack the father. Nazneem's father, for whom she claimed she was the favourite child, had refused to help her to get redress for the crime against her (rape) because of its nature. Subsequently for her husband's family to reject her was to obliterate her very self – she said 'they made me nothing'. At this point in Rozie's development, four to five months old, we could conjecture that in ordinary circumstances a baby will be becoming aware of the father's presence, different from the mother and possibly in early triangulation, apprehending the parental couple, the mother of the night as the French psychoanalysts (Braunschweig & Fain, 1975) describe this early intimation of maternal sexuality and the paternal order. For Nazneem and now Rozie the paternal was contaminated, not just with tragedy but with horror and rejection. Rozie had to contend with her mother's obliterated self, linked to the violation of her sexual body, in which in Nazneem's fantasy there was no difference between her body and her daughter's. Thus Rozie, in the collapsed ('resolved') paradoxical state of psychosomatic duality/unity with her mother, was also obliterated. I suggest that this was the meaning of her symptom of *petit mal* absences.

The therapeutic endeavour

I continued to work with Nazneem and Rozie weekly for a further 20 months following the first sign of Rozie's symptoms, and continued to see them on a monthly basis for a considerable time. I have to acknowledge the great importance of a very sensitive psychiatric crisis intervention team, who were remarkably helpful and supportive during some of this time. They enabled Nazneem to remain out of hospital and supported in the community while I worked with the mother–infant pair and prepared Nazneem for her own individual therapy. As had been evident from the beginning, Nazneem was very aware that her mental states impacted on her daughter and she struggled to protect her from them while also trying to deal with them internally herself. The therapeutic space with me was for both of them together, and in this I was able to support baby Rozie's own struggles to deal with the impingements of her mother's mind but also to address directly Nazneem's mental states as they were manifest in the room. Many times, for instance, I would observe Rozie cutting out, staring out of the window as her mother, head bowed and face immobile, sat silent. I actively intervened addressing the baby, talking to Rozie about her turning away because she sensed her mother's pain. Nazneem would hear this and see Rozie turning to me, looking intently and responding to my tone of voice. Gradually this transformed itself into her making more active bids for her mother, more ordinary demands for Nazneem to attend to and relinquish whatever in her mind interfered with this. Rozie began to be noisy and protest, often expressed not by a scream but a growl, 'GRRRRR', which Nazneem found very dismaying. She was afraid of this growing evidence of her daughter's strength and talked about her fear of it being turned against her (Nazneem) as punishment for all that had happened. Legitimate anger that Nazneem struggled to find in relation to her own trauma was expressed terrifyingly in Rozie. As well as attending to the meaning of this for her, I also played with the interaction in the room. When Rozie would growl, expressing angry feelings, I would imitate her: 'GRRRRR'. At first she was astonished, as was her mother. But then she found it funny and the angry protest could be borne – not dismissed but acknowledged and woven into our interaction together. It became a game, and through this Nazneem could begin to see the value of Rozie's expression of feeling. It didn't have to be so feared, split off and dissociated in a way that fed the defensive reaction of a *petit mal* fit.

Another manifestation of this little girl's struggle for psychosomatic integrity was the gait she developed as she began to walk. In contrast to her early precocious motor development, she would plod along awkwardly, and then tumble as if her whole sense of herself fell apart. This of course was complicated by the medication she was on for the epilepsy, but it reminded me of Winnicott's description in 'Primitive Emotional Development' (1945) of the woman who had never developed 'eyes in her feet' because her sense of her place in the world was so impaired. Rozie's sense of her place in the world, her achievement of 'personalisation' (Winnicott, 1945), remained very tentative for a long time. However, she gradually developed more of a grasp of it, more able to be herself in the room with her mother in an ordinary toddler way, not falling all the time, being able to be naughty because the consequences could be managed, and moving towards using her mother as a base

for exploration and comfort. She gradually developed a security of attachment that became a source of safety and pleasure for both child and mother.

Conclusion

In this chapter I have explored the consequences for a young baby when the
ordinary paradoxical state of merger and separateness of early postnatal life
periodically collapsed in conjunction with her mother's traumatised states of
mind. A development of Winnicott's ideas about primitive emotional development, this notion of the paradoxical dyadic potential space is helpful
in understanding the meanings of the bodily states observable in infants,
especially when they have to manage impingements from the maternal
environment. The regulation of affective states is a central aspect of the
psychosomatic connection between mother and baby. This mother and baby
were overwhelmed by trauma and its aftermath, and their psychosomatic
connections the arena for expressing what could not be borne in mind, nor
elaborated imaginatively. The accidental complication of a lesion in the
baby's brain promoted further the bodily realm as a conduit for excessive
affect; when this mother could not keep her states within manageable bounds
her baby was also flooded. The intervention of parent–infant psychotherapy
to some degree enabled this mother–infant couple to bear these unbearable
states, augmenting the more conventional medical intervention for infantile
epilepsy, such that the symptoms were largely kept at bay.

References

Akhtar, S.A. (1995) Third individuation: Immigration, identity, and the psycho-
    analytic process. *Journal of the American Psychoanalytic Association*, 43:
    1051–1084.
Beebe, B. (2004) Co-constructing mother–infant distress in face to face interactions:
    Contributions of microanalysis. *Zero to Three*, May 2004: 40–48; and *Psycho-
    analytic Inquiry*, 2000, 20(3): 421–440.
Berg, A. (2002) Beyond the dyad: Parent–infant psychotherapy in a multicultural
    society – reflections from a South African Perspective. *Journal of Infant Mental
    Health*, 24(3): 265–277.
Braunschweig, D. & Fain, M. (1975) *La nuit, le jour: Essai psychanalytique sur le
    fonctionnement mental*. Paris: PUR.
Freud, S. (1923) The ego and the id. *Standard Edition of the Complete Works
    of Sigmund Freud*, Vol. 19 (1961). London: Hogarth Press.
James, M. (1960) Premature ego development: Some observations on disturbances in
    the first three months of life. *International Journal of Psycho-Analysis*, 41: 288–294.
James, M. (1962) Infantile narcissistic trauma: Observations on Winnicott's work
    in infant care and child development. *International Journal of Psycho-Analysis*,
    43: 69–79.
Joyce, A. (2002) Prince Blackthorn and the Wizard: Fantasying and thinking in the

psychoanalysis of a ten year old boy. In L. Caldwell (Ed.), *The elusive child*. London: Karnac.

Khan, M.M.R. (1963) The concept of cumulative trauma. *Psychoanalytic Study of the Child*, 18: 286–306.

Lee, G. (1997) Alone among three: The father and the Oedipus complex. In *Fathers and families*. London: Karnac.

Ogden, T. (1989) *Primitive edge of experience*. London: Karnac.

Perry, B.D., Pollard, R., Blakely, R., Baher, W. & Vigilante, D. (1995) Childhood trauma, the neurobiology of adaptation, and user-dependent development of the brain, how 'states' become 'traits'. *Infant Mental Health Journal*, 16: 271–291.

Schore, A. (2001) Effects of early relational trauma on right brain development, affect regulation and infant mental health. *Infant Mental Health Journal*, 22(1–2): 201–269.

Stern, D. (1985) *The interpersonal world of the infant*. New York: Basic Books.

Stern, D. (1995) *The motherhood constellation*. New York: Basic Books.

Tustin, F. (1981) *Autistic states in children*. London: Routledge & Kegan Paul.

Tustin, F. (1986) *Autistic barriers in neurotic patients*. New Haven, CT: Yale University Press.

Winnicott, D.W. (1945) Primitive emotional development. In *Collected papers: Through paediatrics to psychoanalysis*. London: Hogarth (1975).

Winnicott, D.W. (1947) Mind and its relation to psyche soma. In *Collected Papers: Through paediatrics to psychoanalysis*. London: Hogarth (1975).

Winnicott, D.W. (1956) Primary maternal pre-occupation. *Collected papers: Through paediatrics to psychoanalysis*. London: Hogarth (1975).

Winnicott, D.W. (1960) The theory of the parent infant relationship. In *Maturational processes and the facilitating environment*. London: Hogarth (1965).

Winnicott, D.W. (1971) *Playing and reality*. Harmondsworth, UK: Penguin.

Winnicott, D.W. (1986) The ordinary devoted mother. In *Babies and their mothers*. Reading, MA: Addison-Wesley.

Chapter 5

The traumatic sequelae of pathological defensive processes in parent–infant relationships

Amanda Jones

It is traumatic for a baby when a parent's defensive processes are extensively aroused. In this chapter I explore the psychoanalytic concept of 'projection' and its intricately related, particularly invasive, form of emotional defence known as 'projective identification' (Freud, 1895; Klein, 1946). Using two cases, I consider the *cumulative relational trauma* (Khan, 1963) that occurs when a parent misrecognizes their baby due to distorted parental projections and simultaneously creates feelings in the baby that actually belong to the parent, rendering the baby saturated with their parent's disturbed experience (Hobson et al., 2005). The latter is how 'projective identification' works. I illustrate how these processes leave the baby at risk of being thwarted from becoming an individual in his or her own right.

In tandem, I look at the risks a baby is exposed to if projective processes are so powerful that a parent cannot enter into the realm of 'as if' thinking. In the first case, in his mother's mind, a baby boy's needs for human contact and closeness were equated with disgusting neediness that needed to be excessively controlled and cleaned. In the second case, a baby daughter was equated with a murderous presence; her mother believed her baby wanted to kill her. These mothers' beliefs/projections had an almost psychotic quality. For the mothers they were real, the truth. I hope to show how Hanna Segal's (1957) distinction between 'symbolic equation' ('My baby's need to be held *is* dirty') and 'symbolic representation' ('My baby's need to be held makes me feel *as if* I can't cope and I don't know why') is helpful when considering complex parent–infant cases.

Finally, given that the collapse of 'as if' thinking is problematic in any case, I consider what kind of defensive structures are more or less likely to respond to psychodynamic parent–infant therapy.

Emotional defences

We all use psychological defences to protect ourselves from emotional and physical pain. Like the seven sins, when distressed we may pathologically project, deny, split, identify, idealize, introject and become high (manic).

What matters is whether, given time, we can know we were behaving defensively: can we mentalize about the impact our responses might have had and try and repair whatever relational damage occurred? It is when ordinary adaptive ways of defending ourselves become rigid and automatic, akin to character traits, that trouble arises. From a diagnostic perspective, the mothers I describe were different: the first had a predominantly narcissistic/paranoid/obsessive defensive organization, with symptoms of depression, obsessive cleaning, and out-of-proportion anger; the second had a more borderline/dependent/histrionic defensive structure, with symptoms of high anxiety, panic attacks, suicidal feelings and chronic low self-esteem. I could not help the first mother, but I could the second. This raises questions as to the patterns of defensive personality 'structures' more or less likely to work therapeutically with 'parent–infant relational trauma' (Sperry, 2003). I hope to develop an (albeit simplified) argument that when narcissistic/paranoid/obsessive tendencies dominate there is a defensive pull *not* to attach to 'another'; whereas when borderline/dependent/histrionic tendencies are prevalent there exists a defensive urge to seek and cling to an attachment figure, albeit in complex ways, so a therapeutic relationship may stand a better chance of developing.

A parent's history informs the way defensive processes manifest in the present parent–baby relationship and in the relationship with the therapist. Sigmund Freud's (1920) concept of the 'repetition compulsion' helps us understand how traumatic ways of relating can pass from one generation to another. He wrote (1909: 122):

> a thing which has not been understood inevitably reappears; like an unlaid ghost, it cannot rest until the mystery has been solved and the spell broken.

In describing how repetition of 'ways of being' in relationships manifested in the patient–analyst transference relationship, Freud paved the way for clinicians to study in detail actual parent–infant relationships, and to start offering treatment for problematic parental transference dynamics that interfere with the baby's healthy development (Baradon et al., 2005; Beebe, 2000; Fraiberg, 1980). The metaphor of a problematic ghost was used by Fraiberg et al. (1975). Their case studies showed how a baby can become confused in the parent's mind with a figure or figures from the parent's past. A mother's relationship with her own mother can accrue particular power (Benedek, 1959). A parent, without knowing, can also *project* into their baby repressed experiences and feelings, or aspects of their own personalities that they need to disown. Such ghosts profoundly affect the parent's mood when interacting with their baby (Fairbairn, 1951).

Case 1

In the first vignette I witnessed a mother, whom I call Vicky, teaching her eight-month-old baby son not to want to be picked up or held. It is an example of a case in which a therapeutic process could not take place, because Vicky also could not imagine closeness between us being anything other than threatening. Her defensive processes protected her by severing connections: connections between feelings and actions, between thinking and feeling, and between people. Although Vicky had acknowledged to her doctor that she was depressed after the birth of both her babies, it was with great reluctance that she accepted a referral for psychotherapy.

The first meeting remains a blur in my mind. Vicky quickly and emphatically told me there was no problem with her baby: other people had a problem in that they would want to hold him. She *would not* allow anyone else, including her son's father, to touch him. The implication was that holding was dangerous. When I probed, it became clearer that if others held her son he would start to want to be picked up. When I asked why this felt risky, she said she needed to clean a lot and she *could not* be disturbed by her baby needing to be held. The look in her eyes was striking. I was not to question this dictum. At some level, Vicky equated needing to be held as dangerous, bad; and her next association was her own need to clean compulsively. Need for human closeness seemed equated with risk and dirt. In the dynamic between us, I felt Vicky's defensive need to reject my interest and concern. Projected into me was her belief I was a threatening figure who needed to be kept at bay.

All the while her overweight baby was straining in the car seat facing me, making strange strangled sounds. His face conveyed anguish. Slightly desperately I invited Vicky to lift him out. She refused and told me that the real problem was her daughter, whom she described as a 'horrible child'. Her baby gave up his attempts to move or communicate, slumping into sleep. He successfully stifled his attachment and exploratory needs, needs his mother misrecognized by treating them as somehow nasty and messy, to be rigorously controlled.

The sequelae of this encounter were hard. I felt hostile feelings, wanting to get rid of Vicky from my mind as she eradicated dirt through her compulsive cleaning. I felt trapped and helpless, like her baby. Her defensive need to keep all out and uphold her way of managing reality felt impermeable: any other view was treated as dangerous. I knew that Vicky must have suffered herself and found ways to manage her own messy neediness, but she seemed determined not to explore such connections and she told me she saw no point in meeting me again. I felt awful: useless and frustrated. I referred her to an experienced colleague in the hope we might engage her if we addressed her concerns about her daughter, whom I knew she wanted 'fixed'. After two troubling sessions my colleague received a message. The mother told the secretary, 'I felt so awful after the last meeting I wanted to slit my wrists'. In these few words she vividly conveyed her wretched position of desperation. After failed attempts to re-engage the mother we felt we had been paralysed by the following conundrum: Vicky's defensive organization had felt so threatened by the fact that the offer of help invited her to connect with us, yet her whole way of protecting herself depended on not connecting. With hindsight I think I also played into her need to disconnect by referring her on to my colleague and not inviting her to see me again.

Vicky seemed to draw on three entrenched defence mechanisms: *denial*, in that she denied she had any problems at all – all difficulties resided in the other, showing her defensive need to *split* the world into good and bad, and I quickly felt I was experienced as bad. Her defensive carapace was enhanced by her capacity to *induce in others* feelings that perhaps she needed to disown, which in psychoanalytic terms would be described as her defensive use of *projective identification*. The clues to this were that her daughter was becoming violent and I felt angry feelings during our meeting, feelings that were incongruent to my general state of mind that day. Furthermore my colleague was accused of making the mother want to slit her wrists, leaving my colleague bewildered and angry. Hobson et al. (2005: 330) offer a succinct contemporary description of this:

> projective identification, through which the individual stirs negative and disturbing feelings in others by evoking states of mind that mirror her own emotional conflicts. If such patterns of relatedness and interpersonal process are a feature of these individuals' relations with their infants, the impact on infant development might be substantial.

Perhaps the compulsive need to clean up dirt and mess was the outward behaviour of how this deeply unhappy woman tried to manage her unthinkable thoughts and feelings linked to perhaps remembered, and more likely forgotten, experiences of her vulnerabilities and needs when little, which she did not feel able to explore. I worry that Freud's concept of the 'repetition compulsion' will mean that her son may become an adult similarly driven to annihilate mutuality in relationships. Vicky equated her son's neediness with messiness/badness, as she experienced her own. Thus her projective processes were so powerful that they did not allow the possibility of 'as if' thinking.

Perhaps cases that are hardest to help are those when the mother's attachment system is addicted to certain compulsive actions and behaviours or substances such as alcohol, food or narcotic drugs. Vicky sounded to be addicted to defensive cleaning. In other words, her emotional energy was not directed towards a potentially responsive other. It was as if the cleaning behaviour had become the primary attachment figure, meeting her attachment needs. Her defensive structure fell more towards narcissistic/paranoid/ obsessional ways of relating. I was unsuccessful in helping Vicky to feel 'as if' her son's needs were dirty, a position that could then invite possible curiosity as to what such a belief might connect to, leading potentially to change. Her belief remained the same. Maybe it is more possible to help mothers where a longing for human contact still survives. Perhaps mothers with more border-line/dependent/histrionic traits have a surviving wish for intimacy; they just cannot create it in relationships, especially with their babies. Early relational trauma is likely to have occurred in all of the above: maybe it is how the defensive organization manifests that matters when considering how to intervene and whether a therapeutic process has a good prognosis. In the next case a therapeutic relationship could develop, and I was able to help the mother move from believing her baby wanted her dead to realising that she related to her baby *as if* she was threatening. This is a critical distinction because it meant the mother was able to gradually recognise the impact of her own powerful projection and reclaim it as her feeling that she was responsible for.

Case 2

This next case explores the projective processes in play between a young mother, whom I call Helen, and her premature twin daughters after they were born. Helen's defensive use of *projection* and *projective identification* were especially dangerous for Maria, her more vulnerable baby. In her mother's mind, six-month-old Maria was equated with a murderous presence. Helen had experienced considerable fear and neglect of her emotional needs throughout her childhood and adolescence. (Though I focus on Helen's experience now, all that I say is also relevant to fathers and other adults responsible to caring for the baby.)

Both of Helen's babies were at risk, for Helen could not enter into the realm of 'as if' thinking. Helen did not feel 'as if' Maria was a threatening presence, which would have been problematic enough; she felt that Maria wanted her dead, thus Helen would often vomit with fear when faced with her perception of Maria's screaming, angry face. Helen described Maria as *possessed*. In a way, for Maria, this was so: she was taken over by the force of intergenerational projections, unspoken and unthinkable influences in operation long before she was born.

When Helen started weekly parent–infant psychotherapy at The Anna Freud Centre (London) she was living on the edge of perpetual panic. Before becoming pregnant she had been living an outwardly normal life, in a relationship with her partner and with friendships she enjoyed. She was responsible: she had a job and was taking contraception. Helen had no plans to become a mother; her relationship with her mother had been 'awful'.

When Helen found out she was pregnant she had a delusional feeling that her mother had caused her to become pregnant in order to ruin her life again. Her partner persuaded her not to terminate. The conception was experienced as traumatic long before Helen discovered she had twins growing inside her. The pregnancy had already felt like a physical assault – towards the end it felt life-threatening. She had panic attacks and felt claustrophobic. Finally she had an emergency caesarean which made her feel out of control. Helen was very alone: she had a troubled internal world already; she then had to cope with twins with no family to help.

As Helen started her first session, she quickly conveyed how out of control she was feeling. Both babies were screaming.

Helen: ... when I go to sleep ... it's strange, I'm remembering a lot of things. I don't know why, things come like a rush in my mind, whizzing around.

Therapist: You're feeling out of control ...

Helen: Yes, stuff I've kind of closed off, and now it's all zooming back ... everything's out of my control and I've always had an issue with control ... my childhood, nothing, I could never predict anything, no structure, then I got my life in control and now, I never know what's going to happen. I REALLY don't like it. I don't feel safe.

Therapist: It's frightening ...

Helen: Yes ... like I used to be obsessive about locking doors and things because I didn't feel safe and I'm feeling like that again, like I'm in danger which I don't really know why. Ever since the pregnancy ... everything's just coming pouring in ...

I felt the force of Helen's fear. Maria was screaming with her arms rigidly held up, as if enacting what Helen was describing, out of control terror. When quiet Maria was disconnected, preferring to look at materials rather than faces. It was lonely being with her; I think she felt lonely. Maria treated us as if we were potential assailants. This shows how projective processes, and the use of projective identification, so quickly become *co-constructed*. At other times Maria fell asleep, another way of escaping.

Maria and her sister had had a tough time. They were traumatized in pregnancy, during birth, and in the early postnatal period. They left their mother's body too soon and were exposed to a Special Care Baby Unit environment. Maria was especially sensitive because she had suffered more *in utero*. But they were both hard to soothe and would probably have made any parent feel exhausted, worried, useless and desperate, especially first-time parents. Even though their father was depressed, he was also sensitive. The fact that he was present, offering an alternative experience to Helen's terror, was important in terms of the babies' later capacities to recover from the difficulties with their mother. I think he made it possible for the twins to use me as a helpful 'third' figure.

Helen described how, when given Pippa to hold, she felt 'amazed' and an 'overwhelming sense of love'. But when she was given Maria to hold, the following day, she said 'the beepers went off, I gave her back to the nurse' and

Helen, unconsciously driven by a defensive need to split, experienced Maria as 'hating her'. I think Maria's exquisite vulnerability overwhelmed Helen; looking at Maria was like looking into her own unconscious, a terrifying mirror. Perhaps what Helen saw reflected back was her vulnerable, helpless self whom she despised and wanted to flee from.

Helen was given the chance to change Maria's nappy while Maria was in the incubator. She was anxious, already believing Maria hated her. Maria released more pooh, which squirted everywhere. Possibly the nurse sighed, knowing it would take a long time to clean the incubator. Helen heard her sigh as an angry shout, as if in the presence of a critical and dangerous parent. The nurse and Maria became conflated: Helen felt thereafter in the presence of a threatening figure. She left the unit and impulsively took a handful of paracetamol and codeine. The nurse, to this day, probably has no idea what her understandable communication of irritation led to.

Thereafter Helen wanted to flee from her feelings and because she could not, she was hitting herself and making herself sick many times a day. Helen was also having nightmares of being chased by her mother. Soon into the first session I felt anxious and overwhelmed by the risks for Helen, Maria and Pippa. But Helen gave me some signs that she might be able to respond to the treatment we could offer. The following is an excerpt from the middle of the first session.

Helen: I think Maria absolutely hates me, the way she looks at me – I don't blame her because I'd hate me as well, but the way she looks . . . she scares me.

Therapist: What do you see? What do you see in the look?

Helen: Just resentment . . . I don't know. She looks possessed – sometimes when she looks at me it scares me, like she wants me to die or something, I don't know – then when she comes near me, she cries sometimes and I just . . .

Therapist: So sometimes maybe she feels confused with the part of you that can understandably resent them and perhaps even sometimes think 'Oh gosh, I wish she weren't alive . . .'

Helen: Yes . . . and I think she feels that about me.

I felt hopeful at this point because Helen allowed me to suggest that maybe she felt resentment and she did not become persecuted when I named her hostility. She seemed relieved. I said to Helen that it sounded as if she was feeling as frightened as Maria and Pippa felt when they got into fearful states. She agreed. It was impossible, when on her own, for Helen to explore the meaning of how she felt: she just felt.

My challenge was to introduce the notion of 'as if', and to see if this could facilitate a shift for Helen and Maria. In order to do this I had to be available as simultaneously a maternal/receiving and paternal/distinguishing 'other'.

The next excerpt shows how we brought an unconscious influence/ghost into Helen's consciousness so that it could be symbolised: in other words, named. We diluted Helen's belief that Maria wanted her dead. Having been primarily in the receptive/maternal mode, in which I had received and reeled in response to Helen's feelings, I then spoke as the paternal/third presence, able to comment on and add a different perspective (Britton, 1989; Birksted-Breen, 1996). Three-quarters of the way through the first session I said it sounded like Helen had felt very physically traumatised by the pregnancy and birth (maternal mode) and that it was *as if* she felt trapped with a very punishing presence all the time (paternal mode). I still knew nothing of her history but I used my own countertransference feeling of fear. Helen was then able to use my words to start to make some important links about Maria of which she had previously been unaware.

Therapist: So Maria feels most risky to you when you feel she's looking at you with a look that possibly reminds you of how you've been looked at before (*Helen nods*) – a kind of 'you're a hateful person, I'm going to get you'.

Helen: Yes . . .

Therapist: And when you see that coming from Maria it . . .

Helen: I do feel scared . . . I feel scared of, look at the size of her, she's tiny – I do feel scared of her . . . not many people can understand that, if I say that to Pete he says don't be silly . . . I feel like I'm being stupid, but what am I supposed to do, I don't know why I feel that way . . . like if I go in at night time, say if one of them is crying, she looks at me and I do feel really scared. I feel there's someone in the wardrobe watching me . . . and . . .

Therapist: So it's almost like [i.e. 'as if'] Maria's haunted by something . . .

Helen: YES, my mum, she does LOOK like my mum sometimes with her eyes . . . I . . . when my mum was hitting me or doing something it would be her eyes that were the most evil thing about her . . .

Therapist: And you see those eyes looking . . .

Helen: (*swallows hard*) Sometimes . . . yes . . . and that's a really scary thing, whenever I have nightmares about my mum it's always her eyes . . . which is . . .

Therapist: So it's hard for you to separate out then that Maria . . .

Helen: (*nods*) That she's not my mum . . .

Therapist: Mmm . . . Yes . . . that makes sense.

This was the first time Helen had seen a possible link between how she felt when with Maria and how she had felt when with her mother. She needed me, acting as the 'third', to help her do this. Helen's description of feeling someone was in the wardrobe watching her had a worryingly psychotic feel to it. I asked if she had had mental health treatment before. She told me that when fifteen she had been in a psychiatric unit for nine months. She felt secure there. She could not speak more of this in the first session.

In the second session, Helen described her psychiatric breakdown. The session was terrible because Helen started to have a panic attack. Helen and her sister had been subjected to years of violence from their alcohol-dependent mother. This culminated in a life-threatening physical assault from her mother when Helen was fifteen. Helen was subsequently hospitalized medically and then psychiatrically. Her mother fled the country. In the unit, Helen was diagnosed as having post-traumatic stress disorder with psychotic features, an unstable personality disorder, and clinical depression. Her self-harm was, indeed, serious and she was suicidal. Her psychotic belief was that she felt her mother was everywhere, trying to kill her. But she responded well to the treatment available and slowly rebuilt her life. These are the feelings that came back again after the babies were born, for the birth of her twins shattered this recovery.

Although Helen was still feeling terrible, over the following weeks it seemed a relief to talk about her fears that she could become violent like her mother, or that Maria would kill her or her mother would come and find her now and kill her babies. As we were able to talk about these fears, I think Helen had an experience of me imagining what she had gone through and putting into words what she might have felt. In tandem, I noticed how Helen began to show signs of being able to put herself in her babies' bodies, and more awareness that Maria might be affected by her mother's state. Helen was shifting from *equating* Maria with a murderous presence ('symbolic equation' functioning) to recognizing that she *represented* Maria in particular ways; ways that might not, actually, be congruent with Maria's experience. Over the months Maria gradually became, more often than not, experienced as a little baby who cried when she needed comfort ('symbolic representation' mode).

Most importantly, Maria's previously rigid arms began to be able to reach for her mother. As Helen's projections were reclaimed and worked through, Maria could be comforted when held and, in one very moving session, I saw Maria tentatively explore her mother's face with her hand, causing Helen to smile softly which, in turn, gave Maria the signal that she could explore more. She looked into her mother's eyes which were, maybe for the first time, less haunted. This experience offered a breakthrough for them. Maria continued to touch and look and her touch elicited the most beautiful, warm smiles of delight from Helen.

To conclude their story, I return to a difference between her and Vicky, namely that Helen had a surviving desire to attach to humans. Her defensive structure included more borderline/dependent/histrionic traits – although she had been very self-destructive, she was not predominantly invested in addictive behaviours or substances. She wanted to feel safe and to be protected.

Given the history with her mother and father, how come this urge was still alive?

The clues emerged in the transference relationship between us. Several months into therapy I had become a stable person that Helen relied upon. Helen started to experience panicky feelings at the end of sessions. It made sense to me that she could not manage a whole week between sessions without contact. When desperate, Helen would telephone in between sessions. Her suicidal states still terrified her and when she was in the grip of them my absence felt cruel. She needed the reassurance of hearing my voice. The suicidal feelings were specifically linked to the feeling of not being able to reach me. As Maria was able to reach for, and find, her mother, Helen's own needs to reach and find became so painful.

I did not know at this stage that Helen had suffered a major loss in her early childhood, so I was unaware that the pain she was experiencing saying goodbye to me each week was a traumatic reverberation of this earlier loss. For Helen to be separated from me – the person she experienced as calm and steady and wanting to understand – became heart-wrenching. After six months, Helen described walking past the home she lived in when a teenager and the awful feelings associated with that. I strongly felt that I had not been able to protect her from such feelings. She said her whole life had been a disaster. She then said, as if in passing, that her babies were the one good thing that had happened to her. At the beginning of therapy Helen felt becoming pregnant was yet another punishment bestowed on her body by her mother. She did not realise how this perception had changed. Later in the session I noticed how gently Helen handled Maria and Pippa's bodies when changing them, how natural it seemed to be for her to talk to them and play while handling such intimate moments, *and* talk about difficult feelings. I asked whether there might have been someone around when she was little who, perhaps, enjoyed her and also coped with her horrid feelings. She paused. Then she said 'Someone, I don't . . . don't remember . . . can't picture her . . . she was called Maid. I was born when mum and dad lived abroad . . . she looked after me . . . mum left dad when I was three. I don't remember her at all.'

The mystery now made sense. What was noticeable about Helen was how she could evoke loving feelings in others – professionals, friends and her partners. She also loved. I say this because Helen was able to value the treatment she was offered with me. Her motivation to give her babies what she had not had was a powerful ally to the therapy, as was her – until now – unconscious searching for the love of Maid.

I came to understand that Helen had not only experienced a frightening mother, she had also lost a more loving mother-figure when she was three. I now understood how the end of sessions triggered a dreadful feeling of abandonment. Helen would feel understood and then pushed into a desolate world. Even though I could see she was feeling slightly better about her babies, I found myself preoccupied with Helen's safety: rightly so.

Fortunately Helen and I could talk about her feeling cruelly treated, not protected, and abandoned by me. I think the nine months of inpatient care she received had offered her care and containment during her psychotic regression and allowed for her violence and anger to be gradually expressed towards the team rather than against herself.

Helen used the therapy to do many things:

- she began the process of mourning her unhappiness in relation to her own parents, and the loss of Maid
- she started to reclaim aspects of her own hated and disowned self
- she tentatively internalized aspects of our relationship in which she felt accepted – especially when suicidal and desperate – cared for, and understood
- she lessened her use of primitive defensive processes when faced with her babies' cries, perhaps because she experienced me as able to withstand her cries
- Helen stopped seeing Maria as either an all-powerful malignant presence or so vulnerable that her cries evoked feelings of panic in her mother.

At the start of therapy Helen knew she was repeating another unhappy mother–daughter relationship, and she felt unable to change her feelings. Helen's capacity to link to 'another' indicated a deep resilience in her that allowed her compulsion to repeat hatred and trauma to become something different.

It is a major problem when a baby becomes a 'bad object' for the mother. I have linked this to the theme of pathological repetition (Freud, 1914). The psychoanalyst Ronald Fairbairn is worth considering here:

> *It is also to a massive return of repressed bad objects that we must largely look for the explanation of the phenomenon which Freud described as 'the repetition compulsion'* . . . it is not so much a case of compulsively repeating traumatic situations as *of being haunted by bad objects against the return of which all defences have broken down.*
>
> (1951: 166, emphasis added)

Fairbairn's description of being 'haunted by bad objects' echoes the metaphor of ghosts mentioned earlier. When considering Helen and her babies, the danger was that the return of the 'bad objects' in Helen would need to be projected. Her babies became the repositories for these projections and were thus related to in traumatic ways. Having the babies present in the therapy brought these pressing transference dynamics into the room to work with: the 'bad objects' could be discovered, named and – ultimately – changed. For Maria and Pippa, it was critical that, in tandem with working with the 'bad internal objects', we discovered their mother's 'good internal object': her early experience of being loved by Maid.

Helen remains in ongoing individual therapy with me; her daughters are non-symptomatic ('well'). I anticipate that Helen's therapy will go on for many years. The horrors she faces are still considerable yet more manageable. I think her love for her daughters, and me, keeps her coming. She talks often of her conviction that I *should* adopt her, and her fury, despair, sadness and reluctant acceptance that I cannot, a fact that is hard for her to bear, and for me at times. But I know that a certain kind of parental love is actually central to the work because pivotal to parental/therapeutic love is the capacity to take pleasure in the development of the other. In the beginning when Helen experienced my want for her and her babies to develop she was utterly confused. She then began to feel relief as she realized she was with a therapist–mother–father figure who did not want to destroy her, who could withstand her anger and disappointment, and who could take pleasure in her, and in her babies' development.

Now two and a half years old, her daughters symbolize something much more hopeful for Helen. Helen can now take genuine pleasure in them and perhaps this is where the compulsion to repeat malignant projective processes has changed. Helen's mother unfortunately could not take pleasure in her, or her development, nor could she manage her murderous hostility and, unfortunately, Helen's father could not protect her. The compulsion to repeat destruction is changing. Psychodynamic parent–infant therapy has perhaps managed to prevent maternal envy, exacerbated by paternal absence, from continuing to wreak emotional havoc through the generations. Pleasure in development, fortunately, can now predominate.

In the first case there was no 'angel in the nursery' (see Chapter 13), no internalized experience of being lovable. The consequence was a defensive organization that repeated the severance of helpful emotional connection. Vicky cut off help and told us we made her want to slit her wrists. Her way of functioning was structured by narcissistic/paranoid/obsessive ways of relating. For Helen it was different. Although deeply traumatized by her experiences of terror and of being hated, other experiences of making someone's eyes light up with pleasure were, I think, present. In the session when Maria looked into her mother's eyes and elicited a smile of delight, something hopeful ignited again: therapy restored Helen's healthy capacity to trust that it was possible to reach out and cling, and to seek comfort and understanding in an intimate relationship. This finally allowed Maria and Pippa to do the same.

References

Baradon, T., with Broughton, C., Gibbs, I., James, J., Joyce, A. & Woodhead, J. (2005) *The practice of psychoanalytic parent–infant psychotherapy: Claiming the baby.* London: Routledge.

Beebe, B. (2000) Coconstructing mother–infant distress: The microsynchrony of maternal impingement and infant avoidance in the face-to-face encounter. *Psychoanalytic Inquiry*, 20: 412–440.

Benedek, T. (1959) 'Parenthood as a developmental phase – A contribution to the libido theory'. *Journal of the American Psychoanalytic Association*, 7: 389–417.

Birksted-Breen, D. (1996) Phallus, Penis and Mental space. *International Journal of Psycho-Analysis*, 77: 649–657.

Britton, R. (1989) The missing link: parental sexuality in the Oedipus complex. In R. Britton, M. Feldman & E. O'Shaughnessy (Eds.), *The Oedipus complex today: Clinical implications*. London: Karnac.

Fairbairn, W.R. (1951) A synopsis of the development of the author's views regarding the structure of the personality. In *Psychoanalytic Studies of the Personality* (pp. 136–179). London: Tavistock with Routledge and Kegan Paul (1952).

Fraiberg, S. (Ed.) (1980) *Clinical studies in infant mental health*. New York: Basic Books.

Fraiberg, S., Adelson, E. & Shapiro, V. (1975) Ghosts in the nursery: A psychoanalytic approach to the problem of impaired infant–mother relationships. *Journal of the American Academy of Child Psychiatry*, 14: 387–422.

Freud, S. (1895) Draft H – paranoia. In J. Strachey (Ed.), *Standard edition of the complete works of Sigmund Freud* (Vol. 1, pp. 206–212). London: Hogarth Press.

Freud, S. (1909) Analysis of a phobia in a five-year-old boy. In J. Strachey (Ed.), *Standard edition of the complete works of Sigmund Freud* (Vol. 10, pp. 22–148). London: Hogarth Press.

Freud, S. (1914) Remembering, repeating and working through. In J. Strachey (Ed.), *Standard edition of the complete works of Sigmund Freud* (Vol. 12, pp. 255–269). London: Hogarth Press.

Freud, S. (1920) Beyond the pleasure principle. In J. Strachey (Ed.), *Standard edition of the complete works of Sigmund Freud* (Vol. 17, pp. 7–64). London: Hogarth Press.

Hobson, R.P., Patrick, M., Crandell, L, Garcia-Perez, R. & Lee, A. (2005) Personal relatedness and attachment in infants of mothers with borderline personality disorder. *Development and Psychopathology*, 17: 329–347.

Khan, M.M. (1963) The concept of cumulative trauma. *Psychoanalytic Study of the Child*, 18: 286–306.

Klein, M. (1946) Notes on some schizoid mechanisms. In *Envy and Gratitude*. London: Hogarth Press, 1975.

Segal, H. (1957) Notes on symbol formation. *International Journal of Psychoanalysis*, 38: 391–397.

Sperry, L. (2003) *Handbook of diagnosis and treatment of DSM-IV-TR personality disorders* (2nd Ed.). Hove, UK: Brunner-Routledge.

Chapter 6

Infants, relational trauma and homelessness

Therapeutic possibilities through a hostel baby clinic group and research evaluation

Jessica James with Julia Newbury

Homelessness: Impact on infants

A high proportion of infants born into homelessness have ghosts in their nurseries with disrupted attachments and mental health problems. One in four families becomes homeless because of family breakdown, 63% experience domestic violence, and mental health problems are eight times more common (Crisis, 2006). In addition the temporary nature and crowded living conditions of a hostel are likely to exacerbate the ordinary destabilising effects of pregnancy, birth and the postnatal period for the parents. Such internal psychic experiences combine with external realities to suggest that these infants have increased vulnerability to relational trauma.

In the UK today no separate statistics exist about the mental health of homeless infants less than one year old, and the impact seems understated and under-researched. However, it has been established that older children show high levels of behaviour problems including sleep disturbance, feeding difficulties and hyperactivity PTSD (Vonstanis, 2002). It is not hard to imagine that, from infancy, their parents would have often been flooded by their own emotional states and struggled to offer consistent, affectively attuned care.

Many families in hostels are teenagers, single parents, recent arrivals to the UK, refugees, asylum seekers, victims of domestic violence, or have a history of drink or drug use. While a large number will have experienced trauma, their responses to this should not be assumed and there are dangers in pathologising these families as a homogeneous group (Papadopoulos, 2007). There are those who find a hostel a safe haven and those who bring resilience and personal resources to adapting and nurturing babies in these circumstances. Yet the conditions of hostel life are adverse compared to most families', and offer low levels of social capital and high levels of stress, with negative implications for development. For example, residents have little control about noise levels (crying babies or fights between adults in neighbouring rooms) and there are frequent fire alarms at all times of day and night (because of smoking in corridors). Hostel rooms are small and the challenges of ordinary infant-care faced by this client group include setting boundaries when there is no separation, weaning with limited cooking space and concern about germs and infections in high-density living. Many of these families bring a sense of lives on hold while waiting to be housed (even though most stay two years at least), yet their infants cannot afford this wait. The usual support offered frequently fails to meet their needs or to mitigate relational trauma.

Universal services for parents and infants

Baby clinics

All families are invited to attend a baby clinic after an initial home visit by a health visitor at 10 days postpartum. At these clinics babies are weighed, given immunisations, and there is advice on baby care and any concerns. Parents and infants wait their turn while sitting on chairs around the edge of the room. The atmosphere tends to be like a waiting room where parents might chat, but where emphasis is placed on the professional's availability and leaving straight after.

While families appreciate easy access to a knowledgeable expert, many also describe the experience as stressful. They worry about whether their baby will behave himself/herself, about taking up too much of the health visitor's time (clinics are frequently big and busy) and about being checked upon as a good enough parent. Contact with the health visitor tends to revolve around adult conversations, with the baby under discussion being ignored because of time restraints and compelling adult need. Health visitors find themselves repeating advice and, especially with the most vulnerable families, feel at a loss. There is intensified emotional dysregulation and the infants most in need of professional help, such as those living in hostels, are kept away.

Community and specialist psychology projects

Children's Centres and Sure Start schemes offer sessions and classes in the community. These can improve the lives of many families by fostering social contact, reducing isolation and depression, and offering skills for playing and relating with babies. Despite imaginative strategies it remains unproven whether those families most in need and hardest to reach, such as homeless families, are able to use and benefit from them (Sure Start, 2008). This could be to do with expectations to commit, feelings of shame or of not fitting in. Home-visiting projects are available in some areas, and can be enormously helpful both practically and emotionally (Stern, 2008), but are time-restricted and of limited social benefit. Cognitive, psychoanalytic individual and group parent–infant therapies are increasingly available for prevention and treatment of postnatal depression and infant attachment or behavioural difficulties.

These can be valuable for parents who acknowledge their need but, for the most high-risk infants, any relational difficulties tend to be hijacked by the immediacy of external issues, such as money, housing or a violent partner. In addition, parents with childhood histories of trauma can find the treatment situation intolerable, stirring up intense claustrophobic or paranoid anxieties (Garland et al., 2002). Even when referrals are accepted, sustaining commitment is frequently untenable for families who feel let down by the state and lead chaotic lives.

Planning an innovative baby clinic with focus on infant mental health

A specialist health visitor for homeless families and a parent–infant psychotherapist specialising in groups discussed collaborating to develop a new model of baby clinic, both to reach out to homeless families and to be psychoanalytically informed. A new hostel for 140 families, with a communal room in the basement, brought an opportunity where health visiting services could be provided alongside a therapeutic group culture, giving priority to infant mental health. Parents would be encouraged both to meet with the health visitor and 'to drop in to come and play with their babies'. They could have immediate access to a full range of medical services from a team including specialist health visiting (with diagnostic assessment and independent prescribing), weighing, infant feeding, toddler play and parent–infant psychotherapy. Advice on infant care, immunisations, child development reviews and minor illness management are ordinary, concrete and have no stigma attached, all of which are vital for attendance. High proportions of homeless families have no GP, but characterise their difficulties through physical symptoms (Sawtell, 2002).

Description of hostel baby clinic group

The clinic is set out to be conducive to face-to-face interactions with babies, with low chairs and sofas for adults around mats on the floor. This brings everyone to a similar level, with lie-back chairs and supportive foam circles for babies who are not yet sitting, as well as rattles and toys. Both parents and babies are welcomed by a member of the team and are encouraged to go and play by the mats. Discussions take place wherever the family is seated to maintain minimal disruption and give primacy to an infant-centred approach. This also enables observations of infant–parent dyads in action and, rather than just talk about problems, to see them unfolding in the here and now. The parent–infant psychotherapist is introduced as a parent and baby specialist, she stays on the mat and moves among everyone to facilitate positive interactions and group functioning. She joins the health visitor for discussions with an emotional component or recurring behavioural symptoms. However, the group is not seen as the place to give full expression to the parents' many preoccupying emotional and practical traumatic experiences. Those raised in its relaxed atmosphere are responded to empathically, but briefly, to avoid being side-tracked into pressing, often insoluble, adult demand that could take the focus from babies. The setting aims to foster what everyone has: a baby primed to be social and interactive, and a parent keen to do their best for their babies.

This vignette illustrates an ordinary 'positive' group exchange.

> Two young mothers (both 16) and babies are among others on the mats. One is holding her four-week-old baby in her arms so that he can see her face and she supports his head to look around at others as well. He is alert, his eyes sparkly and interested. The therapist comments on how he seems interested in us, and the other mother (whose daughter is four months) says that she didn't think babies could see much at that age. Her baby looks lifeless, she is held flat and her eyes are strikingly empty. The therapist shows her a rattle, talks to her and gets little response. She asks her mother what she enjoys and her mother says nothing really, maybe the TV. The therapist plays with a toy so that both babies, and others, are included, and the teenage mothers chat. Later, the therapist notices that the four-month-old baby is being held supportively to see others and appears a little more engaged. Her mother looks into her face and says that she is going to get her some toys.

The difference between these babies is stark (even though both are subject to a child protection plan). Their social workers (and other professionals) are bound to have given encouragement to play, but this group offers the mothers an unthreatening opportunity to reflect on their own and their baby's experiences, to see others in action and, when coping well, to be boosted in this.

Working as a multidisciplinary team

A team approach is intrinsic to the functioning of this model, with the aim to achieve a joint commitment and support for each other's role. The health visitor is central by taking ultimate responsibility for her case-load, while also being open to conducting interviews on the floor among the infant-led, apparently chaotic, group activity. She shares her expertise with the parent–infant psychotherapist, who brings her particular slant towards psychodynamic thinking and heightened sensitivity to the infants' emotional experience. Potentially this could clash with the medical, symptom-led emphasis of many health professionals, so a mutual desire to value and learn from each other is essential. At the end of clinic sessions all staff share their observations about individual families and the group as a whole.

The following examples illustrate this team approach.

An eight-month-old baby sat frozen and wide-eyed on the mat next to his smiley mother. He took a long time every week to warm up and play. His mother reported that he was settled at home but the team wondered whether his fear and her anxious smiling suggested otherwise. The parent–infant psychotherapist helped her to respond to his need for her reassurance in the group. The health visitor used a postnatal depression questionnaire and talked with her. She was able to disclose domestic violence and, rather than speculating theoretically about the impact on her little boy, they could relate it to their shared observations of his behaviour in the group.

In another instance the health visitor was involved with treating serious eczema in twin baby boys. The parents and professionals stared into their faces with worried expressions to inspect their skin. The parent–infant psychotherapist began to be concerned about the affective experience of these boys, of constant anxious looking and probing. She pointed this out to the team, who moved away from a medical focus and towards seeing beyond the skin surface and into their hearts and souls. The parents were helped to reflect on their own anxiety and how this might impact on their sons as well.

The person weighing the babies is significant, as her remembering and talking with parents and babies enhances their experience and offers a positive model. Once, it was forgotten to explain this role to a stand-in and babies were weighed as though inanimate objects and without eye-contact. The clinic was adversely affected with families staying for shorter periods and an increased number of distressed babies.

Infant feeding peer support and a volunteer to play with the toddlers are also important, bringing their particular skills and coming from the communities represented in the hostel. Team dynamics can be complex and need continuous attention, especially when diverse approaches become conflicted and impact negatively on the clinic's holding capacity. At these times, adult needs tend to dominate, leading to intense discussions and advice-giving, with increased numbers of distressed babies. Any insecure phases of group or team functioning need discussing, and airing openly, and the debriefing at the end of each session provides a forum for this. The clinic tends to regain its momentum in subsequent weeks when staff members are able to reconnect to their purpose. The institutional context of the hostel is influential as well and, unfortunately, such institutions often repeat the experience of passing homeless people from one relevant caregiver to another. This has been borne out in the four years since opening, as hostel managers and staff members have changed frequently. There have also been constant practical problems (including flooding, broken equipment and loss of facilities), adding to low morale. The health visitor and therapist try to keep renewing their personal contact with hostel staff, to be reliable and, as outsiders, not to get caught up in complex institutional dynamics.

The research process

A research psychologist is involved in evaluating this intervention using research tools to evaluate its primary aim: to help parents be attuned to the needs of their babies. The focus is on the parents' perceptions and experiences, the trajectory of infant development and the quality of the parent–infant interaction. The research should show whether infant development is enhanced over a three- to four-month time span, along with the quality of parent–infant interaction compared to a control group of parents and infants in neighbouring hostels without this baby clinic group. Research material was made available to the therapist once interviews and videos were completed and after consent was given to allow material to be used for teaching purposes.

The researcher's experience of conducting this research highlights the hostel context of parent and infant relationships. One of the biggest challenges is people's failure, in both control and intervention groups, to keep appointments despite those appointments taking place in their rooms. Frequently assessments have to be rescheduled and, often, the researcher arrives at the room having confirmed earlier the same day, but with no sign of anyone. Once inside hostel rooms, where the research is conducted, the lack of space is immediately striking with prams blocking the door and the assessment having to take place on the floor or bed. Scattered electronic toys not only make the space more cramped but often distract the infant. Televisions, mobile phone calls and impromptu visitors cause further distractions, along with siblings eager to be involved. These types of conditions instil feelings of discontinuity: having to chop and change activities to fit in with the demands of the situation.

Building a group experience

For these parents and infants, who are frequently living in the context of loss and dislocation, with a sense of helplessness and low social capital, groups have potential to offer a profound sense of belonging and shared solidarity. A group experience can foster emotional connectedness and attachment to an intersubjective matrix, with enhanced endorphin levels when individuals feel supported by social bonds (Schore & Schore, 2007). Creating a group out of a baby clinic involves belief in the group process and a constant reinforcement of its culture as a place with a sense of cohesion. In the model described here, the parent–infant psychotherapist takes overall responsibility for this by promoting constructive group behaviours. She tries to stay within the action on the mat, and to move between individuals and the group as a whole, always keeping the group, as a group, in mind. This is despite sessions that frequently have entirely different parents and babies from previous ones, with many unexpected situations arising.

While families are under no pressure to attend regularly, the group's permanence is made clear as a consistent setting, where both infants and parents are greeted and where departures are marked with goodbyes. The drop-in format enables parents to regulate their involvement, with particular meaning for those who have experienced a prolonged helplessness (Woodhead & James, 2007). As a result they can drop in, but also drop out, and thus take control. This is understood as similar to small babies, whose capacity to manage only short periods of interactive looking results in their regulating intensity through averting their gaze. Like a confident parent, the team try not to feel rejected or become demanding when families stay for short periods or attend sporadically. They endeavour to respect each family's pace and to sustain the group's holding and containing capacities. This involves keeping everyone in mind in team discussions and to be welcoming on their return, even though they might bring the same, or worse, problematic symptoms.

Anti-group processes are inevitable in any therapeutic group enterprise, involving attacks on the group's functioning (Nitsun, 1996). In the baby clinic group all, or some, of the following might occur: families remain around the edge of the mat; babies are held in parents' arms staring into space; professionals are over-actively giving advice, ignoring babies, making suggestions about other services. At these times the value of being together in the here and now of the group can be lost, negative projections can flourish and a sense of difference and despair develops. In the clinic group the balance between constructive and destructive forces can be maintained by having a team able to pull together and a core group of stable families. When anti-group processes are apparent, the therapist holds this in mind and tries to understand them psychodynamically with her therapist colleagues. It is especially important to use discussions within the clinic team to share experiences, acknowledge difficulties and re-focus aims. When these dynamics are addressed openly it usually results in a strengthened group experience.

Forming a group sense of emotional connectedness

A new mother and baby are sitting on the edge of the mat, both staring in different directions apart from each other and the group. The therapist moves over towards them, to try to make contact. She looks into the baby's face, uses an infant-centred tone to her voice and attempts to articulate what it is like for him in this group, such as with lots of new people. She includes his mother, looks to her, asks a few simple questions about both of them and says something affirming. If the baby is only a few weeks old and awake, she may suggest looking together and encouraging her to hold him to face her, going behind them to support this connecting with expressions and sounds. She might include another baby and mother by remembering when they first came and were also unsure and new. For an older baby she may introduce him to another baby, make links between experiences in the current group situation and offer suitable toys or places to sit on the mats between everyone. At stable phases of group functioning, there might be established parents or babies who help this process of including new or hesitant families and the therapist encourages this.

At the beginning her contact is as friendly and attuned as possible with individual dyads, before eliciting common ground. Her assumption is that many arrive at the baby clinic with low expectations and negative transferences towards both authority figures and a clinic setting. Yet she believes that it is possible to create something good out of being together, in the here and now of a group, and aims to convey this. Families already accustomed to this culture can be mobilised as confident group members, both fostering their ego-strength and self- belief and helping those more diffident. Attention to timing is essential, as it is possible to lose connections with a parent or an infant through clumsy, in the moment, impingement (where they feel pressurised to join in and leave hurriedly) or over-sensitivity (where they remain on the sidelines and feel neglected). As in every psychotherapeutic enterprise, it works best if the therapist is able to be authentic and find her own voice. The babies are a port of entry for communications, as in the above example by asking straightforward information about their age, what they enjoy, by engaging in infant-led ways, and by making links between babies and other group members. A benign mini-community builds, like a traditional extended family with genuine interest, but with freedom to dip in and dip out during and between sessions.

Infant-centred atmosphere

Precedence is given to shaping a group rhythm that is responsive to infants, where relating is often without words. The therapist supports a quality of ebbs and flows, nuance, tone, gaze and bodily interactions that has meaning for babies, with emphasis on being together at a quietly attentive pace and an emotionally resonant flow. She uses her own body and voice to try to link into the babies' worlds in authentic and uninhibited ways. Similar conversations are encouraged between parents and their own infants, and with others' infants, and an infant-centred atmosphere grows. There are 'now moments' and 'moments of meeting' (Stern, 2004) and, inevitably, moments of disconnection or not meeting, but even the apparently most fleeting, attuned interacting or expressive gestures are given value. Capturing the gaze of another is enormously significant (Campbell & Salo, 2007), especially for infants whose parents often do not realise that their baby is so capable.

This mother is telling the research psychologist about how she and her baby benefited from this infant-centred focus:

> I've seen L (health visitor) and J (therapist) and the other people in there when I go with her, they'll talk to my baby. First I used to think, she doesn't understand what you're saying. Then I copied them and she does. She responded to me. I used to think you need to talk to babies when they are around this age (four months). I never knew at the beginning, but seeing them doing that I started to do that as well.

On a deeper level, for some infants who may have not have been a gleam in their parent's eye, the clinic group offers new possibilities for relating. The infant's interest in invitations to communicate can provide a turning point in parents' relationships with them: the first 'now moments' that are possible (Reddy, 2008). In sessions where this infant-centred atmosphere develops, there are mutual moments of well-being and feelings of intimacy. There is a sense of an affective connection between everyone, including the team, whose somatic experience also resonates with the families. The therapist draws on her countertransference responses and strives to avoid the constant pull towards adult preoccupation and trauma. Her focus is on building a collaborative rhythm with babies as genuine participants in the group process.

A baby disconnected from her mother

The following example shows the therapist working within this baby clinic context to help a baby, Aisha, who has become avoidant to her mother. There develops an implicit understanding of what has led to this happening and they are actively helped to build their relationship.

When Aisha first comes with her mother to the clinic group at five months, their mutual disconnection is striking. Aisha's gaze goes to anything, or anyone, except her mother. Mother is preoccupied talking about her older son and pointing out positive things about other babies. The health visitor knows the family through social services because of concerns about the boy's behaviour and his mother's mental state. The clinic team have immediate worries for Aisha. Her mother weighs her silently and mechanically and places her in a lie back chair at a distance. They come a few times and not again for some weeks.

After discussing with the team, the therapist decides to ring and be encouraging. Mother says she has been in hospital with a chest infection and the therapist sympathises, but then asks about Aisha. Mother says she should be sleeping but has just woken. The therapist says Aisha must have had a hard time as well and it would be nice for her to come down to play. Mum says OK and they come. *Mum places Aisha (now seven months) on her front on the mat, alone, and she sits on the sofa some way away. The therapist sits nearer to*

Aisha, who starts crying and mother, after a while, having looked towards therapist, picks up Aisha. She holds her and tries to get her to look at her, but Aisha is stiff and looks towards therapist. Therapist says how hard it is sometimes to connect with each other, especially after mum has been ill. Aisha's mother says that mums and daughters don't get on and therapist asks her if that is her experience. She nods and therapist says she has noticed she is close to her son. There is a short discussion where it transpires that Aisha's brother was born in UK while father was still in their African country and that they became very close. Aisha was born nine months after father came to UK and adjusting to the bigger family has been hard. The therapist takes Aisha, talks to her and holds her facing her mother. Aisha relaxes and there is a little smiling between everyone. Mother holds her arms out to Aisha, who allows her to take her in a more cuddly way. The therapist moves to welcome other families.

The therapist is prepared to promote Aisha's experience clearly and firmly: 'Aisha would like to play'. Mother complies by coming to the clinic and 'dumping' Aisha on the mat, but allows herself to open up emotionally with therapist about some of their difficulties. Seeing Aisha in the therapist's lap, she engages in three-way pleasurable interactions and seems to begin to experience Aisha differently, as separate and attractive. She reaches out for Aisha, apparently to claim her, and the therapist leaves them as more families arrive (also modelling the possibility of attending to more than one).

Later in this session, among many families on the mat, Aisha cries out for her mother when her attention is elsewhere. The therapist reinforces this – 'She is saying she wants you' – and mother goes closer. Later they are laughing together and mother is saying 'you're a cheeky girl'. In following weeks they come 'voluntarily' and mother is again talking with Aisha face to face, as mum says 'you cheeky, you cheeky one'. Mum reports that when she was asleep Aisha woke her and that at first she was cross, but then Aisha laughed and she stopped being angry. Aisha sits by mother with stiff outstretched arms held towards her; mother talks about how they are getting closer. They seem to be trying out new ways of being together, both within the group and at home.

The research free-play clips show improvements in their relationship after four months. Mother comments on a change she perceives in herself and consequently the interaction when watching the second video. She talks about feeling and looking more relaxed and remembers the first video as harder for her, not knowing how to handle her daughter's distress. Seeing this change objectively seems to reaffirm her feelings about how the group has helped her get closer to her daughter. She says:

> When I started to go downstairs to the clinic every week it did help. It changed my life really to be honest because I was with Aisha, I was playing with her, you know, Jessica was encouraging me, I had to, you

know, like when she used to go off like crying, like she showed me how to hold her . . . and that's when I did have the confidence of going downstairs alone with my daughter because I could never feel comfortable being alone with her.

Shared ambivalence, disruptions and repairs

The group is fostered as an attachment setting where it becomes possible to acknowledge and survive difficulties and mixed emotions together. Many statements and experiences are potentially joint ones that can be helpful for everyone. A baby's hesitancy may be responded to like this – 'You don't look too sure, do you? But you are safe there on mummy's knee, that's it, take it in gradually' – to label ambivalent feelings bound to be shared by the baby's parents as well as other group members. Direct talking to a baby can be less threatening than addressing similar feelings with an adult (Baradon, 2005) and, in addition, establishes babies as sentient beings for whom the group setting is both significant and challenging. This is especially powerful for hostel parents arriving overwhelmed by their own problems and their baby's symptoms. The hope is to build a culture suggesting that babies are both fascinating and complicated, like all human beings, and that we are in it together. It conveys that parenting is never straightforward, that surviving distress is a natural part of family (and group) life, and that upset babies or frustrated mothers and fathers are inevitable.

When a session is noisy or disconnected, the therapist can make a statement to the air, while knowing only some will hear it, saying 'Gosh, we seem to be quite all over the place today'. Identifying and naming dysregulated emotions, in the here and now, helps to decrease their arousal and creates a 'body shift'. Within a group context everyone potentially benefits, by being offered a hall of mirrors where affects become universal, reducing shame and encouraging openness. The use of the word 'we' helps to reinforce the shared enterprise, to include the team, who are also 'all over the place' on the mat in that moment. Through affective tone and bodily composure, it is hoped to imbue confidence that the session won't escalate out of control, as many of these families' histories lead them to expect. The therapist can also engage face to face with a distressed parent and baby, reaching out as empathically as possible and acting directly, sometimes by holding and touching, to scaffold their experience. Shared experience of disruptions and repairs, turbulence and cohesion, helps to strengthen the group's holding and containing capacities. These are partly the spontaneity and sloppiness of the therapeutic process: 'the manner of negotiating repairs and correcting slippages is one of the more important ways-of-being-with-the- other that become implicitly known' (Stern, 2004). The group offers parents and infants a model for living through and regulating emotions.

Maya, her mother and friends

This final example illustrates a small subgroup of mothers and babies, through their collective use, and testing, of the group's therapeutic capacities. They get to know each other after meeting in the clinic, are all Bengali (some speak fluent English, others not) and seem especially vulnerable, with worrying patterns of relating with their babies. The discussion focuses on one dyad.

Maya arrives at the clinic when she is three months, soon after moving to the hostel and having just spent a week in hospital with feeding problems. Maya is small, still and unresponsive, dressed carefully and beautifully. Her mother seems desperate, talking rapidly and tearfully about their situation, her inability to get Maya to take a bottle and their tiny hostel room. She says she loves her baby but she is so worried and has so many problems, including her own eating difficulties. The health visitor and therapist try their usual advice about feeding, labelling of affects, helping them be together and bringing Maya to life as a little person, but with limited success. Mother and Maya continue coming to the clinic, ostensibly to check Maya's weight which the health visitor does with minimal fuss. Characteristically they arrive and remain standing, with mother saying she has to go, but complaining about Maya's crying and feeding. There is encouragement to sit and play together on the mat. When Maya is shown a toy and an interested face she responds, but mother jumps up for her mobile or because, she says, Maya is tired. The therapist talks for Maya – 'Oh, I was just getting interested' – but mother doesn't hear.

Gradually Maya and her mother meet other Bengali mothers and babies in the clinic and they arrive with three or four others. All of them are dressed up as though going to a party and they get compliments from other families and the staff team. In this phase, in their use of the group, they seem high on the pleasure of finding friends, which is a gratifying function, but their babies are treated like dolls, or accessories, which is painful to watch. Babies are passed around between them looking distressed, being force-fed and having their photos taken. The narcissistic needs of the mothers seem to take precedence and, on occasions, the baby clinic feels invaded by a negative subculture. The team finds itself critical of these mothers and tries to avoid losing sympathy or constructive thinking. Their behaviour can be understood as letting the team know about their lives; perhaps being moved constantly, treated impersonally, force-fed baby care advice and scrutiny as mothers?

Over months the need for these families to come to the clinic all together diminishes as they meet outside. Each, in different ways, lurches between crises, including domestic violence, hospital admissions and loss of contact with families of origin. Maya and her mother appear intermittently, usually with panicky descriptions of physical symptoms that require reassurance. They start to stay slightly longer and Maya has enjoyable moments. Mother might comment on how Maya remembers people in the group or she notices when her eyes light up in pleasure. She is slightly less provocative towards Maya, who continues to look underfed and lacking in vitality. There is reduced anxiety in the staff team, and in the therapist's countertransference, but their second filmed interactions (viewed once research is completed) suggest ongoing difficulty: *Mother takes the bell saying: 'This is no more, no more'; she rings it, hides it behind her back. Mother's tone of voice changes: 'peek-a-boo!' Baby looks for bell, almost falls over and makes squealing noise. Mother presents bell to baby saying 'Aah!' and quickly hides bell behind her back again: 'Where's it gone?' Baby cries and almost falls back, mother catches her and presents her with the bell and then puts it on the floor out of baby's reach.* It goes on like this, until Maya spits up and mother lurches towards her saying 'She is bleeding, oh god, oh god', and the filming stops abruptly. The clip illustrates this mother's relentless teasing and intrusive behaviour towards her infant, and its nadir with bleeding and panic. It is disturbing. It also explains her relationship to the clinic group (as well as to Maya) where her behaviour, as described earlier, is similarly tantalising.

Talking about the clinic to the researcher, Maya's mother says: *They give you the best advice they can do . . . that's probably the one best thing about this hostel to be honest with you, going to the clinic. Everything else is just so rubbish. I mean the lift breaks down . . .* The clinic group lift has apparently not broken down for Maya and her mother, despite their destructive impulses. The staff team, and other families, continue to be involved with them past Maya's first birthday. Simple, possibly profound, things happen like peering beneath Maya's pretty bonnet, into her face, to try to make contact with Maya's infant self. Recently the therapist is able to reinforce an interaction and her speaking for Maya appears meaningful:

> Mother sits next to Maya, who is rocking on a horse and the therapist sits beside them. She says: 'That's lovely, it's nice to have mummy next to me, mummy can be so active just like me, but sometimes it's good to be still and to enjoy each other'. They stay in delighted contact with each other for some time and, from mother's knowing look to the therapist and Maya's pleasure, it seems an important moment.

Progress is limited but this model of clinic group can offer continuity, acceptance and a determination to relate with Maya, her mother and their friends.

Research results and final comments

The full research findings are in the process of being submitted for publication. The preliminary results indicate significant improvements in both mental and motor development for the infants in the intervention group. No such changes were found in the control group. Furthermore, developmental changes did not merely reflect increased ability within already normal limits, but resulted in fewer infants in the intervention group demonstrating delayed development three to four months after initial assessment. This contrasts with those living at control group hostels, where more infants were found to be developmentally delayed after three to four months. The quality of interactions is still in the process of being coded. Free-play filmed sequences and recorded interviews with parents, from the research, have also been helpful in thinking for clinical purposes, as well as for writing this chapter.

These initial research outcomes corroborate the overall positive experience of the baby clinic group. Over weeks, months and, sometimes, years many families sustain involvement despite their difficulties. Their infants are offered opportunities for activity and play through the physical space in the clinic, combined with interested and responsive adults giving priority to babies. Crucial to this success is the integration of health visiting and parent–infant group psychotherapy and a team that is able to work together. The premise is that neither a traditionally run, on-site baby clinic nor a weekly therapeutic 'play with your baby' group would have a similar impact. The ordinariness of the baby clinic, with prompt access to practical advice and medical attention, combines to engage with the infant self in an accessible attachment group setting. This model of parent–infant group psychotherapy shows potential for mitigating relational trauma and could be replicated in other baby clinic settings that have high numbers of infants at risk.

Acknowledgements

Thanks to Lorraine Ibison, Health Visitor, so pivotal in this baby clinic and to Camden Primary Care Trust and Housing. Also to Tessa Baradon and Peter Fonagy, at the Anna Freud Centre, for their support and supervision.

References

Baradon, T., Broughton, C., Gibbs, I., James, J., Joyce, A. & Woodhead, J. (2005) *The practice of psychoanalytic parent–infant psychotherapy: Claiming the baby*. London: Routledge.
Campbell P. & Salo, F. (2007) Babies in groups: The creative role of the babies, mothers and therapists. In M.E. Pozzi-Monzo (Ed.), *Innovations in parent–infant psychotherapy*. London: Karnac.
Crisis (2006) *Fighting for hope for homeless people: Statistics about homelessness*. Available online at: www.crisis.org.uk
Garland, C., Hume, F. & Majid, S. (2002) Remaking connections: Refugees and the development of emotional capital in therapy groups. *Psychoanalytic Psychotherapy*, 15(3): 197–214.
Nitsun, M. (1996) *The anti-group: Destructive forces in the group and their creative potential*. London: Routledge.

Papadopoulos, R.K (2007) Refugees, trauma and adversity-activated development. *European Journal of Psychotherapy and Counselling*, 9(3): 301–312.

Reddy, V. (2008) *How infants know minds*. Cambridge, MA: Harvard University Press.

Sawtell, M. (2002) *Lives on hold: Homeless families*. London: Maternity Alliance.

Schore, J.R. & Schore, A.N. (2007) Modern attachment theory: The central role of affect regulation in development and treatment. *Clinical Social Work Journal*, 36(1): 9–20.

Stern, D. (2004) *The present moment in psychotherapy and everyday life*. New York: W.W. Norton.

Stern, D. (2008) The clinical relevance of infancy: A progress report. *Infant Mental Health Journal*, 29(3): 177–188.

Sure Start (2008) *The impact of sure start local programmes on three year olds and their families*. Available online at: www.surestart.gov.uk/_doc/P0002519.pdf

Vonstanis, P. (2002) Mental health of homeless children and their families. *Advances in Psychiatric Treatment*, 8: 463–469.

Woodhead, J. & James. J. (2007) Transformational process in parent–infant psychotherapy: Provision in community groups. *Innovations in parent–infant psychotherapy*. London: Karnac.

Chapter 7

Babies behind bars

Working with relational trauma with mothers and babies in prison

Ju Tomas-Merrills and Anita Chakraborty

Imprisoned mothers who have care of their babies during their sentence stay in designated Mother Baby Units (MBUs). The units offer a paradoxical experience in having both holding and destabilising elements for the mothers and their babies. The care of staff, the predictability of provision and prison structures provide containment. Other experiences such as the admission to the prison, day-to-day procedures and emergency situations can be unsettling and frightening and have a destabilising effect on what is already a vulnerable and traumatised group (Baradon et al., 2008).

The New Beginnings programme also holds this paradox. It is structured and boundaried and the work is done in a containing manner. However, it raises highly distressing topics for the women, engaging them in a process that challenges their psychic organisation.

In this chapter we describe the delivery of the programme and why we believe it has been beneficial to the mothers and their babies: how in working with the trauma we are not just replaying it but processing it in a way that is beneficial to both.

The prison context

The prison population is high-risk in terms of histories associated with trauma, such as abuse, periods in care, and mental disturbance (Ramsbotham, 2003; Caddle & Crisp, 1997; Birmingham, 2004). Most mothers and babies on the MBU will have also experienced separation from each other prior to admission to the unit. For example, depending on the circumstances of the mother's arrest, her baby may be placed in temporary foster care or remain with the father, other relatives or friends. Some mothers have been separated from a partner, older children, and extended families, and they may or may not have contact with them while in prison. In the prison, mothers may be awaiting possible deportation, sentencing or parole judgments, uncertain about having to stay longer in prison or about the circumstances of their future on release. If a mother's sentence means the child will be in prison past the age of 18 months, separation will usually occur during the first six months of the child's life to prevent undue trauma for the child.

In many ways, the MBU provides a holding and containing environment (Winnicott, 1956) for the mothers and babies with its staffing, and set routine of regular meals, morning and bedtime arrangements, visiting hours, etc. It can provide a context for the mother to experience some stability and more opportunity to be with her baby, a situation that may not have been possible on the outside. Mothers can form attachments to prison officers and other staff working in the MBU and to health and social services professionals who come in on a weekly basis, as well as to each other. Their babies often spend considerable time in the company of other babies and mothers and form relationships with the nursery workers and prison officers whom they see daily. In addition, babies often meet regularly with their mother's partner, friends and other relatives who visit, and may thus have a cumulatively more sociable experience while on the MBUs than might otherwise have been the case.

In our experience, however, the acts of sentencing and process of imprisonment almost always have a significant effect on a mother's wellbeing and can reactivate many troubling aspects of her history. Many mothers for instance do not expect to be imprisoned and are shocked about being sent straight to prison without being able to go home first, expecting some leniency from the court in respect of their pregnancy or young baby. Prison procedures by themselves evoke anxiety for the mother around separation from her baby, as well as from other family members, which can include older children. Her experiences may repeat patterns of trauma she suffered in the past.

Many mothers feel very guilty about the prospect of their babies growing up inside prison, anxious that this may be harmful. Often they project their anger and the perceived responsibility for this on to prison staff and faceless legal and political systems. There is often hostility and resentment from mothers towards those responsible for their care; the relationships with prison officers and the unit manager in particular easily trigger a negative transference underpinned by unresolved conflicts to authority figures and their own child–parent relationship.

This paradox seems to permeate many of the activities related to the prison and imprisonment. A mother who may feel comforted and supported by having an officer accompanying her to the maternity ward or to a hospital visit may also complain at how publicly humiliated she feels by being surrounded by officers with their prison uniforms, making it known to the public that she is a prisoner. Unplanned but necessary legal and medical appointments, unavoidable staffing changes, problems on other prison wings, and disruptions caused by the mothers and their babies themselves, lead to frequent experiences of frustration and sudden changes of plan. Mothers and babies must find ways of dealing with this within their confined circumstances, and often resort to suppression of rage, helplessness and passivity as a means of trying to avoid overt expression of their anger. Even in relatively settled times, when everyone seems to be getting on together, there are frequent disruptions of this kind, consequent on the setting and because impulsive emotional behaviour patterns often seem to characterise this population. For example, we are requested to leave a window uncovered in the group's room at all times so that staff can see and intervene if necessary, for the protection of all. Although we have never witnessed any dramatic incidents where intervention might be necessary, this was a striking reminder that our work was occurring within the prison environment, and that our usual methods of creating safety and privacy in the group had to take this into account.

The *New Beginnings* programme[1]

Acknowledging the possible impact of, and interplay between, past attachment history and current imprisonment on the mother's attachment to her infant, *New Beginnings* aims to facilitate the naturally emerging processes associated with the attachment relationship in the early months of life.

The programme is based on an early-intervention model developed in the Parent–Infant Project at The Anna Freud Centre (Baradon et al., 2005) and aims to improve the mother–baby relationship and to prepare and support the mother and her baby for a future separation, should that be the outcome of sentencing.

The programme consists of eight two-hour sessions, delivered over four consecutive weeks, with a maximum of six dyads. It runs in a group format and is led by two co-facilitators (currently an adult and a child psychotherapist, JTM and AC respectively), who are supervised regularly by a consultant parent–infant psychotherapist.

Sessions are structured around specific themes designed to activate attachment patterns, which can then be utilised to help the mothers think about their babies. The subjects covered include the mother and baby's story from pregnancy to birth to the present day, mother's representation of her own significant childhood experiences and separations, hopes and fears for her baby, and managing strong emotional experiences while maintaining the capacity to parent.

The aim is to create a space in the group where mothers, who are frequently severely traumatised, can think about the baby's behaviour as a communication about needs and feelings and thus to help them to understand their babies better, in turn promoting their babies' healthy development.

A key aspect of the programme is about exploring new ways of mothers relating to their babies. Throughout sessions, playing and being together with

---

1 The *New Beginnings* programme was initiated and designed by Tessa Baradon.

the babies is highly important. The material from the structured programme is woven together with the babies' behaviours as they occur in the group, to facilitate the mothers' thinking about their babies' emotional experience, and ways in which their behaviours communicate about this.

As co-facilitators, we sit on the floor with the mothers and their babies. Being at the same level, we can more easily observe the babies, facilitate interactions and share observations with the mothers. Whenever possible, we sit opposite each other in order to promote eye contact and intuitive negotiation of the running of the group. The mothers are encouraged to bring whatever they might need for themselves and their babies for the whole day to minimise disruptions. In this way we nurture a therapeutic space where they can feel safe for personal and sometimes difficult experiences to be disclosed and discussed.

The group

The MBUs assist in selecting those mothers who will take part in the programme. It is for us as facilitators to assess continually the emotional capacity of all group members to face and reflect on uncomfortable or traumatic thoughts and feelings and to regulate the intensity and depth of the work accordingly. Despite efforts to ensure that the mothers know their participation is voluntary, inevitably there have been occasions where mothers have felt coerced to attend the programme, anxious that non-attendance might count against them in some way. This is something that is then worked with within the group, and between the mothers and prison staff.

The mothers often talk in the group about their experiences on the MBU. They may express anger about the 'prison system', perceiving it as rigid and unpredictable, slow in its response and lacking genuine interest in them or their babies. Some are resentful that their most basic needs such as eating, sleeping, work and exercise are controlled by the regulations and needs of the prison, and they are retaliatory and rebellious against this enforced dependence. Our response is to listen, and to verbalise their affective experience, connecting it with how they then find themselves responding to their babies, and how their babies in turn respond to them. The mothers' behaviour in the group also often reflects current dynamics on the unit, alliances and bullying among the women, and conflict with prison officers that arises on the unit can also re-emerge with us. In the group we can easily move from being perceived as caring and idealised to becoming identified as persecuting and critical, or as useless and unhelpful. The group dynamic can also reflect a sense of helplessness and dependency that some mothers feel about their imprisonment. For example, some mothers suppress their frustration, isolate themselves and keep distant from other mothers. At the same time, in reflection of wider friendships and relationships in the unit, we observe for example some of the older mothers having a supportive role to younger ones, and coalitions among women from the same country of origin. Supportive relationships are also developed with staff members on the unit and they can often become strong attachment figures for the mothers and babies. Attention can be drawn to these dynamics, and links made with the mothers' histories, and with their current relationships with their babies.

In the group we try to model predictability, transparency and empathy. Things that previously could not be talked about, such as the pain and rages of the past, can be shared and discussed to some extent. Sometimes memories or dissociated feelings burst forth as though a dam has been opened, despite an ethos of talking only about what each individual feels comfortable with.

In our experience, problems of affect regulation, low frustration tolerance, aggression, passivity and impulsivity are common in the group. Action, together with a need to destroy and repudiate thinking, for fear of being overwhelmed by affect and loss of control, is typical and persistent.

At times when the mothers' emotions are all-consuming, it leaves little space for them to think about their infants. Indeed, for some mothers the idea of considering the impact of their own emotional state on their babies, or their baby's capacity to experience a range of emotions in such complex ways, is something they have never thought about before. It seems that the weight of the mother's own vulnerability and emotional need often subsumes her ability to notice, let alone think about, her baby's affects and needs.

At the beginning our work with the babies is often regarded with amusement, curiosity or derision. This may change when the mothers start sharing feelings about their childhood experiences. Initially this is often experienced as traumatising and dysregulating, while our enquiries about the babies' experience in connection with the mothers' upset in the group is felt as critical or nonsensical. From their initial anxiety talking about difficult previous experiences, the group can then often find itself enjoying and benefiting from staying with the adult preoccupations, but becomes resistant and defensive in thinking about their infants. In challenging and enquiring about what was previously non-anxiety provoking, the course in effect destabilizes, and can leave some mothers feeling that the process is unhelpful or worse, reducing their capacity to respond to their babies. Gradually the work with the infants, based on an assumption that babies are sentient and intentional, begins to make more sense to them. It is precisely this direct work with the infants, together with the process of interpreting the mothers' own defences and resistance, that allows the mothers to reflect in a more meaningful way. Fraiberg (1980) writes that 'remembering saves a parent from blind repetition because it enables identification with the injured child'.

We help the mothers to see how their own reflective capacity can benefit them in their relationships with their babies, by using 'here and now' moments with the infants in the group that resonate with their own childhood experiences. We make use of those moments when the mother is more able to identify with the infant's vulnerabilities, and help them to observe their infants, promoting and modifying interactions in ways that will directly benefit the infant. For example, a mother told the group that on occasions when she was upset with her baby, she would lock the baby out of the room so that he could not be frightened by her stare as she had been with her mother. She wanted to know what we thought about her actions. We encouraged her to reflect on her baby's experience of being left alone in the corridor, and she was able to identify that her baby might be feeling frightened. This allowed us to explore other ways of managing her angry moments while still remaining available to the baby in a non-threatening way.

At a surface level, the babies are often compliant, remaining quiet and undemanding or asleep. On closer engagement, we begin to see signs of avoidant, passive, or disassociated infants, or ones who are over-aroused and unsoothable. Sometimes the babies seem to be frequently physically ill. As the course progresses, we see how the baby responds to the mother's distress and anxiety, and how the mother responds to the baby when distressed. When this becomes 'material' within the group, it can be used to make links between the mothers' internal representations and the way these influence their present relationships with their babies.

We encourage the mothers to continue the thinking that has been initiated in the group between sessions, to notice and record the babies' communications and their responses to them. In the group we reflect together on those observations made during the week, helping them to distinguish their babies' needs as different from their own, enhancing the attunement of the mother to her baby, and her capacity and range of responses to him.

A constant dynamic is a pull from the mothers for us to join them in a polarised view of the prison staff as persecutory, interfering or neglectful. We find that the interpretation of their disappointment in the prison service and in ourselves as a caring object is often the route both to a more balanced view of the staff and the care that is on offer in the MBU, and to a significant reduction in resistance to thinking together with us. At the end of the programme, some mothers explain that what has been most helpful is that we have just listened to and accepted their feelings of frustration about things that have happened, without taking sides either with them or with the staff.

Case study

The following account describes selected aspects of an interplay between dyadic and group work that took place during a New Beginnings programme in the context of a relatively well-functioning and stable MBU. The unit manager and prison staff had been working together as a team for some time, and a fairly well-established group of mothers and babies was resident on the unit.

On our arrival at the start of the course, the unit manager warned us that we had a challenging group ahead of us with several mothers who had difficult life histories. She told us particularly about Cath (early 20s) and her six-month-old baby, Olu, about whom she felt very concerned. When Cath had been sentenced and sent to prison, Olu, just a few weeks old, had been placed in foster care where he was reported to have been settled. Cath had two older children also living in care. She had been reunited with her baby on the unit in the past month but had been struggling, with Olu becoming extremely distressed and Cath unable to soothe him. This would frequently lead to Cath asking an officer to hold him or threatening to send him back to the foster parent. Cath had recently become provocative, aggressive and inconsiderate towards the other mothers, and in the light of the conflict this had caused, the unit manager felt uncertain whether it would be disruptive for the rest of the group if this dyad took part in the programme.

We were faced with a complicated decision: the course could easily be overwhelming for Cath, who already sounded very uncontained and potentially disruptive. However, we decided to include them as we believed Olu could benefit from being in the group and that working with this dyad within the group could benefit the other members.

On first impressions, Cath and Olu looked like two pieces of a jigsaw that didn't quite fit together. Cath was petite and, even before she first sat down, said Olu was too heavy for her. When introduced to the course, she expressed some concerns about confidentiality and stayed behind afterwards to tell us that she had recently discovered further aspects of her childhood abuse. She linked her current difficulties on the unit to the distress she felt on hearing this new information. While she was telling us this, Olu became extremely distressed. Cath jigged him up and down intensely and repeatedly, becoming angry and distressed herself as Olu's cries heightened. Barely able to register our attempts to help, she handed Olu over to one of the prison officers who was then able to sooth him.

The following week we found Cath occupying the room designed for the group and shouting at a prison officer. Olu was screaming and all the other group members were waiting unhappily outside. Again we experienced a pressure to exclude the dyad, but suspected we would be colluding with dynamics of splitting and projection taking place between Cath and the other mothers. As Cath was very keen to continue with the course, we decided that this was an opportunity for the whole group to work through the difficulties rather than enact them. We therefore worked to integrate Cath and Olu within the group and as we helped to make sense of Cath's own upset and fears about the course, we helped her also to think about how she might explain the morning's events to the other group members. Then we settled the rest of the group in the room, initially in Cath's absence, acknowledging their ambivalent feelings about engaging with us following this disruptive start, and their anger with Cath. We explained how Cath's difficulty in soothing Olu linked to one of the main themes of the course, the question of how to maintain the emotional capacity to respond to your infant when upset yourself. We worked to make links between Cath's current difficulty and the other mothers' experiences of difficulties with their infants. As the group began to engage with us, curious if dismissive about our engagement with their babies, they were able to accept Cath and Olu when they returned. The atmosphere was a little wary but mostly curious, and Cath was able to participate.

Later that day Katie, one of the other mothers, spoke about her difficult pregnancy; her account impacted emotionally on all the others, changing the atmosphere, deepening the sense of people listening, feeling empathic and connecting with aspects of their own experiences. The babies seemed to become quieter. In response Cath began to play with Olu, who seemed to enjoy his mother's attention, gurgling and kicking in response. As she began to increase her volume and activity, Olu's pleasure began to change; his mother responded to his looking away by stimulating him more. Olu became unsettled, while we began to feel a growing sense of irritation and concern. Cath started to tickle Olu, who then started to cry, his face and body looking full and ready to burst. He began to cry in a very upset way, and Cath became very agitated, moving him around from one position to another awkwardly and again jigging him up and down. Both facilitators found it difficult but necessary to intervene at this moment. We were aware that any comment was likely to be experienced by Cath as persecutory, while also aware that her behaviour had appeared quite provocative towards both Olu and the other group members. Treading carefully, we commented about how difficult it seemed in the group right now. We suggested that perhaps Olu's distress now was in some way connected with Katie's very moving story which had affected everyone in the group, and that it was difficult for Cath in this situation trying to soothe and respond to him. We attempted to help Cath in attending to Olu, but she became more agitated and suddenly got up and left the room.

The group reacted with outrage to the disruptions caused that morning, and to other recent incidents involving Cath. This led to a more open discussion about feelings of helplessness and being trapped – feelings that they experienced on the unit, and also in their relationships with their babies. The group became more open with each other, and able to reflect about their babies' behaviours in more complex ways. We were unsure whether their harmony was augmented not only by greater trust within the group but also perhaps by a sense of satisfaction that coincided with the expulsion of the 'bad' group member. Cath didn't return to the group that day, but as we were preparing to leave, she came to talk with us together with her personal officer. In the discussion that followed, Cath was able to think about why she had left earlier that day, linking it with times when her mother used to tell her to shut up and not make a noise. We were able to think with Cath about the impact of Katie's story on her and on her response to Olu, and how this related to her childhood. She also became more able to take on board the idea that Olu responded to her emotional state: as she panicked, so did he; as she became calmer, so could he.

Arriving the following week, we learned that Cath felt that by leaving the group she had deprived herself and Olu from learning something new, and that she very much wanted to continue. She appeared much calmer and contained, and was able to think with us about how the other mothers might feel after the disruptions of the previous week. There was some degree of frostiness initially from the other mothers with their return but this changed considerably as Cath, in response to the morning's programme, was one of the first to speak. She was able to explain how her past experiences of being taken into care might link to her comings and goings in the group and to think about what it might have been like for Olu separating from her, moving into foster care, having to adapt to her presence again and to a new environment.

Others in the group empathized with her situation. Olu began to cry and while Cath still struggled to soothe him, she was more able to respond and allow herself to be helped. The group were more able to tolerate pausing as we took time to think about Olu's experience. One facilitator spoke to Olu directly, verbalising some of the feelings that he might be experiencing when his mother is so upset. Cath observed, watching a different way of relating to her baby, and with the group we were able to think together about what was happening with Olu now and how he was feeling. Later Cath repeated with Olu what she had seen from the interaction with the facilitator. She laid Olu on the floor and began speaking to him slowly, calmly and gently, and Olu in response began to calm and even gave a smile. This experience proved to be a turning point in Cath's recognition of the influence of her speech, tone of voice and behaviour on Olu. It was also a decisive moment for the rest of the group, who became more able to reflect at a deeper level on the impact of their feeling states and behaviour on their babies, including those mothers who had been in denial of having any difficulties at all. Cath was thereafter able to stay in the group without walking out and required significantly less individual attention, ending the programme feeling more accepted, and less isolated and persecuted by the others. Olu remained relatively quiet thereafter, able to make eye-contact and smile, only mildly curious in his surroundings but far less dysregulated during the group time. By the end of the course, the sense of drama and polarisation that we had encountered on the unit in the first few weeks seemed to have dissipated. Instead of hearing concern from the unit manager about what to do about Cath and Olu, we heard reports of all the mothers basically getting along, singing and cooking together.

Clinical formulation: Dyadic and group elements

The clinical example presented is not atypical of that of many mothers and infants that we work with in the prison groups. It illustrates how relational trauma manifests within a dyad and how this can become enacted in the group.

Cath's difficulty in processing the abuse and deprivations of her early life meant that their harmful effects were primed to re-emerge in the relationship between her and Olu. We wondered if Olu's cries reminded Cath of past traumatic experiences, perhaps in identification with the helplessness and vulnerability of her infantile self, and in identification with the abusive mother, filling her with hostility (Fraiberg et al., 1975; Fraiberg, 1980).

As they listened to the other mother's story, we sensed that distressing memories of vulnerability were re-evoked for the whole group, with Cath losing the capacity to differentiate between Olu's needs and her own. It is possible that Olu became a vehicle for her to rid herself of unwanted disturbing affect, a reversal of roles where he carried the responsibility for his mother's state of mind. We suggest that as he became dysregulated, Cath perceived Olu as not wanting to be soothed by her and as deliberately not letting her soothe him, thereby rejecting her. Olu was left traumatized by a mother who could not help him regain equilibrium, and Cath was left carrying unbearable hostility and aggression.

Perhaps being reunited with her baby at the very point in which she faced the reality that her mother had knowingly failed to protect her, placed Cath in a state of conflict between wanting to stay together with Olu and ridding herself of him. Her threat to send Olu back to the foster carer probably had conscious and unconscious meaning. It seemed that she didn't trust herself or felt that others didn't trust her to be a good enough mother to him; perhaps that he would feel safer in foster care just as she had done. At a more unconscious level, perhaps sending him away was an act of retaliation against both her mother and her son who perceivably rejected her.

Initially, the group used Cath to carry all their uncomfortable feelings – hostility, shortcomings as a mother, identifications with victim and aggressor. To exclude the dyad would have been to collude with this split and to create the illusion of a united working group. In accepting them in the group and not colluding with the group's projections into her, ourselves and the prison environment, we refused to fulfil the role of the persecutory rejecting mother. Cath became more capable of receiving our help and intervention, and the group became more capable of genuine reflection, able to own their feelings of negativity and helplessness. The experience of being accepted in this way made it possible for Cath to see the group as a good enough mother, and strengthened her resolve and the potential to be a good mother herself for Olu.

Our aim was to increase the capacity of the group as a whole to recognise the reality of their infants' experience, and thereby promote their ability to respond as mothers, even in the face of their own extreme distress and frustration. The focus of the work with Cath was around enabling her to regulate her infant's affective states and attune to his needs, rather than use him for her own needs. Through the process of the course, the group became less persecutory and Cath's sense of isolation reduced, helping her to see the unit as a more benign place. The course, furthermore, facilitated greater empathy and support between all the mothers, with a consequent improvement in the atmosphere on the unit as a whole.

Discussion: Countertransferential aspects

The programme takes place in a very complex setting and elicits strong and complex emotions in all involved, including the group facilitators. It has thus been very important as co-facilitators to reflect on our own countertransference in understanding and responding to the experiences of staff, mothers and their babies.

Losing our freedom, albeit temporarily, and being dependent on others to take us from the front gate of the prison to the MBU and back again raises feelings in us associated with a lack of autonomy and control. From entering the gates to the moment of final departure, there is a sense that we need to be prepared for the unexpected, with little or no time for reflection or discussion. Commonly we feel frustrated and helpless, particularly in our attempt to maintain an analytic frame, for example in time boundaries, keeping the frequency of disruptions from outside during group time to a minimum and maximizing the mothers and babies' ability to attend all or 'most' of the sessions.

A continual challenge for us is the reverberation of our own past and present attachments with the mothers' primitive emotions and projections. We have needed to watch our own countertransference carefully, specifically our own hopes, frustrations and identifications. One of us might identify more with the baby, the other with the mother; one with the group, the other with the prison staff; both of us may be mindful of a desire born of narcissism or omnipotence to rescue a dyad from its predicament.

We have found repeatedly that paying close attention to the feelings we experience in the setting, and within the group, is vital and instrumental in helping us to stay empathically in touch with the mothers' and babies' cumulative, unprocessed feelings, and to retain our capacity to think. In witnessing the emotional pain, dilemmas and helplessness of the infants, the processing of our own experience has been highly important for both of us in maintaining sufficient genuine emotional resonance with the mother, in order to help her recognise and value empathically her baby's separateness and unique needs as distinct from the infant within her.

We have learnt in delivering this programme that it is crucially important that we model a good thinking couple for the group. This has been vital in containing the destructive tendencies within the group that have pushed towards polarisation and splitting, and it has served as a model for the mothers in maintaining their capacity to parent in the face of high emotional arousal and helplessness. Schore (2001) proposes that the therapist's empathic capacity to regulate the patient's arousal state within the affectively charged non-conscious transference–countertransference relationship is critical to clinical effectiveness. We are aware that when we lose our capacity to think, at times when the group seeks to repudiate linking and begins to act rather than reflect, we find ourselves incapacitated, passive where intervention is required, with the potential to become split as a thinking couple, needing to be extra vigilant not to act out ourselves. Holding onto our analytic frame and the structure of the programme enables us to regain a thinking mind.

Trusting each other and being fluid in the roles we hold has allowed us to have a creative and fruitful working partnership, making the work both challenging and exciting. One of us, for example, can take a lead exploring a family history with a mother while the other keeps a watchful eye on the babies and how what is being said impacts on the rest of the group.

Concluding remarks

In working with the *New Beginnings* groups we constantly reflect on what the mothers experience and gain from the programme and from their relationship with us. We are aware that through our intense work together, we and the group become attachment figures for the mothers and babies (James, 2002). We provide them with the experience of being heard, understood and cared for, and for some this is a significant procedural corrective emotional experience (Beebe et al., 2005). We have seen changes in how some mothers think about and relate to their babies – they start looking at them in a different way and give a different value and more meaning to their baby's behaviour. We experience mothers who at the beginning have a very idealised, denigrated or closed view of the group, and yet who learn to use it as a 'thinking and behaving space' (Baradon et al., 2008) and move more to a position of allowing a more complex and mixed view of themselves as mothers and of their baby. At the same time, in each group we have encountered mothers and babies who have evoked significant concern, and about whom the concern has remained with us after the programme ended.

The feedback given by the mothers is often mixed. One mother reported that she was simply asked to 'divulge these issues without getting anything in return'. Another that it was 'just give, give, give' and we 'didn't provide any solutions' or that it 'felt too much like counselling, going too deep into the past' and 'talking too much about their family' which they didn't find helpful. We have also had feedback that indicates that the programme has led some mothers to begin to relate differently: 'I think more now when [I am] upset to what my baby is thinking'. Another mother was more reflective in terms of attributing reasons for why her baby might be crying (e.g. after she came back from a visit) and this knowledge had also made her feel more calm. One set of mothers wanted the group to be an ongoing one because it was 'such a nice forum to talk about emotions and think about [their] babies'.

We feel that this mixed feedback from mothers encapsulates the paradoxical nature of their experience both of imprisonment and of the programme – intrusive, distressing and destabilising, and at the same time for some (perhaps unexpectedly) also containing and enriching.

It is indeed a challenge to play the role of loved and unloved attachment object in these circumstances, and in concluding this chapter we would like to acknowledge the prison officers, nursery staff and others who provide the containment for these mothers and babies on a regular day-to-day basis. Whatever adaptations we have needed to make in working in this setting, the creation and effectiveness of this applied work have only been possible in the context of the welcome we have received from the prison service, and the MBUs in particular. We would like to thank them for their continual and regular support in keeping us in their minds, and helping us to provide a reliable therapeutic setting. Finally, we would like to express our appreciation to the mothers and babies for their contribution and commitment, without which this work would not have been possible.

References

Baradon, T. with Broughton, C., Gibbs, I., James, J., Joyce A. & Woodhead, J. (2005) *The practice of psychoanalytic parent–infant psychotherapy: Claiming the baby.* London: Routledge.

Baradon, T., Fonagy, P., Bland, K., Lenard, K. & Sleed, M. (2008) New Beginnings – an experience-based programme addressing the attachment relationship between mothers and babies in prisons. *Journal of Child Psychotherapy*, 34(2): 240–258.

Beebe, B., Knoblauch, S., Rustin, J. & Sorter, D. (2005) *Forms of intersubjectivity in infant research and adult treatment.* New York: Other Press

Birmingham, L. (2004) *Psychiatric morbidity and mental health treatment needs among women in prison mother and baby units.* Unpublished paper, University of Southampton, UK.

Caddle, D. & Crisp, D. (1997) *Imprisoned women and mothers.* London: Home Office Research and Statistics Directorate Report, Research Study 162.

Fraiberg, S. (1980) *Clinical studies in infant mental health: The first year of life.* New York: Basic Books.

Fraiberg, S., Adelson, E. & Shapiro, V. (1975) Ghosts in the nursery: A psychoanalytic approach to impaired infant–mother relationships. *Journal of the American Academy of Child Psychiatry*, 14: 387–421.

James, J. (2002) Developing a culture for change in group analytic psychotherapy for mothers and babies. *British Journal of Psychotherapy*, 19: 77–91.

Ramsbotham, D. (2003) *Prison-Gate: The shocking state of Britain's prisons and the need for visionary change.* London: Free Press.

Schore, A.N. (2001) The Seventh Annual John Bowlby Memorial Lecture, Minds in the making: Attachment, the self-organising brain, and developmentally-oriented psychoanalytic psychotherapy. *British Journal of Psychotherapy*, 17, 299–328.

Winnicott, D.W. (1956) Primary maternal preoccupation. In *Collected papers: Through paediatrics to psycho-analysis.* London: Tavistock, 1958.

Chapter 8

Containment of trauma

Working in the community

Tessa Dalley

This chapter will consider parent–infant work in a community with high levels of social and economic deprivation and transient population. The parent–infant psychotherapist worked in both a clinical and a consultation role as a member of the Emotional Support Service, an innovative and unique service set up as part of a Sure Start Local Programme.

The issues of working in this diverse and challenging environment are complex. Using a model of containment in which the mother's mind receives, contains and transforms the projections of the infant, consideration will be given to the role of consultation, wherein the consultant acts as a container for anxiety of practitioners who are exposed to high levels of trauma in this vulnerable client group. Parallels are drawn with the need for containment and attending to the relationship between traumatized mothers and their babies in parent–infant psychotherapy.

Sure Start

Sure Start was set up in 2001 as a cornerstone of the UK Government's drive to tackle child poverty and social exclusion (Tunstill et al., 2005; Fonagy & Higgitt, 2004) and designed to deliver a universal intervention for all children under four and their families. By living in designated areas where Sure Start Local Programmes (SSLPs) were established, all families served as the 'targets' of intervention. This approach limited the stigma that can affect targeted families or specific communities. In this way it was expected that services would help the most hard-to-reach families. SSLPs were expected to provide core services (Anning et al., 2005) and planning and delivery were left to each area to decide for itself (Rutter, 2006).

The Emotional Support Service was an innovative service set up in 2001 by the Sure Start Mental Health Consortium, a partnership between local voluntary and statutory mental health providers and Sure Start Kilburn Priory Locality in London. The aim was to promote the emotional well-being of families with children under five by providing accessible local support services in health centres, community centres and nurseries. Moving some services from clinics to the community improved coordination between existing services, with emphasis placed on joined-up thinking and working collaboratively with other professionals.

The consortium was unique in employing child, adult and infant mental health practitioners, who worked together as a multidisciplinary team offering clinical, outreach and consultation services. The parent–infant psychotherapist worked primarily in one of the health centres with pregnant mothers and those with infants under one. Parents and their babies were seen by individual appointment or they could also attend a drop-in group.

Consultation and working with colleagues

The complexities of offering consultation to teams working in the community have been well documented in the literature (Cregeen, 2008; Obholzer & Roberts, 1994; Emanuel, 2002). Trauma and disturbance associated with severe deprivation and abuse can impact on the professionals involved. Practitioners working closely with traumatized families are repositories for much of the evacuated distress, and this relationship has to bear the strain of cumulative experience of trauma and loss. Their approach to this task is often, unconsciously, influenced by their own experience of trauma and loss and may contribute to a 'disorganized' state of mind being re-enacted by the often conflicting and overwhelming emotional demands of their clients. This interferes with their capacity to provide containment and thereby compounds the situation and the deprivation of the families in their care. 'Disturbing primitive mechanisms and defense against anxiety get "re-enacted" in the system by care professionals who are recipients of these powerful projections' (Emanuel, 2002: 163).

Also within the wider organization, re-enactment becomes a substitute for thought. Workers can become paralysed when caught between conflicting demands of their clients and those of their managers and as this becomes intolerable, it interferes with a capacity to think. Pressure to act is an inevitable response within workers carrying high levels of anxiety from their clients as well as uncontained anxiety permeating through the care system. Burden of work and overwhelming case loads may affect the capacity to make use of outside help, leaving the worker feeling depleted and helpless, which may replicate the experience of deprivation of those families who are most hard to reach, neglected and abused.

Mosse (1994) outlines a model of consultation in which institutions and teams are viewed as social systems with systemic dynamics that have an unconscious life. He argues that social and psychoanalytic perspectives must be deployed together if real change is to be effected. For teams that are largely unfamiliar with psychoanalytic thinking there is a need to create a balance between heightening awareness to unconscious processes and paying attention to the systemic elements that affect the work. Generally, the more distressed the client group, the more unconscious communications are likely to predominate. However, over-emphasis on these may add to frustration and have a negative affect, sometimes leading to teams or individuals feeling in some way criticized or pathologized or what has been called 'character assassination'. 'It can lead to consultants undertaking or presenting their work in a way that pathologised the behaviour and functioning of the institution and its individual members without giving due regard to the effectiveness with which the conscious real-world tasks of the organizations are being pursued' (Mosse, 1994: 7).

Sure Start family support workers form the team of highly committed and enthusiastic practitioners who deliver core services to families in their locality. The team has different responsibilities and a range of expertise in housing, employment, disability, child care and health visiting. They receive and process up to 50 new referrals a week and have a large and complex caseload, many with special needs. Based in one of the Children's Centres, their task is complex and variable in offering support to families and managing the distress of social exclusion, mental illness, economic hardship, poor housing, domestic violence, trauma, unemployment, child abuse, neglect. Helping support these vulnerable families with very young children demands considerable emotional resilience, often working on the threshold of legal child protection.

The parent–infant psychotherapist, who acted as consultant to the family support workers, was part of the overall team employed by Sure Start working with the same client group. Offering a consultation framework not totally outside the institutional dynamics was complex, as maintaining an objective perspective was at times compromised. Mosse (1994) remarks: 'membership of an institution makes it harder to observe and understand that institution; we become caught up in the anxieties inherent in the work and the characteristic defences against those anxieties. This soon leads to shared habitual ways of seeing and a common failure to question 'holy writ' (Mosse, 1994: 8). However, the building of trust and thinking collaboratively as colleagues emerged as important in strengthening ties and professional linking in the understanding of the work.

Establishing a culture for thinking

Consultation took the form of fortnightly meetings for one hour. Regularity of meetings, setting and time established boundaries that were necessary to begin a process of engagement with the team, whose work schedules tended to be chaotic and crisis-driven. Occasionally, the group included professionals from different disciplines. This multidisciplinary composition enabled rich and diverse thinking, but the changeable, unpredictable membership of the group created problems with consistency. The diverse ethnicity added considerable depth and resource to the team. Sharing and understanding language and cultural norms forged tentative links to some of the most isolated, troubled and hard-to-reach families, although some of the team struggled with over-identification of their anxieties and predicaments.

The team was very friendly and seemed to welcome the prospect of engaging in the consultation process. At first, some underlying resistance was expressed by reluctance to leave computers, staff arriving late due to diary errors and at times placing themselves outside the circle, indicating some reluctance to participate fully in the process. Thinking about the meaning of this was important in reflecting on complex anxieties and transference issues that arose in the containment of high levels of risk and trauma. By maintaining the consistent frame and a regular presence, the parent–infant psychotherapist kept in mind the internal struggles of individual team members in bringing emotional pain and conflicts of their clients into the arena for thought.

Over time, the team settled into working and thinking about the powerful and complex dynamics of individuals and the team in general. Sprince (2002) points out the importance of creating an insightful and benign containment at an organizational level, strong enough to withstand the powerful negative projections of distressed and traumatized families. The psychotherapist installs an internalized model of a good and mutually beneficial relationship between container and contained through an open and reflective style. This fosters supportive team dynamics and enables a sense of working together in a joint enterprise, rather than being fragmented and split off from each other.

Cregeen (2008) describes a similar consultation approach to thinking and working using psychoanalytic ideas. Obholzer and Roberts (1994) used the term 'process consultancy'. This is different to advice-based consultancy or providing expertise, and tensions may arise using this approach in that the consultant requires the team to think, take in and absorb the emotional impact of the disturbance rather than provide answers, give advice or give direction.

This dynamic was sometimes present in the Family Support Team if a solution had not been found although understanding had been shared and deepened. Even though the primary task of the consultation was made explicit, this did not mitigate the underlying wish to be alleviated from suffering. This tension eased with acknowledgement of the extent to which internal chaos and projections of their clients were being carried and that action was not the only solution.

The following example was not untypical of the team's caseload.

> A young woman, M, was referred in great distress as she had given birth at home alone with her three-year-old daughter. Although her baby boy was healthy and she had eventually managed to access the necessary medical help, she was finding it difficult to bond with her new baby. On visiting her at home the support worker spoke of how she was struggling

to process the full horror of her story. M had been raped as she fled political violence, and suffered from panic attacks and agoraphobia. She lived alone and found it difficult to go out during her pregnancy except to take her daughter to nursery. She managed to get to the hospital but was turned away as her labour was not far enough advanced. The baby was born on the floor almost as soon as she got home.

The consultation provided time and space to absorb the impact of these terrible events which were hard to hear. Sharing and reflecting on the trauma that reverberated around the room began a process of supporting the worker to work through feelings of violation and cumulative trauma. As well as the mother's distress, there were two small children to consider: a baby struggling to reach his traumatized mother and a small child terrified at what she had witnessed and that her mother would die. The team enabled some reflection by naming and holding onto the feelings in the room rather than allowing these to be fragmented and evacuated through enactment such as apportioning blame or referral to different services in a 'scatter-gun approach'. Experiencing this process helped the worker to establish a feeling of safety and containment for her client. After the initial response, the team was able to think at a deeper level and attribute meaning to what happened, such as whether her home was a place of safety for M which may have prompted the rapid labour, or conversely that the trauma of the rejection from the hospital may have been a significant contributing factor.

In many of the scenarios that were brought regularly to consultation, feelings of inadequacy, inexperience and doubts about competency were central anxieties that emerged. Not feeling 'good enough' was a common theme when particularly traumatic situations were under consideration. It became possible to think about this in relation to the mothers who themselves were not feeling 'good enough'. It was at times a relief to recognize that feelings of distress or inadequacy may come from a mother who passes unbearable feelings of upset or failure to the worker. As mutual trust within the consultation process developed, and this in turn built the idea that sharing difficulties could generate learning from each other. Sharing dilemmas and difficulties meant that the team did not feel so alone in managing the work. This tended to assuage another underlying dynamic: that the need to talk and think about a case was some indication of failure or not coping, and asking for help would lead to exposure of helplessness and hopelessness. 'Under sway of anxious states, an individual or group will become unable to think rationally, reflectively or symbolically and will resort to what are clung to as the "facts" ' (Wadell, 2007: 200).

Gradually the group began to move from seeking the opinion of the consultant to finding their own ways of thinking and understanding. A deeper curiosity developed about the team's capacity to think together, which was a strong dynamic for change. Using a model of the relationship between mother and baby, the concept of containment and the importance of their own containing function with clients became better understood through the experience of the consultation process.

Without adequate support systems, there is always some emotional risk in engaging in consultation work at this level. Frequency of the meetings can be insufficient to process and contain the emotional impact of the discussion. Some individuals within the team may feel further exposed and vulnerable. This in some ways mirrored the situation of the more 'hard to reach' families who were left in similar vulnerable positions without sufficient regular contact. At the end of each session there was a need to ensure that the emotional 'heat' had been worked through and that it was possible for the team to resume their working day. There was also a training function implicit in this approach so that the team could acknowledge how important it was for them to hold boundaries, finish meetings on time and leave their clients in a situation of 'good enough containment'. As well as offering this framework of containment, the parent–infant psychotherapist provided additional training opportunities in highlighting the mental health needs of the infant, postnatal depression, child protection, the impact of trauma and abuse, disability and so on.

Transformation through containment

This model proposed for consultation is similar to the framework of containment established in the clinical setting of parent–infant work where trauma and anxiety are contained and transformed. Transforming work involves the therapist's response to the impact of trauma and is a vital aspect of the parent–infant work in the community setting (Sklarew et al., 2004). Many of the women referred to the Emotional Support Service had suffered considerable trauma or continued to live with trauma (Haw & Dalley, 2008) but tended to present for help with problems located in their infants, such as feeding, sleeping and feeling exhausted and overwhelmed by their demands. Their infant's needs superseded their own and they continued to live with depression, hopelessness and little support in the home.

A traumatized mother may attempt to erase feelings associated with unbearable memory and has an understandable need to protect her infant from exposure to these experiences. Often the therapist has very little knowledge about the mother's past and so the full impact of the story unfolds, as it were, 'live' in the room. If the baby is present, he/she will also be experiencing the impact of this yet again. Holding onto thoughts and feelings and processing of the mother's trauma is central to the therapist's task, as the parent may not be ready to receive this back in any way. Pushing this back prematurely can be re-traumatizing for the mother and baby and continues to confirm their experience.

By tolerating emotional pain, the therapist begins a process of transformation for mother and baby. Elements of traumatic experience become
integrated and a start is made in the process of recovery. Part of the work of
the parent–infant psychotherapist is 'bearing witness' in attending to the
baby and naming aspects of relating in the detailed interaction between
mother and baby (Blackwell, 1997). By slowly working through the complex
feelings until they become bearable, the mother and baby become the focus of
treatment, not the trauma.

Maintaining a containing environment

On meeting with mothers and babies for the first time there was often a
feeling of mistrust, with a tendency to be fearful of questions and authority.
A therapeutic alliance needed to be carefully constructed to evoke a sense of
safety, containment and that the therapist was investing in this relationship
and there was a future. The work was slow and sensitive so that the mother
could begin to understand the extent to which she continued to expose her
infant to her own traumatized and unavailable state of mind. The therapist
remained mindful that it was highly likely that she would not return, as
revisiting painful experience was generally not recognized by the mothers as
having any benefit and tended to raise further anxieties. This phenomenon
was encountered frequently at the outset of the work.

The parent–infant work took place in a health centre with GP's surgery,
health visitors and baby clinics in the same location. This was accessible and
already familiar to most families, which undoubtedly lessened anxiety about
attending. One difficulty of working in this community setting was maintaining consistency of the therapeutic space. In a busy health centre with
multi-purpose rooms, a designated therapy room was hard to maintain.
Consistency of the therapeutic space usually had to be recreated for every
session with the same toys, cushions, mats and furniture and where there were
frequent interruptions from the external frame, such as toys and equipment
being used, double booking of rooms and general noise level. The same
setting maintains the container, consistent and safe, which enables both
mother and baby to anticipate the same room and predictable response from
the therapist. The therapist therefore becomes an important consistent figure
and trust that develops in the relationship between therapist and mother can
come to represent the parental couple in the mediation of mother's trauma,
in the same way as a supportive partner might do at home.

In the following example there was no stable paternal presence, leaving
both mother and baby more vulnerable and exposed to the effects of mother's
trauma.

> Melanie arrived for her first session with baby Laurence, a delightful little
> boy, six months old. The referral from the health visitor simply stated

'sleeping difficulties'. Laurence was an adventurous little boy who seemed curious to explore the toys but stayed very close to his mother. She spoke gently to him and was attentive to the new room, introducing him to the therapist. Melanie explained that Laurence would not sleep away from her, woke constantly in the night and she was worried that he would never be able to separate from her. She was planning to go back to work and could not imagine this scenario continuing as she was exhausted. Laurence's father did not live with them and visited occasionally. Melanie was concerned that Laurence was afraid of his father and responded to him 'like a stranger'. Talking to Laurence, the therapist reflected that she was a stranger to him and he did not need to be afraid but gently enquired about why it might be so hard to leave mummy, go to sleep without her and stay asleep until the morning.

During this first session, Melanie's catalogue of loss unfolded. Her parents had both died from long and drawn-out illnesses when she was adolescent. In her twenties, a long-standing partner was killed in a motorbike accident. During this relationship she had a miscarriage. Although her relationship with Laurence's father was not stable, she was delighted on discovering she was pregnant. The constant threat of miscarriage throughout her pregnancy was traumatic as she faced yet another loss in her life, and made her that more determined to keep her baby.

This session had a dramatic impact on Melanie and Laurence. Melanie wept with relief when she was offered another appointment and the possibility of ongoing contact in this community setting. She feared she would just be offered reassurance but instead felt understood and that her predicament was taken seriously as she became aware how disruption through trauma and her past experience of broken attachments and loss affected them both. This had been reawakened by Laurence's birth. She was an insightful woman but had not made links in her mind about her own experience and that of her predicament as a mother of a small baby. Gaining emotional support and insight from regular parent–infant work, she understood why separation had become so problematic for them both and began to think about her son as a little boy with an evolving sense of self (Stern, 1985).

All fathers and partners were invited to attend sessions even if they were not living at home. Fathers, either present or absent, have a profound impact on the developing relationship between mother and baby. Fathers who are present and supportive can moderate the influence of trauma, not only for the mother but with direct access in their relationship with the developing baby. In the event, very few fathers attended parent–infant sessions in spite of this being raised as an important dynamic in the work. Goldner et al. (1990) suggest that men have a need to define themselves as not being the victim of traumatic events, as this tends to be found in the other sex, i.e. 'not me'. There may be a need by the men in the family to remain powerful and dominant, and this seems to be exacerbated in families where there is deprivation (Woods, 2003: 31).

When Stephanie was referred due to severe depression, isolation and panic attacks, she attended on her own. Her symptoms had become worse since the birth of her third child, Lillian, now three months old. The family lived in a cramped flat on the eighteenth floor and her panic increased when her eldest son threatened to jump out of the window. She was very surprised when the therapist raised the question of her husband attending, as she seemed so alone in her distress. The two parents were from different countries of origin and had no extended family for support.

Peter, who needed some encouragement to attend, was a concerned and thoughtful man overwhelmed with managing the demands of his family and supporting them financially and emotionally. He was traumatized in response to his wife's deterioration and voiced his continual worry that 'something terrible would happen' when he was not there and not being able to get home in time to help. He had recently been immobilized by a knee operation and complained about the lift in the flats constantly breaking down, which increased his anxiety about getting back. Although they were cautious, there was a slow process of engagement with both parents and over the year's work some reflection and understanding of the meaning of Stephanie's difficulties became available to the whole family. Both parents became more able to consider their children's distress rather than being so overwhelmed with their own.

Patterns of attendance for mothers and babies varied considerably and the presence of the partners and the kind of relationship the mothers had with them made a significant difference as to how reliably they attended (Haw & Dalley, 2008). Length of treatment ranged from over a year, as in the cases of Melanie and Laurence, Stephanie and Peter, to one session only. When a mother and baby came for one session only, trauma and intergenerational patterns of relating were sometimes enacted in relation to the therapeutic frame.

> Josephine suffered significant birth trauma. Although she had a healthy baby girl, ten days old, she tore very badly and the extensive stitching added a further violation to her traumatic labour. She described feeling torn in two and, still in a lot of physical pain, was extremely reluctant to face further medical examination of her stitches. The thought of feeling so exposed again was unbearable.
>
> What emerged in the session was a number of significant losses, most significantly her adoption at three days old. The birth had triggered an early sense of being metaphorically 'torn' away from her birth mother. In her own primary maternal preoccupation she could not believe or understand how her birth mother could possibly have given her away. She had

thought she had come to terms with her adoption but realized how her anxieties had in some way become located in her torn and painful body. The trauma was hard to heal. As these events came to light she made links with many complex threads of her life and how these might now be impacting on her relationship with baby Holly. The therapist had made a link in her own mind between Josephine's reluctance to be examined physically and whether she would continue to attend further sessions. The therapist wondered whether she was resisting some dependency and a relationship from which she might once again be torn. In her countertransference, the therapist had a similar experience of being 'torn' away from this brief but profound contact but, through communication with the health visitor, made sure that this proud and capable mother continued to be supported by the other services available to her.

Like Josephine, many mothers who have suffered trauma unwittingly bring 'ghosts' from their past into the relationships with their babies. Fraiberg et al. (1975) suggest that these 'ghosts in the nursery' bring a repetition of painful experiences and unresolved feelings associated with early relational disturbances and trauma in childhood. Josephine's 'ghost' had suddenly reappeared, but it seems that she was now aware of the extent to which this resonated with her own repressed pain and helplessness and intended to give her own baby a different experience of mothering.

Although Josephine lost her primary attachment figure, she described an experience of a loving adoptive family and community in which she grew up. The extent to which the 'ghosts' revisit can depend on the degree of integration or isolation within a community. For mothers who have witnessed or escaped violence, lost extended family and culture of origin, the effects of dislocation, lack of familiar culture and community can adversely impact on the early relationship with their infant. Without a supportive community network of friends and professionals, these vulnerable mothers are more prone to postnatal depression or may express their isolation and despair in other ways, such as maintaining the infant in depressed states and subtly preventing their baby moving and developing (Brown & Harris, 1978).

Mothers in this fragile state of mind tend to anticipate that the therapist will behave in ways in which familiar figures did in the past. When these experiences are not confirmed over time, this allows both mother and babies to experience the therapist as someone who is accepting and empathetic. The parent–infant psychotherapist becomes a new 'object' – someone who can withstand rupture and repair in the therapeutic encounter. Most importantly the therapist becomes available to the infant whose internal world and relationships are so much in flux, and who is in the process of formation.

Pregnancy: The perfect container

Working in a health centre enabled easy access to other health professionals. This was one of the advantages of working in this setting. For example, pregnant women who attended ante-natal clinics felt able to consider accessing emotional support through a referral from a midwife who was already a close and trusted professional. The number of referrals of pregnant women grew substantially during the life of the Emotional Support Service. As the research increasingly suggests, anxiety, distress and trauma of a mother transmits itself to the baby in the womb (Piontelli, 1992), and so early intervention is helpful. In pregnancy, the natural containment of mother's womb is a perfect environment for the growing baby. Raphael-Leff (2003) suggests that this perfect and active space for the baby is like the good enough emotional interaction between mother and her baby. The mother acts as a metaphysical container and transformer of her baby's complex experiences. The extent to which these experiences can be 'metabolized' in the womb was important for many of the pregnant women who were referred and who had suffered trauma.

> Eva, who was six months pregnant, was referred with acute anxiety about the birth of her baby and phobic about hospitals. In the early sessions her initial trauma became manifest as she spoke of being caught up in the tsunami in South-East Asia, escaping almost certain death. The experience continued to haunt her and she was terrified of bringing her child into the world to suffer similar experiences and face disaster and catastrophic anxiety. As work progressed, it was possible to understand the meaning of her fears as she came to think about the impending birth as connected in her mind to the 'flood of water' and being totally out of control.
>
> Other issues emerged, with a number of significant early losses and separation from her own family. It was helpful to begin this work during her pregnancy and to think about the baby's experience *in utero*, so when Tamara was born, Eva could understand her worries about being 'good enough' and bring fewer ghosts into the nursery. As a young mother she lacked confidence with her newborn baby and became anxious that she was not responding to her baby's needs and tuned into her emotional world. The therapeutic framework provided an important and continuous container for the work as Eva had experienced absent and abandoning maternal role models, with no extended family for support in the context of repeated traumatic life experiences.

Conclusion

Containment of trauma mediates enactment by promoting reflection, understanding and thought. Bion (1962) describes the relationship between container and contained as a pattern that is dynamic and constantly recurring.

Working within the community-based service and the complex dynamics between busy staff teams meeting targets and deadlines with overwhelming case loads, thinking and containment requires considerable effort to establish and maintain. The parent–infant psychotherapist worked actively to provide a containing function in the mediation of trauma in the relationship between mother and baby and, in a consultation role, within the wider network of professionals exposed to high levels of risk and trauma.

The therapeutic work with traumatized mothers and babies involved providing a safe place to begin to build a narrative or story by revisiting highly distressing and emotionally charged events. The presence of the parent–infant psychotherapist in the Emotional Support Service enabled the possibility of early intervention, generally responding to referrals within one month, which cut down long waiting times (Haw & Dalley, 2008). The mothers and babies who attended found confidentiality and containment in this accessible and informal but consistent treatment setting. Generally, they were able to build 'emotional capital' (Garland, 1998) by recognizing the impact of external events and trauma as well as the importance of the internal world and the capacity to form emotional connections. 'Ghosts' from the past that were impacting on the mother's relationship with her baby could then be understood and put to rest, preventing transmission of intergenerational patterns of relating.

As a community-based service, the Emotional Support team worked closely with colleagues working in the same health centre, enabling informal discussions about potential referrals. One significant audit finding was that where women were referred for depression, the difficulties of babies were not always mentioned. Referrers tended to respond to mother's distress as the main concern without perceiving psychological and emotional problems in her baby. The parent–infant psychotherapist provided an important training function in helping colleagues to be more aware of the baby's emotional needs in relationship with a depressed, traumatized mother (Haw & Dalley, 2008).

Trauma can reverberate throughout the wider network at an institutional level. The consultation process enabled transformation of anxiety carried by professionals working with high levels of distress and on the threshold of child protection. Building relationships and containment established a framework for thinking. Working on the boundary between conscious and unconscious meaning attended to problems at both levels. A forum for learning from the experience of this containing function enabled meaningful contact to develop at a deeper emotional level with such vulnerable families.

Acknowledgements

I would like to thank the Emotional Support and Sure Start teams for everything I have learnt and the PIP team at The Anna Freud Centre for support and guidance.

References

Anning, A., Chesworth, E., Spurling, L., Partinoudi, K. & National Evaluation of Sure Start Team (2005) *Report 9: The quality of early learning play and childcare services in Sure Start local programmes.* London: HMSO.

Bion, W.R. (1962) *Learning from experience.* London: Heinemann.

Bion, W.R. (1965) *Transformations.* London: Heinemann.

Blackwell, D. (1997) Holding, containing and bearing witness: The problem of helplessness in encounters with torture survivors. *Journal of Social Work Practice* 11(2): 81–89

Brown, G. & Harris, T. (1978) *The social origins of depression.* London: Tavistock.

Cregeen, S. (2008) Workers, groups and gangs: Consultation to residential adolescent teams. *Journal of Child Psychotherapy*, 34(2): 172–189.

Emanuel, L. (2002) Deprivation ×3: The contribution of organizational dynamics to the 'triple deprivation' of looked after children. *Journal of Child Psychotherapy*, 28(2): 163–179.

Fonagy, P. & Higgitt, A. (2004) Early mental health intervention and prevention: The implications for government in the wider community. In B. Sklarew, S.W. Twemlow & S.M. Wilkinson (Eds.), *Analysts in the trenches: Streets, schools and war zones.* Hillsdale, NJ: Analytic Press.

Fraiberg, S., Adelson, E. & Shapiro, V. (1975) Ghosts in the nursery: A psychoanalytic approach to the problem of impaired infant–mother relationships. *Journal of the American Academy of Child Psychiatry*, 14: 387–422.

Garland, C. (Ed.) (1998) *Understanding trauma.* London: Duckworth.

Goldner, V., Penn, P., Scheinberg, M. & Walker, G. (1990) Love and violence. *Family Process*, 29: 343–365.

Haw, C. & Dalley, T. (2008) *An audit and evaluation of the emotional support service 2003–2008.* Unpublished paper.

Mosse, J. (1994) The institutional roots of consulting to institutions. In A. Obholzer & V.G. Roberts (Eds.), *The unconscious at work: Individual and organisational stress in the human services.* Hove, UK: Brunner-Routledge.

Obholzer, A. & Roberts,V.G. (Eds.) (1994) *The unconscious at work: Individual and organisational stress in the human services.* Hove, UK: Brunner-Routledge.

Piontelli, A. (1992) *From fetus to child: An observational and psychoanalytic study.* London: Routledge.

Raphael-Leff, J. (2003) Where the wild things are. In J. Raphael-Leff (Ed.), *Parent–infant psychodynamics: Wild things, mirrors and ghosts.* London: Whurr.

Rutter, M. (2006) 'Is Sure Start an effective preventative intervention?' *Child and Adolescent Mental Health*, 11(3): 135–141.

Sklarew, B., Twemlow, S.W. & Wilkinson S.M. (Eds.) (2004) *Analysts in the trenches: Streets, schools and war zones.* Hillsdale, NJ: Analytic Press.

Sprince, J. (2002) Developing containment: Psychoanalytic consultancy to a therapeutic community for traumatized children. *Journal of Child Psychotherapy*, 28(2): 147–161.

Stern, D. (1985) *The interpersonal world of the infant: A view from psychoanalysis and developmental psychology.* New York: Basic Books.

Tunstill, J., Meadows, P., Akhurst, S., Allnock, D., Chrysanthou, J., Garbers, C. et al.

(2005) *Report 10: Implementing Sure Start local programmes: An integrated overview of the first four years*. London: HMSO.

Wadell, M. (2007) Grouping or ganging: the psychodynamics of bullying. *British Journal of Psychotherapy*, 23(2): 189–204.

Woods, J. (2003) *Boys who have abused: Psychoanalytic psychotherapy with victim/perpetrators of sexual abuse*. London: Jessica Kingsley.

Zaphiriou-Woods, M. (2003) Developmental considerations in an adult analysis. In V. Green (Ed.), *Emotional development in psychoanalysis, attachment theory and neuroscience: Creating connections*. London: Routledge.

Discussion
And what about fathers?

Tessa Baradon

In 1930 Freud wrote: 'I cannot think of any need in childhood as strong as the need for the father's protection' (1930: 72). Reviewing the chapters for the book, I was surprised to find that all the case studies were about trauma in the mother–infant relationship. Yet, paradoxically, the importance of the father is emphasised in the case studies through the therapist's critical positioning of herself as the 'third' for the mother–baby dyad.

The under-representation of fathers in the clinical illustrations reflects trends in the consulting room. Often, single mothers are caring for the baby. Referral patterns for mother and fathers differ as difficulties in mother–baby locus are preferentially identified both by referrers and in self-referral, particularly with the ongoing dominance of the mother as the primary caretaker and love object. Statistics also suggest that men (in the UK) are less likely to access help for psychological problems (Seeman & Gopfert, 2006).

Whether the father is present or absent, traumatised or not, a traumatising or facilitating object, underlying the therapeutic work in this book are assumptions that the father is a (psychoanalytic) love object and attachment figure (Muir, 1989) who has a central place in child development, and therefore in parent–infant psychotherapy.

The following are some of the questions we may ask when thinking about fathers and relational trauma: What roles may a father who is present in the family play when the trauma lies in the mother–infant relationship? Does trauma in the father–infant relationship differ from trauma in the mother–infant relationship? Does the absence of the father constitute a trauma?

The historical role of the father in psychoanalytic literature was that of protectively embracing mother and baby (for a review of the literature, see Target & Fonagy, 2002). On one hand he was seen to provide a buffer for mother from the potentially overwhelming needs and demands of their baby, and on the other to enable the necessary developmental separation of baby from mother. In this role of protector of both mother and infant the presence of a father, when the relationship between mother and baby is deeply troubled, can be critical. It is our clinical experience that in the face of trauma in the mother–infant relationship an emotionally available father, who can hold the baby in mind, may offer the physical and emotional holding normally associated with maternal provision (Winnicott, 1960a, 1960b), and thereby ameliorate the formative relational experiences of the baby. Yet trauma in the mother that is enacted with their baby will come at a point when the father is also highly vulnerable, facing psychic reorganisation to accommodate the new baby. His own earliest relational experiences with his primary love objects are, like the mother's, stirred up. Also, Oedipal issues around coupling and exclusion (initially from the couple his parents formed and now from the mother–baby couple), with accompanying potential for jealousy, hurt, withdrawal, can unsettle psychic solutions that worked for the father until the pregnancy with, and birth of, the baby.

The potential interplay between a father's own issues and his partner's state of mind is shown, for example, in recent research findings that partners of depressed mothers report higher levels of paternal parenting stress and demonstrate less optimal interaction with their infants (Goodman, 2008). The author suggests that the fathers may be influenced not so much by the mother's depression as by mother's attitude to their child: in other words, perhaps a coalescing of internal working models regarding relating with vulnerability and dependence. Couple issues are thrown into relief. Rage, despair, helplessness can resonate between a couple and cluster around the baby. As Barrows (1999, 2004) points out, the relationship between the parenting couple determines the emotional climate into which the infant is born and the relational knowing (Lyons-Ruth, 1998) and representations s/he creates.

For the infant, thus, the father can be an actual 'rescuer', but the potential for disappointment may also be heightened. As one mother (see Chapter 10) described in her AAI with regard to her father, 'I wanted him to save me [from the relationship with mother]'. Yet her kindly but neglectful father was 'blind to what went on in the house when he wasn't there, or he wouldn't accept it'. I imagine that the early longings of this mother were compounded by oedipal disappointment in a father who absented himself from his little daughter. We may speculate in what ways the cumulative trauma (Khan, 1963) over the developmental phases of infancy, childhood and adolescence contributed to her adult psychopathology, which then came into play with her infant son.

In the following discussion I will relate to three kinds of trauma in relation to fathers: trauma directly imposed through the paternal state of mind and interactions with his baby, that which is inflicted via traumatisation of mother by father, and trauma conveyed to the baby via mother's mind in relation to father. As will be immediately obvious, these sections overlap closely.

Trauma directly imposed through the paternal state of mind and interactions with his baby

Paternal interactions with their babies characterised by lack of warmth and affection, rejection, and low sensitivity are associated with unfavourable outcomes to the child, particularly higher rates of externalising behaviours (Rutter & Quinton, 1984; Baker & Heller, 1996; Trautmann-Villalba et al., 2006).

Fathers, like mothers, bring their own ghosts to their baby's nursery. Psychic issues perhaps more specifically facing fathers are to do with procreation on one hand and rivalry on the other. Trowell (2002: 7) writes, 'the force of the drive to impregnate must never be underestimated', but she emphasises the ambivalence of both wanting to create a baby and feeling threatened by it. The unconscious need to bear out his masculinity is inevitably accompanied by having to deal with feelings of rivalry, envy, displacement. Furthermore, the relationship with his own father – positive identifications and unresolved issues – is thrown up by becoming a father.

> Eric was shocked and guilty to find himself repulsed by Sara's thickening body as her pregnancy progressed. When Lily was born he found breast-feeding so distasteful that he had to leave the room. Furthermore, he felt no connection to their planned, previously so much wanted, baby. These were the first cues to Eric's 'post-natal' breakdown, marked by acute anxiety attacks, phobic feelings and severe depression. Adult psychiatry, medication and psychotherapy were put in place, and in parallel the couple and baby attended parent–infant psychotherapy.
>
> In the first session Sara and Eric placed themselves at a distance from each other, with Lily, two weeks old, on a baby-mat between them. Throughout the session Eric was physically and emotionally removed from Lily. He was mechanical in his handling of her, so that his touch contained none of the sensual, embracing passion of a father-in-love-with-his-baby. It seemed to me that that he was brimming with terror at his state and hostility towards his wife and baby, who had an easy intimacy from which he felt excluded. In the process of the treatment what emerged was Eric's loss of his volatile and often frightening father in early childhood, and sense of suffocation in the relationship with his mother. Unconscious, unresolved oedipal longings and mortification, and fears of becoming like his father, underpinned his responses to the pregnancy and then the presence of his baby.

This case also illustrates the interplay between the parents' unconscious phantasies.

> Eric's aversion to her pregnant body resonated with Sara's guilty sense of being greedy and overwhelming to the other. Concomitant with her pain

at the emotional loss of her husband at this point were fears about her own capacity to mother her baby.

The mother's capacity to ameliorate the trauma was present in this case.

> With the birth of Lily her fears were dissipated, as she discovered the good enough mothering within to nurture her baby. Furthermore, the representation of 'father-in-relation-to-baby' in mother's mind was imbued with love alongside the disappointment. In her AAI Sara described her relationship with her father in realistically positive terms. Her conscious feelings for her husband also helped her hold on to her hopes for a close relationship between Eric and Lily. Her ability to put her baby's needs before her own pain, and to hold on to a warm image of fathers (Lily's and her own) mitigated the trauma of Eric's rejection of his baby daughter and provided for repair in their interactions.

Father–infant trauma via traumatisation of mother

Fathers may inflict trauma indirectly through traumatising the mother. In such situations the aggressor–victim dynamic between the parents imbues the environment of the baby with an emotional tone of violence and fear. Elevated levels of arousal in each parent render them incapable of relating to their baby, so that the baby has no protective anchorage. Thus, over and above the specific traumatic events, there is likelihood of chronic traumatisation of the infant through enduring exposure to elevated levels of negative emotion in the household, which is terrifying for the baby. In a study of mothers' clinical presentation, Lieberman and Van Horn (1998) found that all scored within the clinical range for depression and anxiety. These mothers often felt they had failed their babies in terms of the violence and sometimes the loss of the father, and at the same time were struggling to meet the needs of their dysregulated infants. It is not surprising that it has also been found that women who experienced domestic violence had significantly more negative representations of their infants and themselves as mothers and were significantly more likely to be classified as insecurely attached (Huth-Bocks et al., 2004).

A traumatising father in the mind of mother

In the previous section I described exposure of the baby to interactions between the parents which can be overwhelmingly frightening. Additionally, the father–infant relationship may be imbued with toxicity through representations of father and of 'father-in-relation-to-baby' in mother's mind.

An absent father, for example, will be a particular kind of presence for mother and through her to their baby. A father who has deserted may be represented as a traumatising, unresolved absence-cum-presence for mother and infant. In many instances, a forsaking partner resonates with prior experiences of loss of the childhood father figure through abandonment or violence. The mother may show an unremitting need for her infant to identify with her psychic position, so that there is no possibility for the developing child to create a separate notion of father. A particular case of contamination by the mother's representation of father are pregnancies conceived through rape. As Angela Joyce describes in her case study (Chapter 4), the mother believed there to be no difference between her and her daughter in her fantasy about the rape ('they raped me, they raped my baby'). The baby she had once imagined adoring and mothering was replaced by hatred of the pregnancy and lack of love for the baby.

In sum

Trauma in the crucible of the father–infant relationship is multifaceted and often shaped by the representation of father and father-in-relation-to-baby in the mother's mind. In our experience, we work in parent–infant psycho-therapy with fathers as we work with mothers – attending to their states of mind and the impact on the care for the baby. We help the father observe himself in relation to his baby and reflect on the baby's communications. However, the therapist may be positioned differently in the therapeutic encounter. The motherhood constellation, more common when working with a mother and baby, may be replaced when working with a father and infant by a phantasy of therapist as an idealised partner. With a triad – mother, father and infant – the organising role of the trauma within the couple and consequent familial dynamics are actualised in the room, and are as much the focus of the therapy as the dyadic aspects of relational trauma. And lastly, the absence of the father will make the therapist's role as a third 'the more important for the relational dynamics that [the baby] needs to experience for her development' (Judith Woodhead, Chapter 3).

References

Baker, B. & Heller, T. (1996) Preschool children with externalising behaviours: Experi-ence of fathers and mothers. *Journal of Abnormal Child Psychology*, 24: 513–532.
Barrows, P. (1999) Fathers in parent infant psychotherapy. *Infant Mental Health Journal*, 20(3): 333–345.
Barrows, P. (2004) Fathers and families: Locating the ghost in the nursery. *Infant Mental Health Journal*, 25(5): 408–423.
Freud, S. (1930) Civilisation and its discontents. In J. Strachey (Ed.), *Standard edition of the complete works of Sigmund Freud* (Vol. 21, pp. 57–145). London: Hogarth Press.
Goodman, J.H. (2008) Influences of maternal post partum depression on father and on father–infant interactions. *Infant Mental Health Journal*, 2(6): 624–643.

Huth-Bocks, A.C., Levendosky, A.A., Theran, S.A. & Bogat, G.A. (2004) The impact of domestic violence on mothers' prenatal representations of their infants. *Infant Mental Health Journal*, 25(2): 79–98.

Khan, M.M.R. (1963) The concept of cumulative trauma. *Psychoanalytic Study of the Child*, 18: 286–306.

Lieberman, A.F. & van Horn, P. (1998) Attachment, trauma and domestic violence. *Child and Adolescent Psychiatric Clinics of North America*, 7(2): 423–443.

Lyons-Ruth, K. (1998) Implicit relational knowing: Its role in development and psychoanalytic treatment. *Infant Mental Health Journal*, 19(3): 282–289.

Muir, R. (1989) Fatherhood from the perspective of object relations theory and relational systems theory. In S.H. Cath, A. Gurwitt & L. Gunsberg (Eds.) *Fathers and their families* (pp. 47–61). Hillsdale, NJ: Analytic Press.

Rutter, M. & Quinton, D. (1984) Parental psychiatric disorder: Effects on children. *Psychological Medicine*, 14: 853–880.

Seeman, M.V. & Gopfert, M. (2006) Parenthood and adult mental health. In M. Gopfert, J. Webster & M.V. Seeman (Eds.), *Parental psychiatric disorder: Distressed parents and their families* (2nd ed.). Cambridge, UK: Cambridge University Press.

Target, M. & Fonagy, P. (2002) Fathers in modern psychoanalysis and in society: The role of the father in child development. In J. Trowell & A. Etchegoyen (Eds.), *The importance of fathers* (pp. 45–66). Hove, UK: Brunner-Routledge.

Trautmann-Villalba, P., Gschwendt, M., Schmidt, M.H. & Laucht, M. (2006) Father–infant interaction patterns as precursors of children's later externalizing behaviour problems. *European Archive of Psychiatry and Clinical Neuroscience*, 256: 344–349.

Trowell, J. (2002) Setting the scene. In J. Trowell & A. Etchegoyen (Eds.), *The importance of fathers* (pp. 3–19). Hove, UK: Brunner-Routledge.

Winnicott, D.M. (1960a) The relationship of the mother to her baby at the beginning. *The family and individual development*. London: Tavistock, 1965.

Winnicott, D.M. (1960b) The theory of the parent infant relationship. *International Journal of Psycho-Analysis*, 41: 585–595.

Chapter 9

Understanding disruptions in the parent–infant relationship

Do actions speak louder than words?

Michelle Sleed and Peter Fonagy

Trauma within the early parent–child relationship can stem from and be maintained by multiple factors. Early relational trauma has been examined from two different, albeit not independent, perspectives. The first is the observation of parent–infant interactions. This method allows the observer to examine behavioural patterns that might be overtly traumatizing to one or both partners in the relationship, or that may be indicative of traumatogenic relationships. The second perspective involves examination of the mental representations, or internal working models, that each partner brings to the relationship and that are formed within the relationship as it develops.

This chapter will review some of the methods used for assessing the quality of the parent–infant relationship. We will discuss both behavioural and representational methods for understanding the relationship between caregiver and infant, particularly with respect to the development and maintenance of traumatogenic relationships.

Parent–infant interactions

Observations of parent–infant interactive behaviour afford an opportunity to understand and assess the ways in which disruptions in the parent–infant relationship can develop and be maintained. Some observational methods have been developed to delineate particular parental behaviours that can promote healthy social and emotional development in infancy. Others have focused on the behaviours associated with a breakdown of a protective caregiving environment. Several of these are summarized in Table 9.1.

The most widely used construct in the assessment of parent–infant interactions is that of maternal sensitivity. It was first introduced by Mary Ainsworth (1976) and emerged out of her study of 26 middle-class American families in the first year of a baby's life. They carried out monthly home visits and made in-depth naturalistic observations. They found four dimensions of maternal behaviour to be relevant to attachment security: sensitivity, acceptance, cooperation and accessibility. Of these, sensitivity was deemed to be the most important. Maternal sensitivity is conceptualized as a mother's

Table 9.1 Summary of validated measures of parent–infant interactive behaviour

Measure	Author/s	Scales/subscales	Sensitivity	Contiguity of response	Physical contact	Cooperation	Synchrony	Mutuality	Emotional support	Positive attitude	Stimulation
Sensitivity Scale	Ainsworth, 1976	Maternal sensitivity (singe 9-point rating scale)	X	X							
Nursing Child Assessment Teaching/Feeding Scale (NCATS & NCAFS)	Barnard, 1978 Sumner & Spietz, 1995	73 items on the teaching scale, and 76 items on the feeding scale, scored on binary scale: **Parent:** Sensitivity to cues, response to child's distress, social–emotional growth fostering, cognitive growth fostering **Child:** Clarity of cues, responsiveness to caregiver	X	X		X					
Parent–Child Early Relational Assessment (PCERA)	Clark, 1985 Musick et al., 1981	65 variables (scored on 5-point scales) form the following composite subscales: **Parent:** Positive affective involvement and verbalization; negative affect and behaviour; intrusiveness, insensitivity, and inconsistency **Child:** Positive affect and social communicative skills; quality of play, interest, and attentional skills; dysregulation and irritability **Dyad:** Mutual enjoyment and reciprocity; disorganization and tension	X		X	X		X	X	X	

(Continued overleaf)

Table 9.1 Continued

Measure	Author/s	Scales/ subscales	Sensitivity	Contiguity of response	Physical contact	Cooperation	Synchrony	Mutuality	Emotional support	Positive attitude	Stimulation
Parent/Caregiver Involvement Scale (PCIS)	Farran et al., 1986	11 scales (each scored on 5-point rating): **Parent:** Physical and verbal interaction, responsiveness, play, teaching, control of activities, directives-demands, relationship, positive and negative statements, and goal setting **Overall ratings:** Availability, acceptance, atmosphere, enjoyment, and learning environment	X	X	X	X	X		X	X	X
Maternal Behavior Rating Scale (MBRS)	Mahoney et al., 1986 Mahoney, 1999	12 items (rated on 5-point scale) form the following subscales: **Parent:** Responsiveness, affect, achievement, and directiveness		X		X				X	
Parent–Infant Observation Guide (PIOG)	Bernstein, Percansky & Hans, 1987 Hans, Bernstein & Percansky, 1991	Items scored on binary scale (observed/ not observed): **Parent:** Sensitive responsiveness to child's needs, sensitivity to child's interests, affection for infant, helping child to learn **Child:** Expression of needs, use of parent's help, interest in parent, affection for parent	X			X			X	X	

Measure	Reference	Description							
Mannheim Rating System for Mother–Infant Interaction	Esser et al., 1990	Variables coded per minute of interaction: **Parent:** Emotion, physical affect, vocalization, verbal restrictions, congruency, variability, contingency, stimulation **Child:** Emotion, vocalization, looking, reactivity (contingency) and readiness to interact	X	X	X			X	X
Emotional Availability Scales	Biringen et al., 1993, 2000, 2008	**Parent:** Sensitivity, structuring, non-intrusiveness, non-hostility **Child:** Involvement, responsiveness	X		X			X	X
Mellow Parenting Coding System	Puckering et al., 1994	**Parent:** Autonomy, positive affect, negative affect, link-child follow, facilitate before caretake (coded as number of sequences during an interaction situation, mean score used). Warmth, sensitivity and effective control (overall ratings on a 5-point scale)	X		X			X	X
Communications Violations Rating Scale	True, 1994	Ratings (5-point scales): **Parent:** Cooperation, withdrawal, overriding infant negativity, frightened or frightening behaviour **Child:** Directness of signalling, avoidance, resistance, disorganization			X	X	X		
The Parent–Infant Relationship Global Assessment Scale (PIRGAS)	Zero-to-Three, 1994	Global score on a 90-point scale. Three components of the relationship are assessed: behavioural quality of the interaction, affective tone, and psychological involvement	X		X			X	X

(Continued overleaf)

Table 9.1 Continued

Measure	Author/s	Scales/ subscales	Sensitivity	Contiguity of response	Physical contact	Cooperation	Synchrony	Mutuality	Emotional support	Positive attitude	Stimulation
Maternal Behavior Q-set (MBQS)	Pederson & Moran, 1995	90-item Q-set based on home observations: **Parent:** Sensitivity **Child:** Security	X	X					X		
Global Rating Scale for Mother–Infant Interaction	Murray et al., 1996	25 bipolar scales (scored on 5-point ratings): **Parent:** Interactive behaviour, intrusiveness or remoteness, affect **Child:** Interactive behaviour, inertness or fretfulness **Dyad:** Smooth and easy/difficult, fun/ serious, mutually satisfying/unsatisfying, much engagement/no engagement and excited engagement/quiet engagement	X	X		X		X		X	X
Coding Interactive Behavior (CIB)	Feldman, 1998	42 variables (scored on 5-point scales) form the following composite subscales: **Parent:** Sensitivity, intrusiveness, parent limit-setting (for children >12 months) **Child:** Social involvement, negative emotionality, child compliance (for children >12 months) **Dyad:** Dyadic reciprocity, dyadic negative states	X		X	X	X	X	X	X	

The Feeding Scale	Chatoor et al., 1997	46 behaviours (scored on 4-point scale) rated on feeding sessions. Subscales: **Parent:** Maternal non-contingency **Dyad:** Dyadic reciprocity, dyadic conflict, talk and distraction, struggle for control	X	X	X X
Child Adult Relationship Index (CARE-Index)	Crittenden, 2001	**Parent:** Sensitive, controlling, unresponsive **Child:** Cooperative, difficult, compulsive and passive	X	X	X
Microanalysis of parent–infant toy-play	Feldman et al., 2002	Relative time proportions of each behaviour coded on the following scales: **Parent:** Gaze, affect, toy presentation **Child:** Gaze, affect, toy attention		X X	X X

accuracy in perceiving and interpreting her infant's cues and her ability to react in a timely and appropriate manner.

Maternal sensitivity or elements of the concept, such as responsiveness, are recurrent themes in many measures of parent–infant interaction. A major shortcoming of the original sensitivity scale is that it yields only a single global rating, allowing for varying interpretations of the concept across laboratories. The term has often been used quite loosely to describe optimal parental behaviours. For example, a coding system used by Guzell and Vernon-Feagans (2004) yields a rating for 'sensitive behaviour'. This is a composite score for ratings on positive affect, encouragement, interest and empathy. Although these features of the interaction are likely to be linked with Ainsworth's original concept of sensitivity, they are not integral to her definition.

Some more recent assessment tools, such as the Emotional Availability Scales (EAS; Biringen et al., 1993, 2000b, 2008) and the CARE-Index (Crittenden, 2001) have retained the idea of maternal sensitivity as the central construct but have provided more detailed manuals and training procedures. In these coding systems, the sensitivity rating remains very global and is rated alongside a small number of other parental variables considered to be of importance. Other coding systems have taken a more detailed approach to the concept of sensitivity. For example, the Coding Interactive Behaviour Scale (CIB; Feldman, 1998) and the Parent–Child Early Relational Assessment (PCERA; Clark, 1985) rate parent, child and dyadic interactive behaviours on a large number of discrete variables. Both coding systems result in a composite subscale relating to maternal sensitivity, comprising summed scores for a diverse array of individual affects and behaviours, such as 'amount of verbalization' on the PCERA and 'affectionate touch' on the CIB.

The Nursing Child Teaching and Feeding Scales (NCATS/NCAFS; Barnard, 1978) also result in a composite subscale of 'sensitivity to cues'. In this coding system each of the component variables of sensitivity is rated on a binary scale (observed/not observed) rather than a wider scale incorporating both frequency and intensity of behaviours during the interaction. This is a very different approach to the single global ratings of overall sensitivity. In general, the binary rating used in the NCATS/NCAFS and other coding systems does not allow scope for detecting small inconsistencies within the interaction. A mother that is moderately sensitive may at times interpret her baby's cues and respond appropriately, but at other times may not; a mother that smiles once or twice in the interaction is qualitatively different from a mother who demonstrates positive affect throughout the interaction.

It seems that almost all measures of parent–infant interactive behaviour identify sensitivity as a key construct, but they vary somewhat in terms of what is focused on when assessing sensitivity. There is no indication, however, that these variations are material to understanding the nature of inter-active behaviour. The extent to which a parent demonstrates appropriate understanding of and response to the infant's behaviour is a key dimension of individual difference in the quality of parent–child relationships. Clearly, this raises the question of (a) whether the absence of sensitivity could be considered traumatic, or (b) whether its presence provides any kind of protection against traumatic experience that impinges on the parent–infant relationship.

In addition to sensitivity, many other features of parent–infant interactions are common to different coding systems. De Wolff and van IJzendoorn (1997) carried out a comprehensive survey of 55 constructs of parenting behaviour using experts in attachment research. They identified nine conceptually homogeneous groups of concepts: sensitivity, contiguity of response, physical contact, cooperation, synchrony, mutuality, emotional support, positive attitude and stimulation. Table 9.1 provides a rough guide of the extent to which currently available measures tap into these nine constructs. In addition to sensitivity, the most commonly measured features of the interactions are the affective quality of the interaction, cooperation, and the extent to which the parent provides emotional support for the child during the interaction.

Considering all the measures listed in Table 9.1 together, there appears to be considerable agreement about the dimensions of parent–infant interaction that might be relevant in understanding both potentially traumatogenic aspects of parenting and individual differences in dyads' reactions to extreme stress. We will now turn to studies that have evaluated the predictive validity of these instruments.

What do most measures of parent–infant interactions tell us?

Given the strong tradition of behavioural observation of parent–infant relationships from an attachment theory perspective, it is unsurprising that infant attachment security has often been the gold standard against which such measures have been validated. Indeed, early research demonstrated good associations between caregiver behaviour and infant attachment security (e.g. Teti et al., 1991; Ainsworth et al., 1974; Cantero & Cerezo, 2001; Swanson, 1998). Following on from the conceptual grouping of parental behaviour constructs by de Wolff and van IJzendoorn (1997) described above, the authors found that maternal sensitivity was moderately good at predicting infant attachment security but so were the other clusters of behaviours. It therefore seems that maternal sensitivity as well as a number of other aspects of parenting behaviour may be linked with infant attachment security.

Some coding systems have been shown to distinguish between normative and high-risk samples. For example, the Care-Index is able to discriminate between mothers with and without psychiatric disorder (Hughes, 1993), and between irritable and non-irritable infants (Ayissi & Hubin-Gayte, 2006). The criterion validity of the PCERA has been established through a number of studies comparing different populations, such as drug-using parents versus non-drug using controls (Burns et al., 1997) and mothers with psychiatric diagnoses versus those without (Clark, 1983).

Not all measures have performed equally well in studies evaluating the validity of the instruments. For example, Johnson and Lobo (2001) found that NCATS scores did not differ for mothers with and without HIV infection, despite the fact that the mothers with a diagnosis of HIV had more symptoms of depression. Another study showed the NCATS to be related to maternal education and knowledge, but not depression and self-efficacy, indicating that it does not tap into affective quality of interactions (Gross et al., 1993). This raises the question of its suitability for populations where psychopathology is the main risk factor.

It is beyond the scope of this chapter to review validity studies of available measures comprehensively, but they clearly vary in terms of the aspects of parent–infant interaction that they tap, and therefore their sensitivity to different aspects of risk.

Parent–infant interactions and high-level risk

A large number of measures of parent–infant interactive behaviour have been developed with middle-class, low-risk samples. However, in their meta-analysis, de Wolff and van IJzendoorn (1997) found that the link between maternal behaviour and infant attachment is less robust in clinical and lower class samples. Although maternal insensitivity shows some association with attachment insecurity, this may not be a sufficient indicator of risk in and of itself. The discovery of the disorganized attachment classification (Main & Solomon, 1986) has enabled researchers to identify a group of infants most at risk. The high prevalence of disorganized attachment in maltreated children has highlighted the limitations of the original secure–insecure classification system; many of these children were forced into a secure classification before the disorganized category was identified (Carlson et al., 1989). Disorganized attachment has been found to be strongly predictive of later psychopathology (Carlson, 1998; Sroufe et al., 2005; Kobak et al., 2006). A recent meta-analysis (Bodinetz, 2008) found that maltreated children were twice as likely to be classified as insecure–avoidant (odds ratio = 1.99; $p < .001$) and seven times more likely to be classified as disorganized (odds ratio = 6.87; $p < .001$) than non-maltreated children.

Given the powerful relationship between maternal sensitivity and infant security of attachment discussed above, we would expect that sensitivity would also be highly predictive of attachment disorganization in the Strange Situation. Ziv and colleagues (2000) showed that maternal sensitivity on the Emotional Availability Scales could only discriminate between secure and insecure–ambivalent infant classifications, and not avoidant and disorganized infants. Given that it is exactly these two attachment classifications that predict later externalizing problems (Munson et al., 2001) and that are more likely associated with child maltreatment (Bodinetz, 2008), this is a major shortcoming in the assessment process. In a study of predominantly economically disadvantaged adolescent mothers, Ward and Carlson (1995) found no association between attachment security and maternal sensitivity. A meta-analysis focusing on the correlates of disorganized attachment demonstrated a very small effect size relating attachment disorganization and maternal sensitivity (van IJzendoorn et al., 1999). Taken together, these findings indicate the need to identify other aspects of caregiver behaviour that identify the most extreme levels of relational risk within the parent–infant relationship.

Methods of assessing features of parent–infant interactions associated with disorganization

Given the association between trauma and disorganized attachments in infancy, it is essential that we identify aspects of the parent–child relationship that are characteristic of infants who are more likely to manifest this attachment pattern. Two methods for rating parent–infant interactions have been developed specifically for detecting the correlates of disorganized attachments. These are summarized in Table 9.2.

Main and Hesse (1990) have posited that past trauma or loss experienced by the parent, when unresolved, leads to particular anomalous behaviours towards the infant. The unresolved loss or trauma experienced by the parent emerges at times as an alteration of normal consciousness, resulting in behaviours that either frighten the child or indicate that the parent is frightened. As the attachment figure is also normally the source of comfort for the child during times of heightened arousal, the parent becomes at the same time the source of fear and the source of regulation of that fear, adversely affecting the child's ability to form an organized attachment

Table 9.2 Summary of measures of parental behaviour associated with disorganized attachment

The Frightened/ Frightening (FR) coding system	Main & Hesse, 1992–2005	Single 9-point rating **Parent:** Frightening/ threatening, frightened, dissociated, timid/ deferential (role reverting), sexualized, and disorganized/ disoriented
The Atypical Maternal Behavior Instrument for Assessment and Classification (AMBIANCE)	Bronfman et al., 1999	Single rating on 7-point scale based on the following categories of parental behaviour: **Parent:** affective communication errors, role-confusion, disorganized/ disoriented behaviours, negative-intrusive behaviour, and withdrawal

strategy. These frightening or frightened behaviours (termed FR behaviours) form the basis of a coding system to identify such relational processes (Main & Hesse, 1990).

Studies have consistently shown that maternal FR behaviours predict infant disorganization (Schuengel et al., 1999; True et al., 2001), particularly the dissociative and threatening subscales (Abrams et al., 2006). In one study, True et al. (2001) measured both FR behaviour and maternal sensitivity on Ainsworth's rating scale. They found no significant association between these two aspects of maternal behaviour, indicating the independence of these measures. In addition, FR behaviour was a better predictor of infant attachment classification than maternal sensitivity, although the contribution of both measures to explain the variance was very small.

The Atypical Maternal Behavior Instrument for Assessment and Classification (AMBIANCE; Bronfman et al., 1999) is theoretically and functionally related to Main and Hesse's FR coding system. The system includes the frightened and frightening behaviours of the FR coding system. In addition, the work of Lyons-Ruth and colleagues posits a broader range of behavioural correlates that can also link with infant disorganization. Firstly, they propose that parents may display contradictory or competing caregiving strategies, in the same way that the disorganized behaviours of the infant are often contradictory in nature. These behaviours are termed 'affective communication errors' and can be seen as incongruent physical and verbal behaviours, missed cues, or inappropriate responses to infant cues. Secondly, they posit that the parent's overall ability to regulate infant arousal under stressful conditions is important, the breakdown of which can be seen as a 'failure to repair' for the infant. Thus, parental withdrawal or role-reversing behaviours would also inhibit the parent from adequately regulating and responding to the infant's fearful arousal and attachment behaviours. The AMBIANCE has, like the FR scale, been shown in several studies to be significantly related to disorganized attachment in infants (e.g. Lyons-Ruth et al., 1999; Goldberg et al., 2003; Madigan et al., 2006).

It appears that two streams of research into the behavioural aspects of parent–infant interactions can contribute a great deal to our understanding and assessment of the relationship: (1) positive maternal behaviours (falling within the sensitivity domain) that facilitate secure attachments, and (2) breakdowns in the caregiver–child interactions that are indicative of potential disorganized attachment and high levels of risk.

The question is why it is not sensitivity but these particular behaviours outlined in Table 9.2 that are considered causative of disorganized attachment. Even though sensitivity does not predict attachment disorganization, paradoxically, Bakermans-Kranenburg and colleagues (2005) have shown that sensitivity-based interventions can reduce attachment disorganization. In this meta-analysis, the authors also tested whether interventions that reported improvements in sensitivity were more effective at reducing attachment disorganization, but found no significant contrast. So it seems that the use of sensitivity-based therapeutic approaches rather than obtaining measurable improvements in maternal sensitivity is linked with moving children from disorganized to an organized attachment strategy.

None of the interventions included in this analysis focused on influencing parents' frightened or frightening behavior toward their children. These findings might suggest that the behaviours detected by the FR and AMBIANCE coding systems may be correlates rather than causes of a traumatogenic environment. One way of interpreting this pattern of findings is that the FR/AMBIANCE-type behaviours may be indicators of the temporal variability of sensitivity, which is difficult to pick up during relatively brief laboratory observations. It is possible that the behaviours that are coded in AMBIANCE and FR may be indicators, or correlates, of the kind of sensitivity variability that is traumatogenic. For example, a moment of 'dissociation' (frightened behaviour) may not be traumatogenic in itself, but indicates that that caregiver may be capable of behaving differently at other times. It signals that in other circumstances – other than during laboratory observations – the parent might break off completely from the infant. Similarly, the failure to repair, as is coded on the withdrawing component of the AMBIANCE, may be particularly significant in caregiver–infant couples where the requirement for repairing is quite common because of erratic moments of maternal insensitivity. While it has become commonplace to argue that disorganized attachment is independent of sensitivity, it might be that these are only independent during laboratory observations. Extensive periods of naturalistic observation, comparable to those originally carried out by Ainsworth when developing the concept of sensitivity, are still lacking in the literature relating to disorganized attachment relationships. We should be careful not to reify the results of laboratory observations.

Let us now turn to the second major perspective from which we can assess the quality of the parent–child relationship.

Parental representations and relational risk

Parental mental representations, or 'internal working models', have been highlighted as important for determining the quality of the parent–infant relationship for many decades. Several facets of these mental representations are relevant to the early parent–infant relationship, for example the mother's view of the baby, of herself as a mother, and of their relationship with each other and with other significant attachment figures in the past and present.

Assessing maternal representations: Adult attachment

The Adult Attachment Interview

The first detailed studies of the nature and content of maternal representations focused on parents' attachment experiences with their own caregiver(s). The Adult Attachment Interview (AAI; George et al., 1985) is a semi-structured interview that requires adults to provide attachment-related memories from their early childhood and to evaluate these from their current perspective. Individuals can be classified into three major adult attachment categories that are predictive of the infant classifications (Main & Goldwyn, 1993): *autonomous* (secure), *dismissing* (insecure–avoidant), and *preoccupied* (insecure–ambivalent). More relevant to the current discussion, individuals may have an additional classification of *unresolved* (disorganized) in relation to loss or trauma. In describing such experiences, these individuals show lapses in monitoring of reasoning and discourse, demonstrating a lack of resolution to such traumas. These slippages are usually brief and isolated, generally occurring in the presence of an otherwise organized interview (Hesse & Main, 1999). Studies have shown that there is a clear association between mothers' unresolved attachment status on the AAI and FR behaviour towards their infants (Schuengel et al., 1999, Abrams et al., 2006).

Although unresolved loss or trauma has been shown to be strongly related to child disorganized attachment (van IJzendoorn et al., 1999), there are still a large number of disorganized infants whose mothers are not classified as unresolved. One possible reason for the mismatch between some adult and child dyads is that the adult participant needs to disclose an experience of loss or abuse in their past in order for them to be classified as unresolved. This has been criticized as being too narrow a window for capturing the full extent of a parent's attachment-related state of mind (Lyons-Ruth et al., 2005). Hughes and colleagues (2006) prospectively followed mothers who had experienced a traumatic loss (miscarriage of a baby) through pregnancy and the first years of the child's life. This study confirmed the association between unresolved status in relation to the miscarriage or other trauma and disorganization of the infant. However, they also reported indications of factors that moderated the impact of disorganization. Specifically, they found that unresolved mothers whose children were not classified as disorganized reported significantly higher levels of depression and of intrusive thoughts during pregnancy, and showed higher levels of intrusive thoughts when the infant was one year old than unresolved mothers of disorganized infants. To explain this somewhat surprising finding, the authors suggest that maternal depression and suffering of painful intrusive thoughts may protect the mother from the dissociated state of mind that leads to infant disorganization. This is an interesting finding since maternal depression, often seen as a risk factor within the parent–infant relationship, is also associated with maternal insensitivity

(Trapolini et al., 2008). It may, however, have a more adaptive role in cases of maternal trauma and the subsequent risk to the infant.

Hostile/Helpless states of mind

Lyons-Ruth and colleagues (2005) have developed a different approach to coding the AAI to identify *Hostile–Helpless* (H/H) states of mind. This coding system is particularly interesting in thinking about relational trauma as it was informed by descriptions of defensive processes seen in clinical populations with chronic trauma. This rating system is applied to the whole interview and focuses on extreme forms of segregated mental systems relating to 'dissociation' and 'splitting'. The Hostile subtype is characterized by descriptions of at least one attachment figure in globally negative terms and, in many cases, identification with the devalued attachment figure. These narratives also reveal tendencies to block out feelings of vulnerability through the use of dark humour. The Helpless subtype is characterized by pervasive feelings of helplessness and fearfulness. In these descriptions, interviewees may also appear to have identified with a victimized attachment figure. Hostile and helpless states of mind are considered to be related features of the same H/H internal working model of relationships and interviews are given an overall score for H/H state of mind.

The H/H coding system has been shown to be able to distinguish between dysthymic and borderline patients (Melnick & Patrick, 2003; Lyons-Ruth et al., 2007). It has also been shown to be independent from the Main and Goldwyn (1993) classifications, including the unresolved category (Lyons-Ruth et al., 2005). In this study, the H/H states of mind accounted for more variance in infant disorganization than unresolved states of mind. Further, H/H states of mind were significantly related to disrupted maternal behaviour measured on the AMBIANCE. Maternal disrupted behaviour partially mediated the link between H/H states of mind and infant attachment, although due to the small sample size this study needs replication. Another study reported that H/H states of mind are related to the severity of childhood trauma (Lyons-Ruth et al., 2003), indicating the utility of such a measure in understanding the impact of relational trauma.

The strength of this approach undoubtedly lies in the establishment of a link between a particular pattern of representing past attachment relationships and behavioural indicators of parent–infant interaction, as seen in the AMBIANCE scale. Lyons-Ruth and colleagues offer a compelling theory of attachment disorganization in terms of a hostile or helpless stance that induces a particularly maladaptive set of thoughts and feelings in relation to child-rearing, which may in turn trigger the indicator behaviours discussed above. The pattern of derogation and identification with the aggressor places the mother in a paradoxical role in relation to child-rearing. In devaluing a caregiver, she devalues herself as caregiver. In identifying with a hostile carer, she links her own sense of self-worth to that of a person who did not hold her in high regard. Both these scenarios leave her feeling worthless, specifically in her role as a caregiver and possibly in relation to a particular child.

The H/H measure is particularly helpful in linking disorganized attachment in the infant to the mother's trauma history. It makes sense that those with high H/H scores should necessarily also be coded as unresolved on the AAI. It is less obvious, however, why those who are unresolved do not necessarily score higher on the H/H. It's possible but unparsimonious to assume two independent pathways from traumatized parent to disorganized attachment in the child, all the more so because the pathway (FR/AMBIANCE) and the end-point in infancy (disorganized attachment) may be the same.

From adult attachment representations to parent–child relationships

Parents' current state of mind with respect to attachment during their own childhood provides a significant but not complete picture of the risk in their current relationship with a child. A major shortcoming of the AAI as a predictor of infant attachment is that the same mother can have a disorganized relationship with one child but not another. In fact, twins can have different attachment classifications with the same mother (Bokhorst et al., 2003; Fearon et al., 2006). These findings indicate that there is a relationship-specific effect in the development of disorganized attachment. While the AAI is able to highlight increased potential risk within a current parent–child relationship, it doesn't speak to the mechanism that can cause distinctive attachment patterns between parent–child dyads.

In order to complete the transmission gap and link infant attachment, behavioural observations of parents, and the parent's narrative about their own childhood, we need to know about the working model that the parent uses in relation to the particular child.

Interviews

A number of semi-structured interviews designed to capture maternal representations in relation to a specific parent–child relationship have been developed. The *Parent Attachment Interview* (PAI; Bretherton et al., 1989), the *Working Model of the Child Interview* (WMCI; Zeanah & Benoit, 1995; Zeanah et al., 1986) and the *Parent Development Interview* (PDI; Aber et al., 1985; PDI-R; Slade et al., 2004a) all tap into parents' autobiographical narratives about their child and relationship with him or her.

Coding of parent–child relationship representations

Maternal representations on the PAI have been coded on the Sensitivity/ Insight Scale (Biringen & Bretherton, 1988). This coding system was developed on the basis of attachment theory and assesses the mother's overall sensitivity based on representations of the relationship. The relation between Sensitivity/Insight and infant attachment security has been mixed; one study showed significant associations (Bretherton et al., 1989) but a more recent study did not (Biringen et al., 2000a). The PDI has been adapted for use in multiple contexts and coded in several different ways for affective and behavioural perceptions. The authors now advocate the coding of the PDI for parental reflective functioning (see below) as the preferred method of analysis.

Several parent–child representational coding systems yield classifications that parallel the infant attachment classifications in the Strange Situation. The WMCI interviews are rated on a number of rating scales relating to the quality of descriptions and affective tone. The narratives are assigned to one of three categories based on these ratings. *Balanced* representations, relating to secure attachment, are characterized by maternal emotional warmth, acceptance and sensitivity in response to infant needs. *Disengaged* representations, which parallel avoidant attachment classifications, are characterized by the caregiver's emotional distance from the infant. *Distorted* representations, which relate to ambivalent attachment relationships, are characterized by descriptions of the infant or relationship that appear incoherent, confused, contradictory, or bizarre, and sometimes role-reversed. WMCI classifications have been found to distinguish infant clinical status (Benoit et al., 1997b) and the severity of maternal PTSD has been shown to be significantly associated with non-balanced mental representations within a traumatized sample (Schechter et al., 2005). Studies have shown significant concurrent and predictive concordance between WMCI and infant attachment classifications (Zeanah et al., 1994; Benoit et al., 1997a). However, none of the categories of the WMCI correspond specifically to the disorganized attachment category. One study found no associations between infant disorganized attachment and any of the WMCI classifications (Cox et al., 2000).

An adapted version of the PDI used by George and Solomon, the Caregiving Interview, has been developed with an associated coding system (George & Solomon, 2008b). The system draws heavily on attachment theory and particularly on caregiver defensive processes in relation to attachment representations. The scale involves rating and classifying caregivers on four defensive processing categories that parallel the infant attachment classifications (in parentheses): *flexible integration* (secure), *deactivation* (insecure–avoidant), *cognitive disconnection* (insecure–ambivalent), and *segregated systems* (disorganized). The scales are derived from theory and research and comprise the main defensive positions associated with caregiving and attachment. The first three of these scales are theoretically similar to the WMCI classifications. The fourth category, *segregated systems*, is interesting as it is one of the few operationalizations of the specific sorts of caregiver representations associated with trauma and high levels of relational risk.

The *segregated systems* scale refers to an extreme and brittle defensive stance and is linked with 'assaults to the attachment system', such as loss, separation, maltreatment, or threats of these. These thoughts and feelings are organized into a self-contained system that is completely segregated from consciousness. George and Solomon (2008a) have proposed that situations that activate the caregiving system can potentially unlock memories and experiences from the parent's segregated caregiving representation or their segregated attachment system. When unable to regulate these memories and feelings, they become helpless and out of control. This quality of segregated systems is called 'flooding'. Parents who are rated as 'flooded' often talk about their relationship as being out of control. They may describe power struggles between themselves and their child, frightening content, and there may be an element of helplessness or even a complete abdication from their caregiving role.

The second subtype of the segregated system is called 'constriction'. This is seen as a tight blocking-off so that caregiving experience and affect do not enter conscious awareness, in a way that is akin to a dissociative state. Narratives coded on this subscale may demonstrate role reversal, glorification of the child, and there may be signs that the mother becomes completely constricted or even dissociated during the interview. As the exclusionary processes associated with segregated systems are fragile and at risk of breaking down, constriction often gives way to flooding so that both forms may be seen operating together.

Ratings of mothers' representations on the caregiving interview have been found to be positively correlated with concurrent child security in infancy and at six years of age (George & Solomon, 1989). In particular, mothers' helplessness (segregated systems) on the caregiving interview predicts concurrent child disorganization at age six (Solomon & George, 2006).

Parental reflective functioning

Three programmes of work by Elizabeth Meins, David Oppenheim, and Arietta Slade have attempted to link the parent's attachment history to parent–child interaction via the parent's capacity to represent the child accurately as an intentional being. Although there are slight differences in the language these researchers have used, 'mind-mindedness' (MMM; Meins, 1997), 'insightfulness' (Oppenheim & Koren-Karie, 2002) and 'mentalization' or 'reflective function' (RF; Slade, 2005) all refer to the caregiver's capacity to hold the child's mind in mind. A recent review by Sharp and Fonagy (2008) outlines the different constructs and operationalizations of parental mentalizing and they argue that these apparently diverse constructs may tap into the same underlying neurobiological socio-cognitive system.

Elizabeth Meins has shown that the caregiver's reflections on the child's behaviour, both offline (viewing a video) and online (during free play) predicted attachment security, theory of mind and stream of consciousness performance years after the original observations (Meins & Fernyhough, 1999; Meins et al., 2001, 2002, 2003). These findings suggest that the reflectiveness of the caregiver's narrative may be a stable indicator of maternal attitudes that enhance the development of the child's sense of psychological mindedness. In Oppenheim's work, an offline measure relating to playful interaction is coded and the extent of insight into the child's mind, as assessed by independent judges, was found to be more predictive of infant attachment than global sensitivity (Koren-Karie et al., 2002). Across these two studies, both offline and online maternal mentalizing capacity gives the researcher a handle on the child's unfolding development and behaviour.

An impressive programme of work undertaken by Arietta Slade and her colleagues has successfully linked parental attachment history, parenting behaviour, and the caregiver's focus on the child as an intentional being. They take an autobiographical memory rather than a behavioural sampling approach by asking parents to reflect on their experience with a particular child in the PDI. The narratives are coded on an adaptation of the reflective functioning coding system that was originally developed by Fonagy and colleagues (1997) for use with the AAI (Slade et al., 2004b). They report a strong association between infant attachment and the quality of the parent's reflective functioning (Slade et al., 2005; Grienenberger et al., 2005). In this measure, the parent invariably reports a range of interaction experiences and the measure of mentalizing emerges as an aggregate across multiple interaction episodes. High scores on this measure indicate a greater degree of awareness of the characteristic mental function of the infant as well as a better grasp of the sophisticated interplay between the mother's own mental states and their image of the child's subjective experience.

A recent study examined the link between maternal reflective functioning (RF), maternal mind-minded comments made during interactions, and maternal behaviour (Rosenblum et al., 2008). Although RF and maternal mind-minded comments were related, it was RF that was more predictive of maternal behaviour, over and above the effect of mind-minded comments. This perhaps indicates that a broad autobiographical interview approach is a better predictor of the quality of relationship.

Notably, parental mentalization has been found to identify infant disorganization using the reflective functioning measure (Slade et al., 2005; Grienenberger et al., 2005). Parents of infants with disorganized attachment scored a standard deviation below those whose infants were securely attached. Further, Slade and colleagues were able to show that those with high AMBIANCE scores (less optimal parental behaviour) had lower reflective function and that this statistically accounted for the difference in RF between disorganized and organized infant attachment groups. We might argue that the AMBIANCE measures the mother's responsiveness to the intentions that the infant's communication conveys. Atypical behaviours may occur when the mother experiences gross failures in grasping the infant's intentionality. It is these episodes that are particularly traumatogenic for the infant. These mothers' narratives highlight the limited appreciation that they have for the minds of their particular infants and, in extreme cases, depict the infant as having no thoughts, feelings or wishes.

Linking parental behaviour and representations

In our review of the methods for understanding risk and potentially traumatogenic features of the parent infant relationship, several pertinent behavioural and representational correlates stand out. If we take infant attachment disorganization to be an indicator of potential threat to the quality of relationship, we can draw out those features of parental behaviour and representation that have been shown to relate to the primary relationships these infants have. The frightened/frightening behaviours of the FR scale, as well as the additional withdrawing, role-reversed and disrupted affective communications outlined by the AMBIANCE, appear to be especially pertinent. However, more intensive and lengthy home observations may very well reinforce Ainsworth's early claims that maternal sensitivity plays a vital protective function in the relationship and may be limited in disorganized relationships, which tend to be variable and unpredictable. Research into the intergenerational transmission of relational trauma has resulted in interesting methodological tools and theoretical developments in understanding relational trauma. The work of Main and Hesse, and Lyons-Ruth and her colleagues, has linked parental working models about their own childhood attachment relationships with both parental behaviour and next-generation attachment. Momentary lapses in discourse or reasoning when talking about loss or trauma, hostile and denigrating descriptions of caregivers, and talking of states of helplessness and vulnerability are some of the indicators of traumatogenic relationships. These have also been shown to relate to the maternal behaviours described above, and both modalities may be linked with dissociative states and identification with hostile caregivers. Some interesting recent developments, such as George and Solomon's (2008b) description of the segregated systems, have translated many of the features of traumatogenic relationships from the adult attachment literature to understanding representations of particular parent–child relationships. Once again, the themes of hostility, helplessness, dissociative processes and role-reversal dominate this work. A final and slightly more distinct stream of work has looked into parental mentalizing capacities, and has examined how breakdowns in this core function can impinge on the parent–child relationship. We will now examine the behavioural indices of risk in light of this theory of the protective power of parental reflective function.

We suggest that the same control mechanism may be responsible for the inhibitory regulation of certain aspects of maternal behaviour as those manifested in the mother's organization of her narrative about the infant. At the risk of appearing reductionist, we might argue that a common brain mechanism subserves both tasks. For example, the paracingulate cortex might provide input for the organization of both social interactions and person-centred autobiographical narratives (Gallagher et al., 2002; Frith & Wolpert, 2004; Grezes et al., 2004). Alternatively, a recent neuroimaging study (Strathearn et al., submitted) has demonstrated that the insula of insecurely attached mothers is more strongly activated in observing negative affect on their infants' face than that of insecurely attached mothers, who showed more prefrontal activation. The insula is a part of the brain that has been linked in other studies not just with the experience of negative affect, but also with autobiographical memory (Fink et al., 1996; Montague & Lohrenz, 2007). These patterns of findings are consistent with the suggestion that insecure mothers with low RF are more likely to resonate with negative affect in their infants, which retrieves memories of negatively charged emotions from their own history. By contrast, the prefrontal activation of secure mothers suggests that they may be able to reflect on their child's negative affect and actively explore the potential causes of the child's unhappy reaction. This stance of open, respectful enquiring may make use of the mother's awareness of her own mental state in her understanding of her infant, but stops short of the point where her immersion in her own history might obscure a genuine awareness of her child as an independent being. Insecure mothers may tend to actually feel rather than think about the child's negative emotional state. A mother's awareness of her infant's subjectivity may serve to reduce the frequency of behaviours that might undermine the infant's natural progression towards evolving a sense of self as an independent mental entity through the dialectic of interaction with the mother.

Recent studies suggest that the capacity for change in attachment organization decreases over the course of development (Kobak et al., 2006). Thus, persistent trauma is more likely to lead to long-term disorganization of attachment with associated distortions in self-development, social cognition, and psychological disorder. In arguing that parental mentalizing capacity can protect the child from neglect, gross misattunement, and fearful/frightening behaviour, we are placing the emphasis of explanation not on the behaviours themselves, but rather on the potentially pervasive experience of parental dysfunction that they signal. We agree with Lyons-Ruth, Slade and others that sensitivity, as observed in interaction, is a limited indicator of the extent to which a child may rightfully anticipate a caregiver to be present. It is the disruption of an expectation of a contingent responsiveness on the part of the caregiver that signals the risk of a disorganized self-structure. Infants anticipate that in the interaction with the caregiver they will be able to create a sense of self as an active, intentional agent by triggering contingent emotional reactions from the parent. There is no doubt that for all caregivers the number of occasions on which the infant fails to elicit such a reaction probably exceeds the number of times that the infant is successful. What marks out traumatic relationships is the infant having little expectation of being able to recover contingent responding and turning inwards to assure themselves of their continued existence. In the long-term, as Tronick (2005), Trevarthen (2001), and others have for many years asserted, the self is a social creature, created generation after generation out of the recognition of something familiar and recognizable in someone else. This is the raw material for creating an experience of oneself within. The most profound trauma comes when a neglectful environment gives nothing for the child to work with and when the material for constructing an image of oneself is oneself alone. It is this privation that makes us vulnerable to creating a fragile, poorly symbolized, unmoderated sense of subjectivity and a self state where everything is directly experienced but difficult to regulate and potentially overwhelming.

References

Aber, J.L., Slade, A., Berger, B., Bresgi, I. & Kaplan, M. (1985) *The Parent Development Interview*. Unpublished manuscript.

Abrams, K., Rifkin, A. & Hesse, E. (2006) Dissociative 'FR' parental behaviour observed in a laboratory play session predicts infant disorganization. *Development and Psychopathology*, 18: 345–361.

Ainsworth, M.D.S. (1976) *System for rating maternal-care behavior*. Princeton, NJ: Educational Testing Service Test Collection.

Ainsworth, M.D.S., Bell, S.M. & Stayton, D.J. (1974) Infant mother attachment and social development: Socialisation as a product of reciprocal responsiveness to signals. In M.J.M. Richards (Ed.), *The integration of a child into the social world*. Cambridge: Cambridge University Press.

Ayissi, L. & Hubin-Gayte, M. (2006) Irritabilite du nouveau-ne et depression maternelle du post-partum. *Neuropsychiatrie de l'Enfance et de l'Adolescence*, 54: 125–132.

Bakermans-Kranenburg, M.J., Van IJzendoorn, M.H. & Juffer, F. (2005) Disorganized infant attachment and preventive interventions: A review and meta-analysis. *Infant Mental Health Journal*, 26: 191–216.

Barnard, K.E. (1978) *Nursing Child Assessment Teaching Scale*. Seattle, WA: NCAST Publications, University of Washington.

Benoit, D., Parker, K.C.H. & Zeanah, C.H. (1997a) Mothers' representations of their infants assessed prenatally: Stability and association with infants' attachment classifications. *Journal of Child Psychology and Psychiatry and Allied Disciplines*, 38: 307–313.

Benoit, D., Zeanah, C.H., Parker, K.C.H., Nicholson, E. & Coolbear, J. (1997b) Working model of the Child Interview: Infant clinical status related to maternal perceptions. *Infant Mental Health Journal*, 18: 107–121.

Bernstein, V.J., Percansky, C. & Hans, S.L. (1987) *Screening for social–emotional impairment in infants born to teenage mothers.* Paper presented at the Meetings of the Society for Research in Child Development.

Biringen, Z. & Bretherton, I. (1988) *The Sensitivity/Insight Scale for evaluating the Parent Attachment Interview.* Unpublished manual. Department of Human Development & Family Studies, Colorado State University, Fort Collins, CO.

Biringen, Z., Matheny, A., Bretherton, I., Renouf, A. & Sherman, M. (2000a) Maternal representation of the self as parent: Connections with maternal sensitivity and maternal structuring. *Attachment & Human Development,* 2: 218–232.

Biringen, Z., Robinson, J.L. & Emde, R.N. (1993) Emotional Availability Scales. Denver, CO: University of Colorado, Health Science Center.

Biringen, Z., Robinson, J.L. & Emde, R.N. (2000) Emotional Availability Scales (3rd ed.). *Attachment and Human Development,* 2: 257–270.

Biringen, Z., Robinson, J.L. & Emde, R.N. (2008) Emotional Availability Scales (4th ed.). Denver, CO: University of Colorado.

Bodinetz, M. (2008) The association between childhood maltreatment and insecure–disorganised attachment: A meta-analysis. London: Department of Clinical and Health Psychology, University College London.

Bokhorst, C.L., Bakermans-Kranenburg, M.J., Fearon, R.M., Van IJzendoorn, M.H., Fonagy, P. & Schuengel, C. (2003) The importance of shared environment in mother–infant attachment security: A behavioural genetic study. *Child Development,* 74: 1769–1782.

Bretherton, I., Biringen, Z., Ridgeway, D., Maslin, C. & Sherman, M. (1989) Attachment: The parental perspective. *Infant Mental Health Journal,* 10: 203–221.

Bronfman, E., Parsons, E. & Lyons-Ruth, K. (1999) *Atypical Maternal Behaviour Instrument for Assessment and Classification.* Unpublished manual, Harvard Medical School, Cambridge, MA.

Burns, K., Chethik, L., Burns, W. & Clark, R. (1997) The early relationship of drug abusing mothers and their infants: An assessment at eight to twelve months of age. *Journal of Clinical Psychology,* 53: 279–287.

Cantero, J. & Cerezo, A. (2001) Interaccion madre–hijo como predictora de conductus de apego: Evaluacion de dos modelos causales. *Infancia y Aprendizaje,* 93: 113–132.

Carlson, E.A. (1998) A prospective longitudinal study of attachment disorganization/disorientation. *Child Development,* 69: 1107–1128.

Carlson, J., Cicchetti, D., Barnett, D. & Braunwald, K.G. (1989) Finding order in disorganization: Lessons from research on maltreated infants' attachments to their caregivers. in Cicchetti, D. & Carlson, V. (Eds.) *Child Maltreatment: Theory and Research on the Causes and Consequences of Child Abuse and Neglect.* Cambridge: Cambridge University Press.

Chatoor, I., Getson, P., Menvielle, E., Brasseaux, C., O'Donnell, R., Rivera, Y. et al. (1997) A feeding scale for research and clinical practice to assess mother–infant interactions in the first three years of life. *Infant Mental Health Journal,* 18(1): 76–91.

Clark, R. (1983) *Interactions of psychiatrically ill and well mothers and their young children: Quality of maternal care and child competence,* Evanston, IL: Northwestern University.

Clark, R. (1985) *The Parent–Infant Early Relational Assessment: Instrument and manual*. Madison, WI: University of Wisconsin Medical School, Department of Psychiatry.

Cox, S.M., Hopkins, J. & Hans, S.L. (2000) Attachment in preterm infants and their mothers: Neonatal risk status and maternal representations. *Infant Mental Health Journal*, 21: 464–480.

Crittenden, P.M. (2001) *CARE-Index: Coding Manual*. Miami, FL: Family Relations Institute.

De Wolff, M.S. & Van IJzendoorn, M.H. (1997) Sensitivity and attachment: A meta-analysis on parental antecedents of infant attachment. *Child Development*, 68: 571–591.

Esser, G., Scheven, A., Petrova, A., Laucht, M. & Schmidt, M.H. (1990). Mannheim Rating System for mother–infant face-to-face interaction (MRS-III). *German Journal of Psychology*, 14: 301–302.

Farran, D.C., Kasari, K., Comfort, M. & Jay, S. (1986) *Parent/Caregiver Involvement Scale*. Nashville, TN: Peabody College, Vanderbilt University.

Fearon, P., Van IJzendoorn, M.H., Fonagy, P., Bakermans-Kranenburg, M.J., Schuengel, C. & Bokhorst, C.L. (2006) In search of shared and nonshared environmental factors in security of attachment: A behaviour–genetic study of the association between sensitivity and attachment security. *Developmental Psychology*, 42: 1026–1040.

Feldman, R. (1998) *Coding interactive behaviour manual*. Ramat Gan, Israel: Bar-Ilan University.

Feldman, R., Weller, A., Sirota, L. & Eidelman, A.I. (2002) Skin-to-skin contact (kangaroo care) promotes self-regulation in premature infants: Sleep–wake cyclicity, arousal modulation, and sustained exploration. *Developmental Psychology*, 38(2): 194–207.

Fink, G.R., Markowitsch, H.J., Reinkemeier, M., Bruckbauer, T., Kessler, J. & Heiss, W.D. (1996) Cerebral representation of one's own past: Neural networks involved in autobiographical memory. *Journal of Neuroscience*, 16: 4275–4282.

Fonagy, P., Steele, M., Steele, H. & Target, M. (1997) *Reflective-functioning manual, version 4.1, for application to Adult Attachment Interviews*. London: University College London.

Frith, C.D. & Wolpert, D.M. (2004) *The neuroscience of social interaction: Decoding, imitating and influencing the actions of others*. Oxford, UK: Oxford University Press.

Gallagher, H.L., Jack, A.I., Roepstorff, A. & Frith, C.D. (2002) Imaging the intentional stance in a competitive game. *NeuroImage*, 16: 814–821.

George, C., Kaplan, N. & Main, M. (1985) *The Adult Attachment Interview*. Unpublished manuscript, Department of Psychology, University of California at Berkeley, CA, USA.

George, C. & Solomon, J. (1989) Internal working models of parenting and quality of attachment at age six. *Infant Mental Health Journal*, 10: 222–237.

George, C. & Solomon, J. (Eds.) (2008a) *The caregiving behavioral system: A behavioral system approach to parenting*. New York: Guilford Press.

George, C. & Solomon, J. (2008b) *Internal working models of caregiving rating manual*. Unpublished manuscript, Mills College, Oakland, CA, USA.

Goldberg S., Benoit D., Blokland, K. & Madigan S., (2003) Atypical maternal behaviour, maternal representation and infant disorganised attachment. *Development and Psychopathology*, 15: 239–257.

Grezes, J., Frith, C.D. & Passingham, R.E. (2004) Inferring false beliefs from the actions of oneself and others: An fMRI study. *NeuroImage*, 21: 744–750.

Grienenberger, J., Kelly, K. & Slade, A. (2005) Maternal reflective functioning, mother–infant affective communication, and infant attachment: Exploring the link between mental states and observed caregiving behaviour in the intergenerational transmission of attachment. *Attachment and Human Development*, 7: 299–311.

Gross, D., Conrad, B., Fogg, L., Willis, L. & Garvey, C. (1993) What does the NCATS (Nursing Child Assessment Teaching Scale) measure? *Nursing Research*, 42: 260–265.

Guzell, J.R. & Vernon-Feagans, L. (2004) Parental perceived control over caregiving and its relationship to parent–infant interaction. *Child Development*, 75: 134–146.

Hans, S.L., Bernstein, V.J. & Percansky, C. (1991) Adolescent parenting programs: Assessing parent–infant interaction. *Evaluation and Program Planning*, 14: 87–95.

Hesse, E. & Main, M. (1999) Second-generation effects of unresolved trauma in nonmaltreating parents: Dissociated, frightened, and threatening parental behavior. *Psychoanalytic Inquiry*, 19: 481–540.

Hughes, P., Turton, P., Mcgauley, G.A. & Fonagy, P. (2006) Factors that predict infant disorganization in mothers classified as U in pregnancy. *Attachment & Human Development*, 8: 113–122.

Hughes, S. (1993) *The relationship between maternal psychiatric disorder and mother–child responsivity*. Montreal, Canada: McGill University.

Johnson, M.O. & Lobo, M.L. (2001) Mother–child interactions in the presence of maternal HIV infection. *Journal of the Association of Nurses in AIDS Care*, 12: 40–51.

Kobak, R., Cassidy, J., Lyons-Ruth, K. & Ziv, Y. (2006) Attachment, stress and psychopathology: A developmental pathways model. In Cicchetti, D. & Cohen, D.J. (Eds.), *Development and Psychopathology: Vol. 1: Theory and Method* (2nd ed.). New York: Wiley.

Koren-Karie, N., Oppenheim, D., Dolev, S., Sher, S. & Etzion-Carasso, A. (2002) Mother's insightfulness regarding their infants' internal experience: Relations with maternal sensitivity and infant attachment. *Developmental-Psychology*, 38: 534–542.

Lyons-Ruth, K., Bronfman, E. & Parsons, E. (1999) Maternal frightened, frightening or atypical behaviour and disorganised infant attachment patterns. *Monographs of the Society for Research in Child Development*, 64: 67–96.

Lyons-Ruth, K., Melnick, S., Patrick, M. & Hobson, R.P. (2007) A controlled study of hostile–helpless states of mind among borderline and dysthymic women. *Attachment & Human Development*, 9: 1–16.

Lyons-Ruth, K., Yellin, C., Melnick, S. & Atwood, G. (2005) Expanding the concept of unresolved mental states: hostile/helpless states of mind on the Adult Attachment Interview are associated with disrupted mother–infant communication and infant disorganization. *Development and Psychopathology*, 17: 1–23.

Lyons-Ruth, K., Yellin, C., Melnick, S. & Atwood, G. (2003) Childhood experiences of trauma and loss have different relations to maternal unresolved and hostile–helpless states of mind on the AAI. *Attachment & Human Development*, 5: 330–352.

Madigan, S., Moran, G. & Pederson, D.R. (2006) Unresolved states of mind, disorganized attachment relationships and disrupted mother–infant interactions of adolescent mothers and their infants. *Development and Psychopathology*, 42(2): 293–304.

Mahoney, G.J. (1999) *The Maternal Behavior Rating Scale–Revised*. Unpublished manuscript. (Available from the author at Mandel School of Applied Social Sciences, 11235 Bellflower Road, Cleveland, OH 44106–7164.)

Mahoney, G.J., Powell, A. & Finger, I. (1986) The maternal behaviour rating scale. *Topics in Early Childhood Special Education*, 6: 44–56.

Main, M. & Goldwyn, R. (1993) *Adult attachment classification system*. Berkeley, CA: University of California.

Main, M. & Hesse, E. (1990) Parents' unresolved traumatic experiences are related to infant disorganized attachment status: Is frightened and/or frightening parental behavior the linking mechanism? In M. Greenberg, D. Cicchetti & E.M. Cummings (Eds.), *Attachment in the preschool years: Theory, research and intervention*. Chicago: University of Chicago Press.

Main, M. & Hesse, E. (1992–2005) *Frightened, threatening, dissociative, timid–deferential, sexualized, and disorganized parental behavior: A coding system for frightened/frightening (FR) parent–infant interactions*. Unpublished manuscript, University of California at Berkeley, CA, USA.

Main, M. & Solomon, J. (1986) Discovery of an insecure–disorganized/disoriented attachment pattern. In T.B. Brazelton & M.W. Yogman (Eds.), *Affective development in infancy*. Norwood, NJ: Ablex.

Meins, E. (1997) *Security of attachment and the social development of cognition*. Hove, UK: Psychology Press.

Meins, E. & Fernyhough, C. (1999) Linguistic acquisitional style and mentalising development: The role of maternal mind-mindedness. *Cognitive Development*, 14: 363–380.

Meins, E., Fernyhough, C., Fradley, E. & Tuckey, M. (2001) Rethinking maternal sensitivity: Mothers' comments on infants' mental processes predict security of attachment at 12 months. *Journal of Child Psychology and Psychiatry*, 42: 637–648.

Meins, E., Fernyhough, C., Wainwright, R., Clark-Carter, D., Das Gupta, M., Fradley, E. et al. (2003) Pathways to understanding mind: Construct validity and predictive validity of maternal mind-mindedness. *Child Development*, 74: 1194–1211.

Meins, E., Fernyhough, C., Wainwright, R., Das Gupta, M., Fradley, E. & Tuckey, M. (2002) Maternal mind-mindedness and attachment security as predictors of theory of mind understanding. *Child Development*, 73: 1715–1726.

Melnick, S. & Patrick, M. (2003) *Discriminating borderline states of mind: Operationalizing the concept of affective splitting and pervasively unintegrated states of mind on the adult attachment interview*. Poster presented at the biennial meeting of the Society for Research in Child Development, Tampa, FL, USA.

Montague, P.R. & Lohrenz, T. (2007) To detect and correct: Norm violations and their enforcement. *Neuron*, 56: 14–18.

Munson, J.A., McMahon, R.J. & Spieker, S.J. (2001) Structure and variability in the developmental trajectory of children's externalizing problems: Impact of infant attachment, maternal depressive symptomatology and child sex. *Development and Psychopathology*, 13: 277–296.

Murray, L., Fiori-Cowley, A., Hooper, R. & Cooper, P. (1996) The impact of postnatal depression and associated adversity on early mother–infant interactions and later infant outcome. *Child Development*, 67: 2512–2526.

Musick, J.S., Clark, R. & Cohler, B.J. (1981) The Mothers' Project: A clinical research program for mentally ill mothers and their young children. In B. Weissbourd & J. Musick (Eds.), *The social and caregiving environments of infants* (pp. 111–127). Washington, DC: National Association for the Education of Young Children.

Oppenheim, D. & Koren-Karie, N. (2002) Mothers' insightfulness regarding their children's internal worlds: The capacity underlying secure child–mother relationships. *Infant Mental Health Journal*, 23: 593–605.

Pederson, D.R. & Moran, G. (1995) Caregiving, cultural, and cognitive perspectives on secure-base behavior and working models: New growing points of attachment theory and research. *Monographs of the Society for Research in Child Development*, 60: 247–254.

Puckering, C., Rogers, J., Mills, M., Cox, A.D. & Mattsson-Graff, M. (1994) Process and evaluation of a group intervention for mothers with parenting difficulties. *Child Abuse Review*, 3: 299–310.

Rosenblum, K.L., Mcdonough, S., Sameroff, A. & Muzik, M. (2008) Reflection in thought and action: Maternal parenting reflexivity predicts mind-minded comments and interactive behaviour. *Infant Mental Health Journal*, 29: 362–376.

Schechter, D.S., Coots, T., Zeanah, C.H., Davies, M., Coates, S.W., Trabka, K.A. et al. (2005) Maternal mental representations of the child in an inner-city clinical sample: Violence-related posttraumatic stress and reflective functioning. *Attachment and Human Development*, 7: 313–331.

Schuengel, C., Bakermans-Kranenburg, M. & Van IJzendoorn, M. (1999) Frightening maternal behaviour linking unresolved loss and disorganised infant attachment. *Journal of Consulting and Clinical Psychology*, 67: 54–63.

Sharp, C. & Fonagy, P. (2008) The parent's capacity to treat the child as a psychological agent: Constructs, Measures and implications for developmental psychopathology. *Social Development*, 17: 737–754.

Slade, A. (2005) Parental reflective functioning: An introduction. *Attachment & Human Development*, 7: 269–281.

Slade, A., Aber, J.L., Bresgi, I., Berger, B. & Kaplan, M. (2004a) *The Parent Development Interview – Revised*. Unpublished protocol, The City University of New York, NY, USA.

Slade, A., Bernbach, E., Grienenberger, J., Levy, D. & Locker, A. (2004b) *Addendum to Fonagy, Target, Steele, & Steele reflective functioning scoring manual for use with the Parent Development Interview*. Unpublished manuscript, The City College and Graduate Center of the City University of New York, NY, USA.

Slade, A., Grienenberger, J., Bernbach, E., Levy, D. & Locker, A. (2005) Maternal reflective functioning, attachment, and the transmission gap: A preliminary study. *Attachment & Human Development*, 7: 283–298.

Solomon, J. & George, C. (2006) Intergenerational transmission of dysregulated maternal caregiving: Mothers describe their upbringing and child rearing. In O. Mayseless (Ed.) *Parenting representations: Theory, research, and clinical implications*. New York: Cambridge University Press.

Sroufe, L.A., Egeland, B., Carlson, E. & Collins, W.A. (2005) *The development of the person: The Minnesota study of risk and adaptation from birth to adulthood*. New York: Guilford Press.

Strathearn, L., Fonagy, P., Amico, J. & Montague, R. (submitted for publication) Adult attachment predicts maternal brain and oxytocin response to infant cues.

Sumner, G. & Spietz, A. (1995) *NCAST Caregiver/Parent–Child Interaction Feeding Manual*. Seattle, WA: NCAST Publications, University of Seattle.

Swanson, K. (1998) *Intrusive caregiving and security of attachment in drug exposed toddlers and their primary caregivers*. Los Angeles: Department of Psychology, Fuller Theological Seminary.

Teti, D.M., Nakagawa, M., Das, R. & Wirth, O. (1991) Security of attachment between preschoolers and their mothers: Relations among social interactions, parenting stress and mothers' sorts of the attachment Q-sort. *Developmental Psychology*, 27: 440–447.

Trapolini, T., Ungerer, J.A. & McMahon, C.A. (2008) Maternal depression: Relations with maternal caregiving representations and emotional availability during the preschool years. *Attachment & Human Development*, 10: 73–90.

Trevarthen, C. & Aitken, K.J. (2001) Infant intersubjectivity: Research, theory, and clinical applications. *Journal of Child Psychology and Psychiatry*, 42(1): 3–48.

Tronick, E.Z. (2005) Why is connection with others so critical? The formation of dyadic states of consciousness: Coherence governed selection and the co-creation of meaning out of messy meaning making. In J. Nadel & D. Muir (Eds.), *Emotional development* (pp. 293–315). Oxford, UK: Oxford University Press.

True, M. (1994) *Mother–infant attachment and communication among the Dogon of Mali*. Unpublished doctoral dissertation, University of California at Berkeley, CA, USA.

True, M., Pisani, L. & Oumar, F. (2001) Infant–mother attachment among the Dogon in Mali. *Child Development*, 72(5): 1451–1466.

Van IJzendoorn, M., Scheungel, C. & Bakermanns-Kranenburg, M.J. (1999) Disorganized attachment in early childhood: Meta-analysis of precursors, concomitants and sequelae. *Development and Psychopathology*, 22: 225–249.

Ward, M.J. & Carlson, E.A. (1995) Associations among Adult Attachment representations, maternal sensitivity, and infant–mother attachment in a sample of adolescent mothers. *Child Development*, 66: 69–79.

Zeanah, C.H. & Benoit, D. (1995) Clinical applications of a parent perception interview in infant mental health. *Child and Adolescent Clinics of North America*, 4: 539–554.

Zeanah, C.H., Benoit, D. & Barton, M.L. (1986) *Working model of the Child Interview*. Unpublished manuscript, Brown University Program in Medicine, Providence, RI, USA.

Zeanah, C.H., Benoit, D., Hirshberg, L., Barton, M.L. & Regan, C. (1994) Mothers' representations of their infants are concordant with infant attachment classifications. *Developmental Issues in Psychiatry and Psychology*, 1: 1–14.

Zero-to-Three (1994) *Diagnostic classification: 0–3. Diagnostic classification of mental health and developmental disorders of infancy and early childhood*. Washington, DC: Zero-to-Three.

Ziv, Y., Aviezer, O., Gini, M., Sagi, A. & Koren-Karie, N. (2000) Emotional availability in the mother–infant dyad as related to the quality of infant–mother attachment relationship. *Attachment and Human Development*, 2: 149–169.

Chapter 10

Contributions of, and divergences between, clinical work and research tools relating to trauma and disorganization

Tessa Baradon and Elisa Bronfman

This chapter will consider how research informs clinical practice and how clinical practice validates and informs research in the field of relational trauma in infancy. The importance of a close working relationship between these branches will be emphasized, especially since research and practice often use different lenses to see similar phenomena, such as intergenerational transmission, mental representation, and disorganized attachment.

We will conduct the dialogue between research and applied psychoanalytic practice through examples from a treatment case of a (borderline) mother and her infant whose relationship was characterized by intergenerational trauma. Clinical material will be presented from the therapeutic work,[1] including two brief segments of sessional material that illustrate the back-and-forth of trauma in the interaction between mother and infant. The research tools applied in this case were the Adult Attachment Interview (AAI) of the mother,[2] conducted by the therapist in their second meeting, and the Atypical Maternal Behavior Instrument for Assessment and Classification (AMBIANCE) coding of the presented clinical segments.[3] We will conclude with the questions of whether research – which aims to find generalities across numerous individuals – can assist in the understanding and treatment of a single dyad or individual, and whether looking at one dyad can raise questions pertinent to research.

The research tools

The AAI and the AMBIANCE were chosen because of their current use in the research community to assess child outcomes. The AAI (Main & Goldwyn, 1993) is used to assess parental cognitive and emotional strategies for dealing with relationships. In research studies, the AAI has been shown

---

1 The therapy was conducted by Tessa Baradon.
2 Coded according to Main and Goldwyn (1993) by Dr Mary Target.
3 The AMBIANCE was coded by Dr Elisa Bronfman.

to be highly predictive of the parent's relationship with her own child (van IJzendoorn, 1995), has been used to assess outcome in psychoanalytic treatment (Gullestad, 2003), and has shown links between child attachment classification and adult classification for the same individual (Waters et al., 2003). In terms of potential benefit to clinical work, the AAI asks questions that are relevant to clinical formulation (Steele & Steele, 2008).

The AMBIANCE (Atypical Maternal Behavior Instrument for Assessment and Classification; most current version, Bronfman et al., 2008), which drew from the work of Main and Hesse (1990) and others, identifies maternal behaviours that are seen as influential in creating the dynamics potentially leading to infant disorganization. AMBIANCE includes five dimensions of maternal behaviour, which will be discussed in the context of this case presentation. To date, research with AMBIANCE has shown links between maternal disrupted behaviour and infant attachment status (Lyons-Ruth et al., 1999; Madigan et al., 2006), maternal behaviour and trauma history (Lyons-Ruth et al., 1999) and classification on AMBIANCE and on the AAI (Goldberg et al., 2003). AMBIANCE has also been used to measure treatment outcome with a play-based intervention (Chasoit et al., 2001). Like the AAI, the behaviours seen on the AMBIANCE are the kind of behaviours that therapists see in parent–infant therapy.

The clinical process: Constructing a psychodynamic formulation

Relational trauma places the parent/caregiver centre-stage as a potential source of trauma, through the parent's state of mind and – often unconscious – feelings and intentions towards her infant.

In the case discussed below, the defining emotional state of the mother was ambivalence. The mother's state of mind swung unpredictably from benign to malevolent in her intentionalities towards her baby. Consequently, the baby experienced a sometimes caring, responsive mother and, at other times, an emotionally dysregulated parent who was both a source of alarm and absent as a protector. This lack of predictability for the infant can be more frightening and confusing than a consistently negative state, because the baby has incompatible (loving and rejecting) and apparently random experiences with his parent, and cannot build up expectancies of what the next emotional tone will be – that of safety or of danger. One of the key sources of information in the consulting room is the infant's second-to-second affective and behavioural responses to the changes in the parent's state of mind. Careful observation of the traumatizing 'dance' between parent and infant, and of the therapist's countertransference, privileges the domain of implicit relational knowing (Stern et al., 1998). In other words, resonating traumatizing transactions take place not only outside consciousness, but also in the spheres of affect and action (see also McLaughlin, 1991).

At a clinical level of making sense of phenomena observed and experienced in the here-and-now of the consulting room, the therapist is often working with a dynamic formulation about possible causal links between states of mind and behaviours at both the implicit and declarative levels (Baradon, 2002; Baradon et al., 2005). Reflecting on the intrapsychic experiences of each participant – including the countertransference of the therapist – and the interpersonal processes between them may elucidate nuances of representation, affect, gesture, and behaviour that play a role in the transmission loop.

Case material

First session: Tessa Baradon, therapist

Stacey and Chas were referred for parent–infant psychotherapy when Chas was four months old. When asked what had brought them to seek help, Stacey replied 'Well . . . I just don't want to be like my mother to Chas. She was really violent, made me feel worthless, which I still do. I just don't feel for him as much as I should, I'm scared to love him in case he's horrible to me when he grows up.' These comments suggest that Stacey intuitively recognized the potential for intergenerational transmission and, at the same time, the clear difficulty of overcoming this threat despite her understanding of its presence.

In the consulting room they immediately presented a complex picture for the therapist. When Stacey laid Chas down on the baby mat she spontaneously cooed at him and he gave her a big smile. Yet immediately after this, he averted his head and his gaze remained fixed to the right of his mother's face, avoidant of further visual exchange. At the same time, in a voice devoid of affect, Stacey presented a list of the substances she had used to obliterate pain. Chas's slumped body tone suggested that his vitality was cut off and I, too, was affected by the destructiveness of Stacey's life-story. When Chas fretted, she bottle-fed him. He took, then rejected, the milk and 'fell into' desperate crying. We were in a predicament as mother and baby heightened each other's emotional dysregulation. My tentative formulation was that Chas desperately wanted the bottle/mother but could not take in food 'toxified' by her projections. His apparent rejection confirmed her dread that she was bad for him, and also her fear that her baby would recreate the traumatic patterns of her own childhood with her parents. Stacey appeared helpless in the face of Chas's distress, stating: 'I really don't know what to do'. Chas then experienced a maternal mind that could not receive his feelings into her reverie (Bion, 1962), and it became for him a psychosomatic experience of 'catastrophe'.

The AAI

The AAI was conducted by the therapist in the next meeting. Stacey described a very unhappy childhood characterized by physical and emotional abuse by her mother and neglect by her father. Adjectives given for her relationship with her mother were: controlling, evil, scary, embarrassing, unloving. When asked for an illustration of 'evil' her response was 'Um [7 seconds]. The whole childhood . . . and it was just evil – the look in her face and you can't, you couldn't tell what mood she was in, whether she was in a good mood or a bad mood, and she'd switch and she'd become . . . she could be really nice and then she'd be just evil.' Stacey described her dependency on, and inability to separate from, her mother: 'When I was away from her I craved for her, I had to be at home . . . I'm so scared to be anywhere else but at home, but I didn't want to be there when I was there, I wanted to die.'

For her father the adjectives were: kind, blind (to what was happening in the family), separate, controlling. She was unable to give any examples, claiming she had blocked out all memories except the pain, but recalled always wishing for her father's recognition and protection.

Commentary of the clinician (TB) regarding the AAI

The AAI was a powerful experience for both of us. There was a 'surprising of the unconscious' (an aim of the AAI) and Stacey's emotions were spontaneous and raw, with a strong sense that she remained in the grip of the past fears and grievances. I was moved by the frightened child within her and her feelings of helplessness in relation to her baby, whom she already regarded as a potential abuser. This felt important in order for me to remain empathic to Stacey when observing Chas suffering in her care. I was left deeply concerned for both of them.

The outstanding feature pertaining to relational trauma in Stacey's narrative was her experience of emotional abuse interspersed with care. Particularly moving was Stacey's recognition of the paradox of her traumatic attachment – her fear of being with mother and fear of being away from her. Furthermore, Stacey felt abandoned by her father and left alone with this traumatizing relationship with her mother.

Commentary of AAI coder 1 (Main coding system)[4]

This is quite an extreme transcript, incoherent with contradictory ineffective strategies to deal with attachment feelings and memories. There is clear-cut disorganization with respect particularly to trauma (abuse) but also to

4 We are grateful to Dr Mary Target for her coding and comments on this AAI.

loss (deaths); the main indicator of this is repeated speaking of the dead mother in the present tense. This does not seem to be a technical violation of narrative – it seems that mother is still an actively threatening figure, to whom the subject speaks and with whom she is currently angry as well as frightened. The main (more) organized strategies (reflected in the long list of contributing classifications) are: angry grievance, derogation of attachment and of attachment figures, fearful intrusive thoughts of trauma, and dismissing of attachment/repression of memory. The CC classification (Cannot Classify means that there are contradictory strategies) is given because of her preoccupation and dismissal. It means that coherence is very low and reflective function necessarily compromised – undercut by unintegrated and incompatible thoughts. The intergenerational patterns are obvious in the final section.

Classification: U/CC/E2 /Ds2 (E3/D).

Mother–infant interactions within the therapeutic encounter

The following two-minute excerpt is taken from session 10; Chas was six months old. The material illustrates the rapid movement, in the minute-to-minute interactions, between responsivity and hostility in the mother and experiences of intersubjectivity and collapse as expressed in the responses of the infant.

We have incorporated the clinician's commentary and the AMBIANCE coding to illustrate the approaches of each. A selection of the AMBIANCE coded behaviour is noted along the five dimensions: Affective communication errors (1), Role/boundary confusion (2), Disorientation (3), Intrusiveness/ Negativity (4), and Withdrawal (5). At the conclusion of the interactive segment, the more global ratings on the AMBIANCE will be discussed. While individual behavioural codes are important, the main purpose of these individual scores is to inform the coder's decisions regarding the overall patterns of behaviour and assignment of global scores (see Table 10.1).

Clinical commentary on the parent–infant interactions (TB)

Parent–infant interactions that take place within the therapeutic setting are framed by the singular tension between emotional containment offered by the therapist's mentalizing stance, the challenge and disruption of working with painful material, and the need to be a participant–observer while such painful material unfolds in the form of present-day potentially traumatizing interactions. In the interaction described above, Stacey and Chas have attended 10 parent–infant psychotherapy sessions. They are already acquainted with the framework and rhythm of the therapeutic encounter and have a strong bond with, and expectations of, me. Whereas Chas more consistently turns to me as a benign third object/alternative attachment figure,

Table 10.1 Clinician's commentary and AMBIANCE coding

Observation	Therapist's thinking	AMBIANCE
Chas is arching in mother's embrace. He cries fretfully.	Chas is cueing that he is dysregulated and needs his mother's help.	Distanced position (5)
Stacey says in a loud, rather accusatory voice, 'You're a tired baby . . . Shh . . . you're tired.'	There is an attempt to quiet rather than soothe Chas, and a lack of mentalization on mother's part. I experience Stacey's voice and gestures as brittle.	Fails to soothe crying infant (1) Harsh voice (4) Makes negative comment about infant (4)
She rocks him hard with her legs and replaces the dummy firmly in his mouth but, at the same time, she holds the dummy in place and strokes his hair.	On a bodily level, too, Stacey expresses her negativity in trying to silence Chas. I am wondering whether Stacey is conscious of the anger in her voice?	Behaves aggressively toward the infant (4)
Chas waves his arms and pulls the dummy from his mouth while arching, again with the loud cry.	Chas's levels of dysregulation rise in response to mother's anger.	Infant cue. Not coded in AMBIANCE directly but important to note parent's response
Stacey rebukes Chas: 'Why do you pull it out when you know it's going to upset you? Shh . . .'	Mother attributes intentionality to Chas's actions – in her mind he is making himself more upset. She doesn't see her potential role as a soother herself.	Criticizes (4) Hushes crying infant (4)
She holds the dummy in place briefly, then strokes his hair.	There are contradictory messages of silencing and soothing.	
Chas's head is turned towards the therapist.	He is avoiding his mother and seeking out the benign adult. I try to hold his feelings with my gaze.	Infant cue
Stacey to therapist: 'She [Aunt] made me leave him alone when he was screaming and crying.'	Stacey sounds indignant with her aunt and protective of her baby.	Therapy content not coded, although suggestive of Stacey's struggle to find ways to be with her infant
There is a momentary pause.	An opening for mother to recognize Chas's cues and pre-empt escalation. Will she turn her mind to Chas?	

Chas squirms in her arms and she looks down.		Infant cue. Ignores infant cue (1)
She continues to represent Aunt: 'Like "we'll break him of that".' Her tone of voice is angry.	Although Stacey consciously disagrees with her Aunt's attitudes, she may unconsciously be identified with the wish to 'break' Chas of his crying.	Negative comment about the infant (4) Fearful face (3)
Chas wails again, his body becoming rigid.	Stacey has missed the opportunity to regulate before his distress escalates, and Chas responds to her tone of voice as directed towards himself.	Infant cue
Stacey replaces the dummy in his mouth and rocks him . . .	She is using the dummy to quiet and her rocking to soothe.	Uses prop to soothe infant (5)
. . . but continues to look at the therapist and returns to her complaints about Aunt: 'I couldn't bear it, he wasn't well. We pick him up too much is what she's saying . . . I don't care.'	There is a contradiction between Stacey's stated concern for Chas and her overriding of his distress in the here-and-now of the session.	Therapy content – not coded
Chas bunches his legs, arms flailing.	He seems to be fragmenting, communicating distress with his whole body.	Infant cue
Stacey looks down and adjusts the dummy that is already in his mouth.	Stacey intrudes on Chas's use of the dummy, perhaps to soothe or silence herself as well as him?	Uses prop to soothe infant (5)
Chas turns his head away, sucking hard on the dummy.	He withdraws from mother and uses his dummy to self-regulate, perhaps feeling he has lost me too.	Infant cue
The therapist leans forward.	I offer myself to Chas as another attachment figure at that point.	Therapy content
Chas turns his head to look at her.	He moves towards engagement with the familiar, non-threatening adult.	Therapy content

(*Continued overleaf*)

Table 10.1 Continued

Observation	Therapist's thinking	AMBIANCE
The therapist says to Chas in a low, crooning voice: 'But you need help, don't you, you're very small, you need help to be calmed.'	I use my voice to regulate Chas and my words to help mother consider his dependency and need for her protection.	Therapy content
Chas looks at the therapist, rocked more gently now by mother's legs, seeming calmer.	Chas responds to my scaffolding and emotional holding.	Therapy content
Stacey, also crooning now, says 'I love my baby.'	Stacey is also responding to my intervention, and her negativity softens.	Ameliorating behaviour – noted but not directly coded
The therapist continues to talk rhythmically to him: 'Yes? Mummy's rocking you . . .'	I privilege Chas's vulnerability, but also confirm Stacey's identity as mother-with-baby. I am using my voice to regulate Chas and my words to represent to Stacey his infantile dependency and need for her protection.	Therapist–child interaction
Stacey looks at Chas, a smile flickering around her lips.	Stacey emotionally reengages with Chas.	Ameliorating behaviour – noted but not directly coded
Chas lies soothed and relaxed in his mother's lap, gazing at the therapist.	There is a moment of close rapport between the three of us.	
Stacey interjects: 'My legs are tired because you're so . . . you're a big heavy smelly baby boy . . . you do some big smelly poo poos now . . .' Her voice has softened as she says this.	I am taken aback by the content of this remark.	Negative comment about the infant (4) Contradictory signal – derogatory message with a sweet voice (1)
She laughs.		Laughs at infant (4)
Chas is still looking at the therapist. Stacey continues with more urgency: 'I don't care, I still eat them cos I love you.'	I continue to offer myself as a predictable 'third'. I speculate that there is a breakthrough of a primitive fantasy.	Bizarre comment (3)

Chas looks fleetingly into her face.	Chas is highly sensitized to changes in his mother's state of mind and is immediately on his guard again.	
She goes on: 'Yeah, I love you', caressing his face repeatedly and stroking his hair.	Her caresses seem intrusive.	Touches infant in a way that appears affectionate but is annoying to the infant (4)
Chas looks away crying, the dummy falls from his mouth.	He is highly dysregulated, not able to use me either.	Infant cue. Ignores infant cue (1)
The therapist looks on intently.	My posture and gaze convey that I am an emotional presence.	
He lifts his head and upper body off his mother's legs.	A strong body movement towards escape, suggesting that he is frightened by mother.	Infant cue
The therapist involuntarily draws back from her highly engaged physical position and straightens her back.	Chas's move to flee is echoed in my momentary physical withdrawal. I feel that we are all poised above an abyss.	
Stacey replaces the dummy in his mouth and repositions Chas more comfortably on her knees.	She seems to be reading his cues and trying to respond to them.	Uses a prop to soothe infant (5)
Chas arches briefly then seems to sink back into her lap.	He resists, then allows her to reach out.	Infant cue
Stacey looks down at him and speaks in a crooning voice: 'No no no OH.'	She seems to have responded to his cues in a more attuned way.	
He glances up at her and their gazes lock for a few moments.	A moment of interactive repair takes place between them.	
Mother and Chas and I sit quietly for a few moments.		

Stacey brings complex transference feelings, as is to be expected from the AAI material.

In her AAI Stacey is unresolved with regard to the relational trauma she experienced with her mother. It would be expected, because of the nature of unresolved states of mind and the psychic compulsion to repeat (Freud, 1920; Sandler, 1987; see also Chapter 5, this volume), that Stacey's represented attachment experiences with her mother would be repeated in some measure in other attachment relationships. Indeed, her description of the dependency and humiliation with the Aunt, a current caretaking figure, have the quality of rumination – like unresolved trauma. Her incongruent, dissonant behaviours that so dysregulate Chas (as in her multiple uses of the dummy – as an aggressive object, a soothing object, and as a way of escaping from the intimacy of the relationship with Chas) suggest also an unconscious identification with the aggressors (Freud, 1936) in Mother and Aunt.

Stacey has a number of conscious and unconscious agendas in this brief interaction. On one hand, she is placed in the role of comforting adult by her baby, who is in a state of emotional turmoil. On the other, she is deeply preoccupied with her child-like relationship with her Aunt/substitute mother. The raw experiences with the Aunt, as the unresolved relational trauma with her mother, mean that the negative transference feelings to her baby are constantly triggered. I observe that when Stacey's hostility is provoked Chas is no longer seen as her small, vulnerable and rewarding baby. Rather he himself becomes a traumatizing object, already powerful enough to make 'big poo poos', eliciting fearful facial expressions and voice tones that resonate with her early statement of fearing to love him 'in case he's horrible to me when he grows up'.

The breakthrough of negative representational and procedural material from the past interferes with the ongoing relationship between mother and baby, with interactional contributions from both. Despite conscious intention to the contrary, early relational procedures of being with the other, as well as the return of the repressed, are enacted in those interactions with her baby that are characterized by moments of fear (Boston Change Process Study Group, 2008). When Stacey is in a state of emotional turmoil herself, Chas experiences her dysregulation on a physiological level – through her body tone, heartbeat, agitated gestures.

Chas's extreme sensitivity to changes in his mother's states of mind, and the rapidity with which he becomes highly dysregulated, indicate that he has been frightened by her hostility before and that, also because of the unpredictability of when she will be hostile again, he is not able to 'prepare' for it. In a state of dependency on her (Winnicott, 1960) and lacking predictably responsive experiences with her, he is constantly on the verge of disintegrating. Moreover, Chas, himself further destabilizes his mother both in his inconsolable current state and as subject of the intergenerational 'ghost in the nursery' (Fraiberg et al., 1975) which returns to persecute her with his demands and fragility. Thus their negative affective states escalate (Beebe, 2000, 2005). Yet, contrary to earlier sessions in which Chas fell into states of dissociation in retreat from inconsolability, by this session he has developed some ways of adapting to his mother's failures. He uses me (I have been experienced as helpful before) as a regulating object; when I fail him, he capitalizes on his dummy to self-soothe.

Commentary by the AMBIANCE Coder (EB)

Although many researchers are now expanding AMBIANCE to other play-based situations (Madigan et al., 2006), the therapy segment discussed in this paper was unusual for AMBIANCE coding in that rather than coding the infant–parent dyad alone, there was a 'trio', including the mother, therapist, and infant. AMBIANCE is most effectively coded when the parent is in a condition of 'attachment stress' such as produced by the Strange Situation. In this case, the parent was in a condition of 'attachment support', with her therapist on several occasions assisting the mother in reading her child's cues, supporting the infant's needs, and preventing situations from spinning further out of control. Although the therapist primarily provides attachment support, she also induces stress with some of her comments that are aimed at helping Stacey gain greater understanding of her baby and privilege his needs. Despite the uniqueness of the setting, interesting information and relevant behaviours were exhibited in the sessions that allowed for coding.

The interaction piece described in this chapter was only a portion of the segment that was coded with the AMBIANCE. In the entire clip, Stacey had codes on each dimension of AMBIANCE. There were also numerous behaviours that were very concerning. The *disoriented behaviours* were the most striking, with many fearful facial expressions, fearful voice tones, and a few odd/disconnected comments, such as eating her child's faeces. Even with the individual codes aside, there was a generally helpless/fearful quality to this parent that pervaded the entire clip. Her *affective errors* involved several contradictory signals (such as delivering negative messages with sweet voices) and a difficulty soothing her child when he indicated distress. The *role confusion* issues were less clear but suggested a view of the infant as powerful and her own vulnerability and fear of him. She achieved many codes on the *intrusiveness/negativity* dimension. These were for personalizing the infant's behaviour as negative and more powerful than he actually could be as an infant. These seemed more in the service of battling her own helplessness rather than in any true aggression toward her child. The *withdrawal* involved adopting postures designed to keep her child at a distance as well as directing him to both toys and his pacifier (dummy) rather than using her self to provide comfort. The overall pattern of the interaction suggested a lack of predictable response and support, leading to an overall assignment of the 'Disrupted: Fearful Subtype Level 6' category for Stacey, which suggests that the 'parent demonstrates a significant lack of responsiveness to infant cues, confusion, disorientation, withdrawal, or fearful behaviours in response to her infant' (AMBIANCE manual; Bronfman et al., 2008).

We will now compare the above with a later session. Session 30 is quite different to the earlier session – both in what is present in the mother's supportive and playful behaviours, and in what is absent in terms of previous hostility and lack of responsivity.

Excerpt from session 30, baby aged one year

The following summarizes a two-minute segment of the session (taken from the therapist's session notes, supplemented by video recording):

> Chas is lying on his back facing mother, babbling, but also trying to get up into a sitting position. Stacey sends me a look of amusement and when Chas pulls himself quite high, Stacey and I (TB) gasp admiringly at the same moment and both of us laugh. She holds out her arms, calling his name in an inviting tone, but is still out of his reach so he cannot get to her hand for him to grasp. Stacey then leans in further and gently pulls him into a sitting position. Chas re-orients himself, and then looks out of the big picture window he is facing
>
> Stacey follows his gaze: Are you looking at the trees?
>
> Stacey turns to tell me about their weekend. Chas is babbling and looking between the window and his mother.
>
> He makes a movement and Stacey stabilizes him. She holds his hand briefly. Chas angles his head with a smile. Stacey smiles back and also angles her head. She asks him: 'Oh, should I look upside down?' but continues to talk to me. Chas again angles his head and waits for his mother. She does not copy him so he angles his head again, looking at her expectantly. Stacey laughs and looks at me. I am also enjoying Chas's playfulness and I smile back in acknowledgement. Stacey copies Chas and they share a moment.

Clinical commentary, session 30 (TB)

Chas holds centre stage in Stacey's mind and she is more drawn to playing with him than she is to talking with me about her grievances. He is seen as separate and adored in his own right, a source of pride and pleasure – no longer carries a 'ghost' in his mother's mind. Chas certainly relates to Stacey as his love object and he initiates humorous, playful interactions with her with obvious expectations that she will respond positively. I am considerably less active. My role at the particular moment is to observe and affirm. There is a 'motherhood constellation' (Stern, 1995) in Stacey's mind whereby I am the mother she never had.

AMBIANCE coding, session 30 (EB)

In session 10, the therapist was much more active than she was in session 30, as the parent–infant interaction required more of her interventions. Session 30 is striking for an absence of contradictory signalling, withdrawal, and negativity in mother, and it is also much different in the manner in which Stacey is able to be present and engage. In dramatic contrast to session 10, in session 30 the mother is facing her baby, actively playing with him. She is making direct eye contact, smiling and truly enjoying her child. Rather than using a dummy or toy to be with her baby, she plays directly with him using her self through her voice and body. However, there is still a remnant of fear (when speaking of the weekend), which is seen in the disorientation codes that remain codable in the session. The summary coding for session 30 was 'level 2, not disrupted', which suggests very minimal behavioural misses in the context of a *parent who is generally sensitive to her infant's signals*.

Discussion

As this chapter demonstrates, in many ways research and clinical lenses are focusing on the same phenomena. At a clinical level, a traumatized infant is one who repeatedly experiences prolonged overwhelming, unregulated psychobiological states of 'fear–terror'. From our clinical observations at the AFC we would suggest that all states of prolonged dysregulation overwhelm the infant and are traumatizing when not alleviated by the adult. The overwhelming emotion may be that of fear of the parent, when the parent is actually frightening to the infant as described by Main and Hesse (1990) and often – through identification – also to the therapist. There are also instances where the parent may become a 'bad object' in the internal world of the infant through the failure to regulate the infant's state. The AMBIANCE manual, based on research regarding trauma and problematic mother–infant dyads, describes: 'In the conception underlying the AMBIANCE coding system, disorganized infant attachment results when the caregiver consistently fails as a source of protection against overwhelming arousal. In this view, without reasonably effective caregiver modulation of arousal, the infant is unable to organize a consistent strategy for using the parent as a source of comfort when under stress. In particular, the disruption of communication between parent and infant in attachment-eliciting contexts should be fear-arousing in itself because the infant will have little sense of influence over the caregiver at times of heightened fear or stress (Bronfman et al., 2008; Lyons-Ruth et al., 1999a, 1999b; Madigan et al., 2006). Both the clinical and research interests are, thus, in the traumatizing 'dance', with shared interest to elucidate further the transmission loop.

What can dyads like this tell researchers? What does this family have to say in terms of limitations in overarching types?

The research agenda of 'furthering science' and gaining knowledge about such dyads may, at times, seem to ignore the needs of the individual subjects involved. It was a unique opportunity for me (EB) to be able to code one dyad at two points in time. Normally research integrity and maintaining a neutral/blind stance in a larger study would prevent such an undertaking. The dyad, Stacey and Chas, fits nicely into the patterns of behaviour that have been seen before in my (EB) coding of larger samples. It is a validation that these patterns can be demonstrated outside artificially created interactions such as the Strange Situation. It is evidence that in daily interactions, such as this therapeutic encounter, it is possible to discern researched patterns of behaviour. It was extremely useful to be able to look at not only the inter-action itself but, as a single example, to see how the therapist's observations, maternal history, AMBIANCE and AAI all fit together. Looking at all the details and tools for single cases may ultimately refine how tools such as AMBIANCE and the AAI are used when descriptors are found that help fully elucidate the nature of the sample. For example, the nature of blind coding means that only a small part of the overall picture of the sample is perceived at the time of coding. Even if later details are revealed, it is after the scene has been surveyed. While the coding in this instance was also completed with no information, there was the unique opportunity to watch it again with details from the different perspectives available – the history, the therapist's commentary, the AAI, the outcome. This ability to watch 'nonblind' may truly allow researchers/coders really to see the dyad.

By coding two points in time for a dyad, it was interesting to see that, with skilful intervention, patterns can be altered. Such information provides hope-fulness for the future of distressed parents and infants. At the same time, the challenge continues with the disoriented remnants of behaviour that were still observable in Stacey despite her marked improvements.

What can research tools and investigative results add to clinical practice?

The AAI's sensitivity as a clinical tool is increasingly acknowledged (for a recent analysis, see Steele & Steele, 2008). In a focused manner and through both content and narrative structure, the AAI provides critical information regarding the parent's mental state in terms of coherence of thought, reflective function, defences against intimacy and dependency. It assists the parent–infant clinician in assessing the internal balance between 'ghosts' and 'angels' (Lieberman et al., 2005) in the nursery (see Chapter 13) and other areas where intergenerational trauma may seep into the relationship with the new baby and the transference to the therapist.

The AMBIANCE carries this process further. In delineating parental behaviours associated with disorganized attachment, i.e. the probable behavioural components of the transmission loop, this tool offers the clin-ician clear criteria with which to assess pathology and risk. In particular it describes the parent's behaviours that potentially make for the infant's overwhelming experience and details the behaviours that essentially negate infantile needs for safety, solace, predictability, playfulness. These are parental affective and behavioural interactions that the clinician will be attending to observationally and through her countertransference. At the same time, the AMBIANCE takes account of ameliorating behaviour, much as the clinician would do in considering the infant's total experience (such as 'parent appears to take genuine pleasure in interacting with child, physical contact is tender and comfortable, parent responds to most of baby's cues promptly and appropriately').

The translation from clinical 'hunch' into more transparent, 'evidence-based' information can give further coherence to the therapeutic process. In the AFC parent–infant psychotherapy we have found that explicit detailed knowledge is bolstered by clinical nuance to enhance both the therapist's psychodynamic formulation and the therapeutic dialogue with the patients – parent(s) and infant.

Yet, clinical 'wisdom' is necessary for the research 'data' to be integrated smoothly into the therapeutic process. Moreover, for the moment the research tools do not incorporate the baby as key co-constructor of the process. What the baby 'says' affectively and behaviourally, alongside the therapist's countertransference, informs the clinician of the baby's experience and emergent representations. In a sense, the clinician is straddling observations of baby's communications about his internal experiences with hypotheses about current states and potential precursors to distorted development (e.g. is the baby who continuously sleeps in the consulting room also indicating predisposition to avoidant defences?). In carrying the hypotheses forward the clinician is reliant on collaboration with the researcher to test the thinking.

In sum

The conclusion in this paper is that from the collaborative analysis of a single dyad by clinicians and researchers, much can be learned. Putting together the pieces of the research/clinical puzzle – here in the form of AAI, AMBIANCE and therapist observation and formulation – shows that each perspective adds something new and tells the same story as well. A central contribution of the research tools is in translation of clinical hunches and unconscious processes into standardized language. In tandem, clinical fluidity and 'turn-taking' between patients and therapist enhance the accuracy of description of the individually nuanced, psychological process the researchers are trying to study and describe. The end result may be greater sensitivity and efficacy of our understanding and ability to help parents and infants in trouble.

References

Baradon, T. (2002) Psychotherapeutic work with parents and infants – psychoanalytic and attachment perspectives. *Journal of Attachment and Human Development*, 4(1): 25–38.

Baradon, T. with Broughton, C., Gibbs, I., James, J. Joyce, A. & Woodhead, J. (2005) *The practice of psycho-analytic parent–infant psychotherapy: Claiming the baby*. London: Routledge.

Beebe, B. (2000) Co-constructing mother–infant distress: The microsynchrony of maternal impingement and infant avoidance in the face-to-face encounter. *Psychoanalytic Enquiry*, 20(3): 421–440.

Beebe, B., Knoblauch, S., Rustin, J. & Sorter, D. (2005) *Forms of intersubjectivity in infant research and adult treatment*. New York: Other Press.

Bion, W.R (1962) *Learning from experience*. London: Heinemann.

Boston Change Process Study Group (2008) The foundational level of psychoanalytic meaning: Implicit processes in relation to conflict, defense and the dynamic unconscious. *International Journal of Psychoanalysis*, 88(4): 843–860.

Bronfman, E., Madigan, S. & Lyons-Ruth, K. (2008) *Atypical Maternal Behavior Instrument for Assessment and Classification (AMBIANCE): Manual for coding disrupted affective communication Version 2.0*. Unpublished manual.

Chasoit, D., Madigan, S., Lecce, S., Shea, B. & Goldberg, S. (2001) Atypical maternal behavior before and after intervention. *Infant Mental Health Journal*, 22: 611–626.

Fraiberg, S.H. (1982) Pathological defenses in infancy. *Psychoanalytic Quarterly*, 4(51): 612–635.

Fraiberg, S., Adelson, E. & Shapiro, V. (1975) Ghosts in the nursery: A psychoanalytic approach to the problems of impaired infant–mother relationships. *Journal of the American Academy of Psychiatry*, 14: 387–421.

Freud, A. (1936) The ego and the mechanisms of defense. In *The writings of Anna Freud* (Vol. 2). New York: International Universities Press.

Freud, A. & Burlingham, D. (1943) *War and children*. New York: Medical War Books.

Freud, S. (1920) Beyond the pleasure principle. *Standard Edition* (Vol. 1). London: Hogarth Press.

Goldberg, S., Chasoit, D., Blokland, K. & Madigan, S. (2003) Atypical maternal behavior, maternal representations, and infant disorganized attachment. *Development and Psychopathology*, 15: 239–257.

Gullestad, S.E. (2003) The Adult Attachment Interview and psychoanalytic outcome studies. *International Journal of Psychoanalysis*, 84(3): 651–668.

Kelly, K.M., Ueng-McHale, J., Grienberger, J. & Slade, A. (2003) *Atypical maternal behaviours at 4 months of age and their relation to infant attachment disorganization*. Presented at the biennial meeting of the Society for Research in Child Development, Tampa, FL, USA.

Lieberman, A.F., Padron, E., Van Horn, P. & Harris, W.W. (2005) Angels in the nursery: Intergenerational transmission of benevolent parental influences. *Infant Mental Health Journal*, 26(6): 504–520.

Lyons-Ruth, K., Bronfman, E. & Atwood, G. (1999a) A relational diathesis model of hostile–helpless states of mind: Expressions in mother–infant interaction. In J. Solomon & C. George (Eds.), *Attachment disorganization*. New York: Guilford Press.

Lyons-Ruth, K., Bronfman, E. & Parsons, E. (1999b) Maternal frightened, frightening, or atypical behaviour and disorganized infant attachment patterns. *Monographs of the Society for Research in Child Development*, 64: 67–96.

Madigan, S., Bakermans-Kranenburg, M.J., van IJzendoorn, M.H., Moran, G.,

Pederson, D.R. & Chasoit, D. (2006) Unresolved states of mind, anomalous parental behavior, and disorganized attachment: A review and meta-analysis of a transmission gap. *Attachment & Human Development*, 8: 89–111.

Madigan, S., Moran, G. & Pederson, D.R. (2006) Unresolved states of mind, disorganised attachment relationships, and disrupted interactions of adolescent mothers and their infants. *Developmental Psychopathology*, 42(2): 293–304.

Main, M. & Goldwyn, R. (1993) *The Adult Attachment Classification System*. Unpublished manuscript, University of California, CA, USA.

Main, M. & Hesse, E. (1990) Parents' unresolved traumatic experiences are related to infant disorganized attachment status: Is frightened and/or frightening parental behaviour the linking mechanism? In M.T. Greenberg, D. Cichhetti & E.M. Cummings (Eds.), *Attachment in the preschool years: Theory, research, and intervention* (pp. 161–182). Chicago: University of Chicago Press.

McLaughlin, J.T. (1991) Clinical and theoretical aspects of enactment. *Journal of the American Psychoanalytic Association*, 39: 595–614.

Perry, B.D., Pollard, R.A., Blakely, T.L., Baker, W.L. & Vigilante, D. (1995) Childhood trauma, the neurobiology of adaptation and use-dependent development of the brain: How states become traits. *Infant Mental Health Journal*, 164(4): 271–291.

Sandler, J. (1987) *From safety to superego*. London: Karnac.

Schore, A.N. (2003) *Affect disregulation and disorders of the self*. New York: W.W. Norton.

Schore, J. & Schore, A.N. (2008) Modern attachment theory: The central role of affect in development and treatment. *Clinical Social Work Journal*, 36(1): 9–20.

Spitz, R. (1961) Some early prototypes of ego defenses. *Journal of the American Psychoanalytic Association*, 9: 626–651.

Steele, H. & Steele, M. (2008) *The Adult Attachment Interview in clinical context*. London: Guilford Press.

Stern, D.N. (1995) *The motherhood constellation*. New York: Basic Books.

Stern, D.N. (2004) *The present moment in psychotherapy and everyday life*. New York: W.W. Norton.

Stern, D., Sander, L., Nahum, J., Harrison, A., Lyons-Ruth, K., Morgan, A., et al. (1998) Non-interpretive mechanisms in psychoanalytic therapy: The 'something more' than interpretation. *International Journal of Psychoanalysis*, 79: 903–921.

Van IJzendoorn, M. (1995) Adult attachment representations, parental responsiveness and infant attachment: A meta-analysis of the predictive validity of the Adult Attachment Interview. *Psychological Bulletin*, 117(3): 387–403.

Waters, E., Merrick, S., Treboux, D., Crowell, J. & Albersheim, L. (2003) Attachment security in infancy and early adulthood: A twenty year longitudinal study. *Child Development*, 71(3): 684–689.

Winnicott, D.M. (1960) The theory of the parent infant relationship. In *The maturational process and facilitating environment*. London: Hogarth Press and the Institute of Psycho-Analysis, 1965.

Winnicott, D.M. (1962) Ego integration in child development. In *The maturational process and facilitating environment*. London: Hogarth Press and the Institute of Psycho-Analysis, 1965.

Chapter 11

The Adult Attachment Interview and relational trauma

Implications for parent–infant psychotherapy

Miriam Steele, Howard Steele and Anne Murphy

The burgeoning field of infant mental health is by its very nature multidisciplinary, with influences from adult and child psychiatry, psychoanalytically based theory and treatment, and empirical studies in contemporary developmental research. The dialectic that exists in the exchange of ideas and practice between these disparate but related fields is usefully exemplified by looking at how attachment theory and research is currently being applied to ongoing intervention work with distressed families participating in a parent–infant psychotherapy programme (Steele et al., in press). This chapter will focus on the knowledge gained from the use of a set series of questions concerning what happened during an adult's childhood, and how those childhood experiences are represented in the mind of the adult, namely the Adult Attachment Interview (AAI; Main et al., 1985). This tool is of special interest because of the detailed rating and classification system most recently summarized in Main et al. (2008) that permits, among other clinically relevant phenomena, identification of adults for whom past loss and trauma represents an ongoing bereavement problem.

Thus, for those working with families suffering from current 'relational trauma' there is great value to be gained from having reliable information about the meaning of past trauma in the mind of the parent. This will permit mapping of a current clinical case in the mental and emotional landscape established by published research with the AAI, and, more importantly, this will be a valuable potential guide to understanding and responding to central issues in the ongoing clinical work. Thus, reviewing past work with the AAI, and framing its relevance to parent–infant work involving relational trauma, constitutes the first part of this chapter. The second section will describe an attachment-based intervention programme specifically designed for families suffering from relational trauma where the use of the AAI has been an important tool in helping to facilitate the clinical process and in demonstrating the efficacy of the intervention.

There is an expanding field of clinically relevant research that utilizes the AAI (Steele & Steele, 2008a). The interest in the AAI began with its unique capacity to provide the empirical flesh to the long-held psychoanalytic belief that the most robust predictor of current parent–child relationships is the adult's own experience of having been parented. A landmark finding for the field of parent–infant work was produced by Mary Main and Erik Hesse (1990), who first showed that parents whose AAIs were classified as Unresolved with regard to their own experiences of loss and/or trauma were more likely to have children classified as Disorganized in the Strange Situation. This finding has been replicated multiple times with its robustness confirmed by meta-analytic summaries (van IJzendoorn, 1995). For clinicians working in parent–infant psychotherapy, against the backdrop of Selma Fraiberg's (1980) words and work on the infamous 'ghosts in the nursery', with the AAI a means became available to measure the ghosts (Fonagy et al., 1993).

The Adult Attachment interview

The AAI is structured entirely around the topic of attachment, principally the individual's relationship to their mother and father (and/or to alternative caregivers) during childhood. The interview protocol was recently described as having been 'designed and structured to bring into relief individual differences in deeply internalized strategies for regulating emotion and attention response to the discussion of attachment' (Main et al., 2008: 37). Interviewees are asked both to describe their relationship with their parents during childhood and to provide specific memories to support global evaluations. The interviewer asks directly about childhood experiences of rejection; being upset, ill, and hurt; as well as about loss, abuse, and separations. In addition, subjects are asked to offer explanations for their parents' behaviour, and to describe the current relationship with their parents as well as the influence they consider their childhood experiences to have had on their adult personality. These questions specifically are ones that offer the interviewee an opportunity to demonstrate their capacity for 'reflective functioning', which may be briefly defined as a being able to put oneself in one's parents' shoes, and understand the thoughts, feelings and intentions of the other (Steele & Steele, 2008b).

Adult patterns of attachment, identifiable in spoken (recorded and transcribed) responses to the AAI, refer to different strategies adults rely on when faced with the task of making sense of their childhood relations with adult caregivers. The signal features of the 'secure–autonomous' strategy are coherence and a strong valuing of attachment. The dismissing and preoccupied patterns each represent different forms of insecurity arising out of negative attachment experiences that *do not* appear integrated evenly into the adult's sense of self. The dismissing strategy is typically seen in an incoherent narrative characterized by global idealized statements about a good or normal childhood that cannot be supported by relevant memories. The preoccupied strategy is typically seen in an incoherent narrative characterized by global statements about a difficult childhood that are accompanied by an overabundance of memories and affects from childhood and adulthood, which lead the speaker to express current feelings of anger, or a sense of resignation to difficulties that cannot be overcome. Finally, the unresolved pattern, which may be present in an otherwise dismissing, preoccupied, or autonomous interview, is evident when an adult shows signs of ongoing grief and disorientation concerning some past loss or trauma. Narratives that are assigned a classification of 'unresolved' with respect to loss and/or trauma include an excessive attention to detail when discussing loss, delayed bereavement reactions, lapses in the monitoring of speech that go uncorrected, and lapses in the monitoring of reason, as when dead loved ones are spoken about in the present tense as if they were still alive.

It is a remarkably hopeful and positive sign when a speaker refers to past trauma without slipping into the abovementioned quagmire of absorption and confusion. In the nonclinical population, in cases where childhood experiences have involved trauma, it is not uncommon for the speaker to convey a sense of having moved beyond the fear they felt so often as a child. Additionally, such speakers are capable of progressing towards understanding, though not necessarily forgiving, caregiving figure(s) who once perpetrated abuse against them. For the field of clinicians working to interrupt the deleterious effects of 'relational trauma' in the parent for the sake of improving the quality of parenting of their young infants, it is useful to be reminded of a recent paper from Busch et al. (2008), who refer to the AAI as 'an observational measure of post-bereavement functioning'. This definition conveys the essence of the AAI in respect of trauma, that is, what is critical is not that the individual was exposed to relational trauma but whether there is ongoing evidence of bereavement and lack of resolution of trauma. Importantly, the AAI provides direct clues as to the specific content of an individual's bereavement difficulties, providing openings for clinical work aimed at healing the deep wounds of past relational trauma. Achieving this goal is vital so that fear in the life of the present infant may be contained and minimized, as opposed to becoming exacerbated into an atypical pattern of attachment disorganization.

Links with disorganized attachment patterns

Organized child–parent relationships typically adhere to one of three patterns: (1) the optimal 'secure' or evenly regulated pattern, the majority (55–65%) of low-risk samples, is widely documented to serve as a protective factor for the child's current and future mental health; (2) the insecure–avoidant or excessively 'down-regulating' pattern, typically 20–25% of low-risk samples; and (3) the insecure–resistant or excessively 'up-regulating' pattern, typically 10–15% of low-risk samples. These patterns were first identified by Ainsworth et al. (1978) and their links to emotion regulation have since been elaborated (e.g. Main & Hesse, 1990; Thompson, 2008; Bretherton & Munholland, 2008).

A fourth group, already identifiable at one year of age in response to two

brief separations from the attachment figure (Ainsworth et al., 1978), show
the effects of relational trauma by way of freezing in the presence of the
mother for 20 seconds or more, hiding from the mother, hitting the mother,
alternately displaying avoidance (moving away) with resistance (crying
uncontrollably) – and all the time the mother appears at a loss as to what to
do to settle her child (Main & Solomon, 1986, 1990). Anomalous behaviour
such as this is termed 'disorganized/disoriented' and has many correlates in
maternal behaviour. Infants with disorganization are significantly likely to
have mothers noted for the display of frightening or frightened behaviour
with their infants or marked signs of withdrawal and more generally profoundly insensitive behaviour, well beyond a hint of rejection or interference
(Lyons-Ruth & Jacobvitz, 2008).

In high-risk samples, like those where relational trauma was a feature of
the parent's history, 50–80% of samples are observed to show attachment
disorganization (Lyons-Ruth & Jacobvitz, 2008). The long-term correlates
of disorganized attachment prominently include childhood externalizing
behaviours such as elevated levels of aggression and disruptive behaviour
(Lyons-Ruth et al., 1997; Main & Cassidy, 1988; Shaw et al., 1996). Shaw
et al. (1996) examined disorganized attachment at 12 months and maternal
personality and child-rearing disagreements during the second year as
predictors of disruptive behaviour at age five. They found that these early risk
factors predicted aggressive behaviour at age three years and disruptive
behaviour at age five. A meta-analysis confirmed these findings, showing
that disorganized attachment in infancy predicts aggression in school-aged
children, with an effect size of .29 across 12 studies (Schuengel et al., 1999).

A related outcome of infant disorganization, highlighted most clearly in
the large longitudinal Minnesota study of high-risk families, is a range of
clinical outcomes linked to dissociation and cognitive confusion. For
example, it was found that infant disorganization predicted psychopathology
as assessed with the Kiddie Schedule for Affective Disorders and Schizo-
phrenia (K-SADS) at age 17 years (Weinfeld et al., 2000). Specific dissociative
symptoms in adolescence have also been linked to earlier assessments of
infant disorganization (Ogawa et al., 1997), with similarities drawn between
the fear-infused stances evidenced in the Strange Situation and the corollary
indices of dissociative qualities in young adulthood. Recently, an independent longitudinal study that included observations of attachment disorganization with mother at 12 months has shown that such early relational trauma is
linked to PTSD symptoms in later childhood, specifically in the ninth year of
life (Macdonald et al., 2008). In this latter work with 78 8.5-year-olds, of
whom 16 (21%) had been disorganized as infants, those with disorganization
in their past were significantly more likely than non-disorganized children to
show both higher avoidance cluster PTSD symptoms and higher re-
experiencing cluster PTSD symptoms.

Given these long-term clinical correlates of infant–mother attachment
disorganization, it is all the more impressive that an assessment of the mother

(potentially conducted before the birth of the child) can forecast the likelihood of disorganization. A meta-analysis of nine studies (N = 548) revealed an effect size of d = 0.65 (r = .31) for the relation between child disorganization and parental unresolved status (van IJzendoorn, 1995). That these two disparate measures are linked places them even more squarely in the centre stage of what is of interest to clinicians working with parents where there is evidence of relational trauma. That traumatic experiences are relational in context is critical. This has been demonstrated by a recent well-designed and innovative study (Sagi-Schwartz et al., 2003) where the potential transmission of attachment patterns was studied in individuals known to have suffered enormous trauma (from the Second World War), namely a group of 48 Holocaust survivors, their daughters and grandchildren. When the research team looked at the extent of transmission of unresolved trauma across generations, they found that it was much less than what is typically found when the trauma emanates from *within* relationships. The researchers posit that this was the case for two reasons: (1) firstly some of these individuals would have experienced pre-war secure attachment relationships with their attachment figures providing them with a resilient capacity; and (2) even for those who did not have these optimal experiences, the most frightening experiences were probably associated with forces outside their family.

Thus, relational trauma is inherently within the family and carries the power to stay with an individual long into the future, impacting the next generation. Empirical evidence of this fact has followed from the observations of Main and Hesse (1990), who showed that unresolved trauma (stemming from abuse or loss within the family) leads to frightened or frightening behaviour overwhelming to the infant which can result in the infant displaying disorganized and/or disoriented behaviour. For the infant, this puzzling and paradoxical situation of being faced with the at times loving parent who is alternately frightened and frightening is likely to lead to several incompatible models of self and other in the immature child's mind. These incompatible models linked to overwhelming feelings of fear and confusion herald the hallmark behaviours of disorganized attachment such as freezing or approach and simultaneous avoidance. Further, these multiple models leave the infant at risk for failing to cope with future affect-laden events that require the availability of integrated effective strategies. Yet post-infancy experiences may actually hold the potential to introduce organization where there was previously disorganization. At the same time, early disorganization makes later dissociative experiences more likely. For example, Ogawa et al. (1997) compared scores on the Dissociate Experiences Scale of young adults previously classified as disorganized during infancy who had not faced trauma (N = 10); young adults classified as disorganized in infancy who were faced with later trauma (N = 35); and other young adults not previously classified as disorganized (N = 83). A significant elevation in dissociation scores was found only among those who both were disorganized and had experienced later trauma. It is also notable that 78% of those classified as disorganized during infancy had experienced later trauma. This high rate suggests that the caregiving environment associated with infant disorganization places an infant at risk for further exposure to trauma or loss.

The Adult Attachment Interview as assessment tool

The use of the AAI in evidence-based studies within the context of parent–infant psychotherapy has a demonstrated efficacy across many domains which include the setting up of the therapeutic frame, uncovering traumatic experiences and important losses, permitting the reliable observation of reflective functioning and assessing therapeutic outcome (Steele & Steele, 2008a).

The AAI can also help predict which clients may be most amenable to the therapeutic process based on their attachment states of mind. For example, Christoph Heinicke and Monica Levine (2008) found that mothers' prebirth AAIs 'anticipated' their involvement in a relation-based home visiting programme as well as features of the developing mother–child relationship and the child's emotional development. Specifically they found that the mothers whose AAIs were classified as Secure–Autonomous had the best outcomes both in terms of involvement in the clinical process and with regard to the best child outcomes. This was the case even when the mother's AAI was judged unresolved but secure/coherent as contrasted with those that were unresolved but incoherent/insecure. This speaks to the protective value of an organized secure state of mind, even in the presence of ongoing bereavement issues.

Complementary findings arose from an independent conducted by Douglas Teti and colleagues (2008), who used the AAI as a potential predictor of engagement in the therapeutic process with mothers of premature infants. They found stronger maternal commitment from women whose AAIs were classified Autonomous–Secure as compared to these whose interviews were non-autonomous/dismissing. These recent studies add to earlier work which also found that autonomous states of mind in mothers were associated with greater receptivity to parent–infant intervention (Korfmacher et al., 1997).

Against this backdrop of research findings using the AAI, we will present a clinical example highlighting its use in a specifically designed, attachment-based intervention for families known to 'preventive services' where there is a documented concern about whether children can remain with their birth mothers. Thus, the intervention is aimed both at improving the quality of the mother–child relationship, against the background of much past and current trauma, and with the fundamental task of family preservation. In this context, the AAI may be a particularly useful tool for identifying not only 'ghosts' in the nursery but also perhaps barely remembered 'angels' who may offer some much-needed protection (Jones, 2008; Lieberman & Van Horn, 2008; Steele et al., in press).

The Center for Babies, Toddlers and Families of the Early Childhood Center at the Children's Evaluation and Rehabilitation Center of Albert Einstein College of Medicine

Context of intervention

The Center as whole has a range of functions including multidisciplinary assessments, individual treatment, pediatric mental health, family court, foster care and preschool consultation and the parent–child psychotherapy programme (Briggs et al., 2007). Over 400 families are treated at the Center annually. The parent–child psychotherapy group model was developed and has evolved over the past five years to meet the needs of a very isolated group of parents who are referred because of their own history of multiple adverse childhood experiences. Importantly, these parents are seeking help in becoming a 'different kind of parent' from that which they experienced as children growing up. Many express histories of abuse and neglect during their childhoods in the 1980s, in the Bronx, New York, a time when substance abuse peaked. Accordingly, many of these young parents report experiences of parental substance abuse which caused disruption in their young lives, placing them in unprotected situations where they were abused and neglected, often leading to multiple foster placements. Many report dropping out of school to care for younger siblings. All the families fill out the Adverse Childhood Experiences questionnaire[1] (ACE). This measure is included as a way of helping to describe the background from which these parents come. This measure was first used in a large epidemiological study of a managed care health group in California, showing the long-term deleterious physical and mental health effects of child maltreatment (Dube et al., 2003; Felitti et al., 1998).

While preventing disorganization and promoting security is an immediate goal of the therapeutic intervention, it is the longer-term social, behavioural and mental health problems for both the child and the parent that this intervention is aimed at ameliorating. The intervention was specifically designed for the high-risk parents and children who live in the Bronx, New York. The intervention and research programme associated with it are both infused with attachment-based theory and assessment measures, as will be described in detail below.

The parent group serves multiple purposes. The group format has been designed for a high-risk population referred to as families 'on the outside' (Osofsky et al., 1988) where the effects of poverty are exacerbated by homelessness, greater exposure to community and domestic violence, drug use, single-parent families and less access to medical care. The group format is

---

1 The questionnaire was modified through personal communication with Shanta Dube, one of the study's authors.

especially helpful for these families with such impoverished social support, as the group provides the possibility to forge new relationships with peers both during and outside the intervention context (Niccols, 2008). Importantly, group formats have also been demonstrated to be one half as expensive as home-visiting interventions (Niccols, 2008). Observing behaviour by co-participants in the group also facilitates therapeutic goals as it is often a catalyst to change to identify strengths and difficulties in others. A secondary but clearly related benefit of a group format is the advent for the children of offering a safe and well-regulated environment for them to build their skills at socialization.

Case illustration: The repetition compulsion and the wish to change

The following case illustrates well the utility of using the AAI in a clinical context. The material revealed in the parent's response to the AAI protocol enhanced the therapist's understanding of the particular attachment issues, and vulnerabilities of the parent, most salient in the ongoing work. Further, the parent's AAI alerted the therapist to potential allies of positive change in the inner world of the parent evident from her account of past support, however brief or fleeting, received.

The case presented here is one of many arising from the ongoing collaborative work between the Early Childhood Center for Babies, Toddlers and Families at the Albert Einstein College of Medicine, and the Center for Attachment Research at the New School for Social Research. In the context of supporting the ongoing clinical work, led by Anne Murphy, we have been assessing a sample of the at-risk families using a range of state-of-the-art attachment measures. Central among this list is the AAI. Dejanae, aged 22 years, was referred to the Center when her son, Jamal, was almost three months old. The referral was precipitated by concern for the infant due to the mother's significant mental health history, current isolation and lack of social support. Dejanae herself was born to a 14-year-old mother at the height of crack-cocaine epidemic that haunted New York City in the 1990s. Dejanae was raised by different relatives and her father has been incarcerated for the past seven years. She had been sexually abused since early childhood. She was diagnosed as suffering from borderline personality disorder/bipolar disorder and posttraumatic stress disorder, but since the pregnancy with Kamal has been off medication and desisted from a previous pattern of multiple suicide attempts and cutting behaviours.

Dejanae's narrative responses to the AAI corroborate her difficult past, yet studying her narrative has been helpful, if not altogether illuminating, in terms of giving us important clues as to the landscape of her inner world, her strategies for regulating arousal and distress, and her hopes for herself and her child. For example, when asked to give five adjectives to describe her early relationship with mother she provides the following: '*Weird, fast, confusing, independent, lonely'*. When asked to elaborate on how the relationship was 'confusing', she responds: '*Confusing, I don't ever think that she really accepted me as her daughter, I am just like the younger sister that she pushed out. I remember my grandmother doing most of the stuff at one point and then it just like and everything went blink. And then there was a different grandmother, then there was a grandfather, then there was an aunt, then there was an uncle, then different schools. I went to so many different schools . . .*'

When asked 'When you were upset as a child what would you do?' Dejanae responds in a clearly dismissing way, derogating of attachment: '*Nothing, it wasn't my place to be upset. A child has no real feelings.*' Interestingly, she shows a reliance on identification with the aggressor (Freud, 1936), here the aggressor being the parent who took no notice of the child's feelings, and the child has become a parent who endorses this view of children. This harshness of viewpoint and overall derogation of attachment can also be seen in response to the question that sparks a reflective stance in some but not in this respondent: 'Why do you think your parents behaved as they did when you were a child? "*Because they were young and dumb and hot in their pants, they had nuthin' else better to do".*'

Despite the overall quality of the narrative as being characteristic of the insecure–dismissing type, there are small glimmers of understanding and sparks of reflective thinking. For example, when asked about her experience of sexual abuse she reports '*he [mother's boyfriend] started at two and a half with touching at first and it started going into other things. When I got older I realized that I felt I had no voice because when I told, nobody believed me and I got beaten . . . it could be once or twice a day.*' The words 'when I got older I realized that I felt I had no voice' speak to D's capacity for adopting a developmental perspective. They leave one to wonder what other realizations await for her so that she become more integrated, and more available to her son.

When asked about her relationship with her father – 'When you think of the relationship with your father in which there is guilt, do any specific memories come to mind? – Dejanae says: '*In a way I feel a little bit guilty about it because the little girl that he knew so long ago is dead and lost a long, long time ago and he is never ever going to get that part of me back. Cause I even lost touch with that person.*' This is a compelling sign of how the speaker is in the process of developing a coherent narrative concerning the abuse and loss she suffered as a child as distinct from the adult she is now striving to be. For the therapist, this is a most hopeful sign. Coherence and reflection of this sort, beginning to be articulated by Dejanae, is the antidote to unresolved mourning and unthinking repetition of a painful past.

The AAI often reveals that there were attachment figures other than parents who had an important role in a person's development. The positive influence of an aunt was evident in Dejanae's history. When she was asked 'How has the death of your aunt affected how you approach your own son?', she replied as follows:

I mean she taught me to be a little bit more loving but I guess my own fears pushes what she taught me aside a little bit. I try to strive for at least near perfection. Because that is just something that has been instilled in me but my fear is that I'll screw my son up and it freaks me out like bathing him and touching him. I am very precise about it and you know, time limits about it, the hugging, cause I be afraid that you know I'll be doing something to him unconsciously and I don't want to like freak him out.

Here Dejanae describes openly her appropriate hopes for her son, and her struggles with past demons that interfere with her ability to respond appropriately to her son. We can perhaps hear something of how the therapeutic work is impacting on her when Dejanae shows an awareness of the powerful pull of unconscious forces on her behaviour. At the time of the interview being conducted, Dejanae had been working as a member of the weekly individual and group therapy process for nearly one year.

The Administration of Child Services (ACS) was alerted to this case at the time of Jamal's birth. Indeed, very early on Dejanae projected intense negative attributions to her young son such as the beliefs that he was '*greedy*' and '*aggressive*'. When asked to elaborate she made the complaint that '*he is a pervert, just like his father*' as his one-month-old hand brushed against her breast as he was feeding. The therapist contained much of Dejanae's anxieties in both individual and group sessions. Critical to the treatment was the therapist's ability to keep Dejanae in mind and to convey to her that despite her often expressed anger and rage with the therapist, the therapist would remain her ally and made herself available for ongoing consultation. Given the paucity of 'good enough parenting' in her own childhood experience, Dejanae felt challenged by her own internal struggle and a wish to be a different kind of parent for her young son. This was expressed both in her AAI responses as cited above and her crude assertions that she '*doesn't care how he* [Jamal] *feels*', that she would easily '*pop him*' (strike him in the mouth) if he touches something he shouldn't, and that children his age (18 months) need to respect their parents. Further progress on the part of this parent will be considered, in part, through re-administrations of the AAI 12–18 months from the original interview (above) in order to detect (hopefully) an increase in coherence and an appreciation of the age-appropriate needs of her son, together with an anticipated diminishment of fear and anger.

Interestingly, at the time this AAI was collected, Jamal was one year old and we looked at his response to mother in the Strange Situation (Ainsworth et al., 1978). Jamal made repeated approaches to his mother, mainly to show her the toys in a bid to get some help from her in figuring them out. As is often the case for mothers unfamiliar with the situation and coping with enormous emotional burdens, Dejanae behaved as if Jamal's task was to play on his own and so she rebuffed him a number of times. Jamal's pattern of attachment could not be called secure, but this was not for lack of trying on his part! Impressive was the observation of an organized avoidant response, and no signs of disorganization as we would certainly have expected had the pair not benefited from a year of therapeutic work.

In the case of Dejanae, her AAI was collected many months after her involvement with the Center for Babies, Toddlers and Families, and so the signs of coherence and reflection that were noted may well have been the outcome of therapy rather than an indication that she would respond well to the intervention. Clearly, though, the experience of being interviewed with the AAI provided fresh insights as to Dejanae's state of mind concerning attachment, and motivational support for her to consolidate the gains she was making through therapy.

Conclusion

Early intervention work holds out the promise of preventing or repairing the wounds that accompany relational trauma. Understanding the consequences of relational trauma in the adult mind, and pursuing the prevention of relational trauma in an infant's life, may be greatly supported by familiarity with, and use of, the AAI. In fact, the AAI can be relied on as one very useful measure of the efficacy of our interventions. Why? Because, as so poignantly phrased by Mary Main and colleagues, 'coherence can change, whereas life-history cannot' (Main et al., 2008: 48).

Acknowledgements

We are grateful to the families participating in the ongoing work. Much appreciation is to be extended for funding from Einstein-Montefiore Institute for Clinical and Translational Research, the Children's Evaluation and Rehabilitation Center, and the Robin Hood Foundation. At the Center for Attachment Research, the group of graduate students who have been exceptionally helpful with data collection and coding include Allison Splaun, Francisca Herreros, Ellie Neuman, Julia Broder, Kiara Schlesinger, Kathleen Hartwig, Erica Rosenthal, Kim Nguyen, Kristen Stephenson, Kristen Capps, James Grimaldi and Alex Kriss.

References

Ainsworth, M.D.S., Blehar, M.C., Waters, E. & Wall, S. (1978) *Patterns of attachment: Assessed in the Strange Situation and at home.* Hillsdale, NJ: Lawence Erlbaum Associates, Inc.
Baradon, T. & Steele, M. (2008) Integrating the AAI in the clinical process of psychoanalytic parent–infant psychotherapy in a case of relational trauma. In H. Steele & M. Steele (Eds.), *Clinical applications of the Adult Attachment Interview* (pp. 195–212). New York: Guilford Press.

Bowlby, J. (1988) *A secure base: Clinical applications of attachment theory*. London: Routledge.

Bretherton, I. & Munholland, K. (1999) Internal working models in attachment relationships: Elaborating a central construct in attachment theory. In J. Cassidy & P.R. Shaver (Eds.), *Handbook of attachment: Theory, research and clinical applications* (pp. 102–130). New York: Guilford Press.

Briggs, R.D., Racine, A. & Chinitz, S. (2007) Preventive pediatric mental health care: A collocation model. *Infant Mental Health Journal*, 28(5): 481–495.

Busch, A., Cowan, P. & Cowan, C. (2008) Unresolved loss in the Adult Attachment Interview: Implications for marital and parenting relationships *Development and Psychopathology*, 20: 717–735.

Dube, S.R., Felitti, V.J., Dong, M., Giles, W.H. & Anda, R.F. (2003) The impact of adverse childhood experiences on health problems: Evidence from four birth cohorts dating back to 1900. *Preventive Medicine*, 37(3): 268–277.

Felitti, V.J., Anda, R.F., Nordenberg, D., Williamson, D.F., Spitz, A.M., Edwards, V. et al. (1998) Relationship of childhood abuse and household dysfunction to many leading causes of death in adults: The adverse childhood experiences (ACE) study. *American Journal of Preventive Medicine*, 14: 245–258.

Fonagy, P., Steele, M., Moran, G.S., Steele, H. & Higgitt, A. (1993) Measuring the ghost in the nursery: An empirical study of the relation between parents' mental representations of childhood experiences and their infants' security of attachment. *Journal of the American Psychoanalytic Association*, 41: 957–989.

Fonagy, P., Target, M., Steele, H. & Steele, M. (1998) *Reflective-Functioning Manual, version 5.2, for application to Adult Attachment Interviews*. Unpublished document, University College London and New School for Social Research, New York, NY, USA.

Fraiberg, S. (Ed.) (1980) *Clinical studies in infant mental health*. New York: Basic Books.

Freud, A. (1936) *The ego and the mechanisms of defence*. New York: International Universities Press.

George, C., Kaplan, N. & Main, M. (1996) *Adult Attachment Interview* (3rd ed.). Unpublished manuscript, University of California at Berkeley, CA, USA.

Heinicke, C.M. & Levine, M.S. (2008) The AAI anticipates the outcome of a relation-based early intervention. In H. Steele & M. Steele (Eds.), *Clinical applications of the Adult Attachment Interview* (pp. 99–125). New York: Guilford Press.

Jones, A. (2008) The AAI as a clinical tool. In H. Steele & M. Steele (Eds.), *Clinical applications of the Adult Attachment Interview* (pp. 175–194). New York: Guilford Press.

Korfmacher, J., Adam, E., Ogawa, J. & Egeland, B. (1997) Adult attachment: Implications for the therapeutic process in a home visiting intervention. *Applied Developmental Science*, 1: 43–52.

Lieberman, A. & Van Horn, P. (2008) *Psychotherapy with infants and young children: Repairing the effects of stress and trauma on early attachment*. New York: Guilford Press.

Lyons-Ruth, K. (2008) Contributions of the mother–infant relationship to dissociative, borderline, and conduct symptoms in young adulthood. *Infant Mental Health Journal*, 29: 203–218.

Lyons-Ruth, K., Easterbrooks, M.A. & Cibelli, C.D. (1997) Infant attachment strategies, infant mental lag, and maternal depressive symptoms: Predictors of internalizing and externalizing problems at age 7. *Developmental Psychology*, 33: 681–692.

Lyons-Ruth, K. & Jacobvitz, D. (2008) Attachment disorganization: Genetic factors, parenting contexts, and developmental transformation from infancy to adulthood. In J. Cassidy & P.R. Shaver (Eds.), *Handbook of attachment: Theory, research and clinical applications* (pp. 666–697). New York: Guilford Press.

Macdonald, H.Z., Beeghly, M., Grant-Knight, W., Augustyn, M., Woods, R.W., Cabral, H. et al. (2008) Longitudinal association between infants disorganized attachment and childhood posttraumatic stress symptoms. *Development and Psychopathology*, 20: 493–508.

Main, M. & Cassidy, J. (1988) Categories of response to reunion with the parent at age 6: Predicted from infant attachment classifications and stable over a 1-month period. *Developmental Psychology*, 24: 415–426.

Main, M., Goldwyn, R. & Hesse, E. (2003) *Adult Attachment Classification System Version 7.2*. Unpublished manuscript, University of California at Berkeley, USA.

Main, M. & Hesse, E. (1990) Parents' unresolved traumatic experiences are related to infant disorganized attachment status: Is frightening and/or frightened parental behavior the linking mechanism? In M. Greenberg, D. Cicchetti & E.M. Cummings (Eds.), *Attachment in the preschool years: Theory, research and intervention* (pp. 161–182). Chicago: University of Chicago Press.

Main, M., Hesse, E. & Goldwyn, R. (2008) Studying differences in language use in recounting attachment history. In H. Steele & M. Steele (Eds.), *Clinical applications of the Adult Attachment Interview* (pp. 31–68). New York: Guilford Press.

Main, M., Kaplan, N. & Cassidy, J. (1985) Security in infancy, childhood and adulthood: A move to the level of representation (Growing points in attachment: Theory and research). *Monographs of the Society for Research in Child Development*, 50(1–2): 66–104.

Main, M., & Solomon, J. (1986) Discovery of a new, insecure–disorganized/disoriented attachment pattern. In T.B. Brazlenton & M. Yogman (Eds.), *Affective development in infancy* (pp. 95–124). Norwood, NJ: Ablex.

Main, M. & Solomon, J. (1990) Procedures for identifying infants as disorganized/disoriented during the Ainsworth Strange Situation. In M.T. Greenberg, D. Cicchetti & E.M. Cummings (Eds.), *Attachment in the preschool years: Theory, research and intervention* (pp. 121–160). Chicago: University of Chicago Press.

Niccols, A. (2008) 'Right from the Start': Randomized trial comparing an attachment group intervention to supportive home visiting. *Journal of Child Psychology and Psychiatry*, 49: 754–764.

Ogawa, J., Sroufe, L.A., Weinfield, N., Carlson, E. & Egeland, B. (1997) Development and the fragmented self: Longitudinal study of dissociative symptomatology in a nonclinical sample. *Development and Psychopathology*, 9: 855–879.

Osofsky, J.D., Culp, A.M. & Ware, L.M. (1988) Intervention challenges with adolescent mothers and their infants. *Psychiatry*, 51: 236–241.

Sagi-Schwartz, A., van IJzendoorn, M., Grosmann, K., Joels, T., Grossmann, K., Scarf, M. et al. (2003) Attachment and traumatic stress in female Holocaust child survivors and their daughters. *American Journal of Psychiatry*, 160: 1086–1092.

Sameroff, A.J., McDonough, S.C. & Rosenbaum, K.L. (Eds.) (2004) *Treating parent–infant relationship problems*. New York: Guilford Press.

Schuengel, C., van IJzendoorn, M., Bakermans-Kranenburg, M. & Bloom, M. (1999)

Frightening, frightened and/or dissociated behaviour, unresolved loss, and infant disorganization. *Journal of Consulting and Clinical Psychology*, 67: 54–63.

Shaw, D., Keenan, K., Vondra, J., Delliquadri, E. & Giovannelli, J. (1997) Antecedents of preschool children's internalizing problems: A longitudinal study of low-income families. *Journal of the American Academy of Child and Adolescent Psychiatry*, 36: 1760–1767.

Shaw, D., Owens, E., Vondra, J., Keenan, K. & Winslow, E.B. (1996) Early risk factors and pathways in the development of early disruptive behaviour problems. *Development and Psychopathology*, 8: 679–699.

Spangler, G. & Grossman, K.E. (1993) Biobehavioural organization in securely and insecurely attached infants. *Child Development*, 64: 1439–1450.

Sroufe, L.A. (2005) Attachment and development: A prospective, longitudinal study from birth to adulthood. *Attachment & Human Development*, 7: 349–367.

Sroufe, L.A., Egeland, B., Carlson, E. & Collins, W.A. (2005) *The development of the person: The Minnesota study of risk and adaptation from birth to adulthood.* New York: Guilford Press.

Steele, M., Murphy, A. & Steele, H. (in press) Identifying therapeutic action in an attachment based intervention. *Journal of Clinical Social Work*.

Steele, H. & Steele, M. (2008a) *Clinical applications of the Adult Attachment Interview.* New York: Guilford Press.

Steele, H. & Steele, M. (2008b) 10 clinical uses of the Adult Attachment Interview. In H. Steele & M. Steele (Eds.), *Clinical applications of the Adult Attachment Interview* (pp. 3–30). New York: Guilford Press.

Steele, H., Steele, M. & Fonagy, P. (1996) Associations among attachment classifications of mothers, fathers, and their infants. *Child Development*, 67: 541–555.

Teti, D., Killeen, L., Candelaria, M., Miller, W., Hess, C. & O'Connell, M. (2008) Adult attachment, parental commitment to early intervention, and developmental outcomes in an African American sample. In H. Steele & M. Steele (Eds.), *Clinical applications of the Adult Attachment Interview* (pp. 126–153). New York: Guilford Press.

Thompson, R. (2008) Early attachment and later development: Familiar questions, new answers. In J. Cassidy & P.R. Shaver (Eds.), *Handbook of attachment: Theory, research and clinical applications* (pp. 348–366). New York: Guilford Press.

van IJzendoorn, M.H. (1995) Adult attachment representations, parental responsiveness, and infant attachment: A meta-analysis on the predictive validity of the Adult Attachment Interview. *Psychological Bulletin*, 117: 387–403.

van IJzendoorn, M.H. & Bakermans-Kranenburg, M.J. (2008) The distribution of adult attachment representations in clinical groups: Meta-analytic search for patterns of attachment. In H. Steele & M. Steele (Eds.), *Clinical applications of the Adult Attachment Interview* (pp. 69–96). New York: Guilford Press.

Weinfield, N., Sroufe, L.A. & Egeland, B. (2000) Attachment from infancy to young adulthood in a high risk sample: Continuity, discontinuity and their correlates. *Child Development*, 71: 695–702.

Chapter 12

Measuring trauma in the primary relationship

The parent–infant relational assessment tool (PIRAT)

Carol Broughton

This chapter presents a study of trauma in the primary relationship as it was identified and explicated through coding the interactions between a mother and six-week-old baby using an observational risk assessment tool: the Parent–Infant Relational Assessment Tool (PIRAT).

PIRAT had its beginnings in the Parent–Infant Project (PIP) at The Anna Freud Centre when the clinicians in the Project were apprised by health visitors and other workers in the professional network of their need for a tool to identify risk in the parent–infant relationship which was standardised and reliable but also flexible and easy to use in their everyday work setting: clinic, consulting room, home visiting. I will briefly describe the rationale for the tool and its subsequent development before presenting material relating to its use in the case of a traumatised mother and infant.

PIRAT: Rationale

The Parent–Infant Project offers psychotherapy to parents and infants experiencing relationship difficulties, either individually to parent–infant dyads or triads or in the form of groups for mother and infants in different settings. Initially, PIRAT took the form of an in-house tool grounded in the clinical practice of the project psychotherapists and their wish to systematise their thinking on the qualities of the parent–infant relationship. It was hoped that such a tool would subsequently leave the clinician's room and facilitate the transfer of knowledge about infancy research into the broader professional milieu.

The importance of early identification of difficulties in the parent–infant relationship is now widely accepted as a result of findings in developmental neuroscience and infancy research (Perry et al., 1995; Panksepp, 2001; Schore, 2005). A vital adjunct to the need for early intervention is access to treatment modalities that address such difficulties. A number of parent–infant psychotherapies based on psychodynamic thinking are available to practitioners (see, for example, Muir, 1992; Beebe, 2006; Baradon et al., 2005).

PIRAT: Genesis and development

Through their work, members of the parent–infant psychotherapy (PIP) team identified common themes and behaviours that formed the basis of an agreement about what constitutes difficulty in the parent–infant relationship. These behaviours were compiled into table form under the headings parent–infant behaviours and infant–parent behaviours. This resulted in two separate sections to the coding scheme, e.g. infant's seeking of contact/parent's initiation of physical contact (see Figure 12.1). A manual was compiled providing descriptors of parent–infant and infant–parent behaviours that would constitute no concern, some concern or significant concern. A reliability study was conducted with the six members of the PIP team, and once it was established that good levels of agreement could be achieved among the clinicians using the tool, we felt able to implement the next stage of the process.

We needed to know if other health professionals could be trained to use the assessment tool and whether reliability could be established among a panel of health professionals. As a first stage in the research project, the original manual had to be rewritten to meet the needs of workers outside the PIP team. It was judged necessary to provide fuller, more comprehensive definitions of each of the categories in the coding scheme. At the same time, the revised manual needed to be sufficiently concise for health professionals to use during the course of their work in various clinical settings. Detail and specificity had to be set against economy and flexibility. Each of the items on the coding scheme was revised in terms of its content for the three categories: significant concern, some concern, no concern. Figures 12.2 and 12.3 give examples of manual descriptors for infant–parent interactions and parent–infant interactions.

Ten participants were involved in the training and reliability study, comprising two health visitors, two midwives, one clinical psychologist, one clinical psychologist in training, one speech and language therapist, one child

Infant–parent interaction	Parent–infant interaction
Infant's seeking of contact	Parent's initiation of physical contact
Responsiveness to contact	Parent's emotional contact
Ability to communicate needs	Parent's playfulness in relation to infant
Ability to be comforted	Pleasure in parenting
Quality of contact:	Quality of contact:
aggressive/attacking	intrusive/controlling
clinging	frightening
frightened/wary	sexualised
lack of pleasure	avoidant
sexualised	consistency/predictability
dissociative	
predictability	

Figure 12.1 Parent–Infant Relational Assessment Tool (PIRAT) coding categories

Manual definitions

0 No concern
Infant shows fear/anxiety/caution that is alleviated by parent in relation to an external event.

1 Some concern
Infant intermittently presents behaviours suggesting fear, e.g. rigid body tone, overcompliance, withdrawal. Infant avoids eye contact but appears wary if eye contact is made. Further evidence is required.

2 Significant concern
Infant shows through feelings/behaviour experiences of being frightened, e.g. stilling, freezing, overcompliance, panic, which is induced by parent.

Figure 12.2 Infant–parent interaction – quality of contact: Frightened/wary

Manual definitions

0 No concern
Parent is able to let infant take control of what he is doing, while maintaining safe boundaries.

1 Some concern
Parent repetitively interferes with infant's exploration and play. Parent withholds toy, blocks infant's play or directs infant to a different activity when infant is clearly interested in what he/she is already doing.
Parent makes infant wait for something he/she wants or needs, e.g. food, bottle, treat.

2 Significant concern
Parent pervasively interferes with infant's exploration and play. Parent controls infant's activity in all respects. Parent forces infant to continue with an activity despite infant's wish to stop, or parent denies infant game or activity of infant's choice.
Parent is intrusive in terms of body functions. Infant is not allowed to regulate his food or drink intake. Parent imposes rigid toileting routine.

Figure 12.3 Parent–infant interaction – quality of contact: Intrusive/controlling

protection social worker, one child and family worker specialising with children with disabilities and their families, and one child and family worker specialising in addiction within the family. All participants were female and, apart from the student clinical psychologist, had more than three years' experience in post.

During the training period the participants familiarised themselves with the PIRAT manual and coding scheme and, using 10-minute segments of videotape, they practised using the manual descriptors to identify behaviours in the mother–infant interactions that they observed. The researcher encouraged discussion in order to explore any difficulties and disagreements and to establish a group culture in which participants recognised their contributions as valuable. The fluency with which the participants came to discuss the nature of the mother–infant interactions that they observed is evidence of the success of the training and can be seen in the transcripts of their discussions presented later in this chapter.

For the reliability study, each of the participants videotaped a consultation with a mother–infant dyad where the infant was under three years of age. Prior parental consent was obtained both verbally and in writing. The videotapes were divided into 10-minute segments. Participants watched 10-minute excerpts and then, using the PIRAT coding sheet and manual, they rated behaviours on the coding sheet according to degree of concern. Post-coding, participants conferenced disagreements and evaluated the usefulness of the descriptors. The post-coding discussion was tape-recorded. In each case, one or two of the participants had prior knowledge of the family involved. Participants did not discuss the circumstances and characteristics of the families involved in order to maintain as far as possible impartiality and objectivity in the rating of specific videotaped excerpts.

The percentage of inter-rater reliability was calculated using 24 excerpts from the videotapes. Since this was a pilot study, acceptable agreement was considered to include same code, 0 and 1, 1 and 2 but not three codes or 0 and 2. The overall percentage of acceptable agreement was 86.2%. The overall percentage of disagreement was 13.8%. The statistical results suggest that healthcare professionals can be trained to use the PIRAT and that good inter-rater reliability can be established. Altogether, 24 videotape excerpts were coded and examination of the results showed that four of those excerpts were problematic in that they had higher levels of disagreement than the others. Two of these excerpts were of the same mother–infant dyad and evoked huge concern in the participants, who gave the most '2's for significant concern of any of the videotapes. Yet they struggled to understand what they were seeing and how to allocate their coding choices.

The following transcripts of the participants conferencing their rating decisions give an unusual insight into the coding process and the way in which the assessment tool allows insight into the relationship between mother and infant without recourse to any external information or case history.

Transgenerational transmission of trauma: A case study using the PIRAT

In the following transcripts, trauma in the mother–infant relationship is identified through coding and conferencing the interactions between a mother and her six-week-old infant using the behavioural observation risk assessment tool PIRAT.

The 10 participants (see above) coded two 10 minute segments of a videotape of the mother and baby at home in their everyday environment. The interaction had been videoed by a colleague of one of the participants, a health visitor who was visiting mother and infant on a professional basis. There was some concern in the professional network surrounding the mother and baby because mother was very young and the baby had been conceived as a result of a rape. Mother had concealed the pregnancy until the 24th week.

I have picked out the salient parts of the discussion among the participants/health professionals in order to elucidate what is happening between mother and baby and the process by which the participants came to understand it. Apart from the health visitor involved, none of the participants has any prior knowledge of the mother–infant pair and were unaware of the circumstances surrounding mother and baby throughout the coding sessions.

In the videotape to begin with, the health visitor is sitting close to the infant who is lying in a crib in the family living room. At one point, the infant begins to cry and the health visitor picks him up. Mother, who is clearly young, comes in after several minutes have elapsed. After a nappy change and feed, baby appears to fall asleep.

For the purposes of this chapter, I will concentrate on two categories that best reveal the participants' thinking, the difficulties involved in coding complex material and the vivid depiction of a primary relationship in which the infant is at risk of emotional derailment. Subsequently, I will outline the participants' coding on other categories to give an overall picture of the mother–infant relationship as assessed by the PIRAT.

Infant–parent interaction: Frightened/wary (Figure 12.2)

Participant 1: Baby didn't look at mum once.

Participant 2: I put '1' but I made some notes about fear and anxiety because I felt that apart from the sort of overcompliance and avoiding eye contact I suppose I didn't feel that he was frightened of his mother. What I felt was that there was this anxiety because he's not being contained and I thought is that fear? Is that how I code it because there's some children that are clearly frightened of their parents? . . . but I didn't see that . . . I did see that this child was anxious . . .

Participant 3: Because of what he wasn't getting rather than aggressive behaviour towards him.

Participant 2: Yes, exactly, because he was being left in this state of who's out there, what's happening, why am I not being responded to?

Participant 4: I couldn't score this because I thought it was more of avoidant rather than frightened because I just felt there was no communication going on because at one point at the beginning he was cooing to himself and you know he seemed to be talking to himself.

Participant 5: I thought that as well. Avoidant I found easy to classify as 2 but then it made me think but what is he so significantly avoiding? What's going on that he's so avoidant and maybe there are times when he is frightened and wary and is it that he's frightened or is it that he's uncontained?

Participant 2:   Yes, I've been struggling with the idea of his not being contained . . . I'm wondering if the mother is being careless.

Participant 5:   More like a non-relationship that we are interpreting as avoidant.

Participant 4:   Maybe if the mum did try to communicate then maybe the baby would have responded.

Participant 3:   But you know it didn't seem like if at all that mother was to hug or try to make any form of communication with that little baby that that little baby wouldn't respond back.

Participant 5:   I actually put '1' there and put down 'inhibited' and 'overcompliance' and 'avoiding eye contact'. They were the two things that I picked out to score it. So are we saying it's a '0'. Is that what you're suggesting?

The discussion here revolves around the understanding of the subjective experience of the infant in relation to his mother's emotional unavailability and possible hostility towards her infant. The participants are struggling to define the infant's affect. From the videotape the infant appears too quiet and undemanding, but should the participants rate inhibition, overcompliance and gaze avoidance as suggesting that he is frightened? Or should they see him as avoidant given that he appears to exclude his mother from his focus of attention? Are the two factors linked? Is he avoidant of his mother because he is frightened? Or does he appear to exclude his mother from his attention because his mother is not emotionally available, being almost entirely cut off from him? Should we be talking more in terms of anxiety in the infant because the primary relationship is not providing him with the containment or growth-facilitating environment (Schore, 1994) that he needs? Or is he, as one participant suggested, able to soothe himself to some degree and to remain open to positive interactions should they be instantiated? They are asking whether anxiety can be equated with fear in a six-week-old infant. Does the infant's innate predisposition to seek companionship (Trevarthen, 2001) and his need for containment leave him fearful when his caregiver is emotionally absent, or does it leave him in a state of anxiety of the sort described by Winnicott (1965) or in psychobiological terms prey to an unregulated stress response (Schore, 1994)? It is difficult to know, given his age, whether the categorical emotion of fear is appropriate as a description of his feeling state. Stern (1985) has suggested an alternative lexicon for feelings, including vitality affects, hedonic tone and activation to encompass quality and intensity of pleasure or unpleasure in infants' feeling states.

The participants also raise the question of the infant's still fluid attachment representations. They feel certain that at this early stage the infant would be able to respond positively to a change in mother's behaviour towards him.

Parent–infant interaction: Intrusive controlling (Figure 12.3)

In the following extract the participants conference their different coding decisions. Participants are divided between '1' (some concern) and '2' (significant concern). They note that the baby does not appear to want the bottle of milk that mother offers. Mother then presents a bottle of water which baby again rejects.

Participant 1:   When she was giving the milk the baby actually refused but then she gave the water. She [baby] didn't want it so she wasn't . . . in terms of bodily functions . . . she wasn't intrusive.

Another participant describes her dilemma in relation to this scenario.

Participant 2:   I gave her a '1'. I was going to give her a '2' for that, because of that, not 'allowed to regulate' but in the end I gave her a '1' and I know it's not quite right because it says 'making infant wait for something' that she wants but she wasn't making her wait. In fact, it was the other way round which is why I didn't give her a '2'.

Participant 3:   But she responded to the baby arching didn't she? She took the bottle away so it might be inexperience. She didn't persist, she responded. Maybe the understanding wasn't there but she responded. That's why I didn't give her a '2'.

Participant 4:   I actually felt that when she gave the milk and baby arched away, then the water, I felt she held the bottle in her mouth for too long. I didn't think she responded to the baby's cue.

Participant 3:   Oh yes! Now I'm beginning to think it should be a '2' after all.

Intrusiveness

The participants in the above dialogue try to make sense of what was happening between mother and infant. They struggle with their perception that mother allows the infant to 'regulate his food or drink intake', making a '2' for 'intrusiveness in terms of bodily functions' appear inappropriate. However, they find '1' problematic too as the parent is not making the infant 'wait for something he wants or needs, e.g. food, bottle, treat'. Equally, there is a problem in giving '0' since the mother is not positively letting the infant take control of what he is doing; rather there is a sense of indifference and detachment:

Participant 1:   . . . I think almost she's so dissociated from this child I don't know if she's intrusive or not aware . . .

Participant 2:   Even if she's not allowing the infant to regulate the food I think the word 'force' . . . there wasn't that feeling.

Participant 3:   I don't think that she had that much investment to force any-body to do anything actually.

Controlling

Other participants consider the issue of control.

Participant 1:   I don't think that she was intrusive but it was to do with the controlling of the infant's activity in all respects in that there was no sense of taking any clue at all or cue from the baby. It was 'right, you've been fed, you're going there, you're staying there'.

Participant 2:   But this baby wasn't giving many clues at all.

Participant 3:   The only protest that baby made was with the bottle, otherwise there was none.

Participant 1:   But this was the opposite of intrusive, wasn't it?

Participant 2:   It was almost controlling by disengagement.

Participant 3:   Which again is another form of control but there weren't any words.

Participant 4:   I couldn't find any words – apart from maybe the controlling – but again it was a control by absence.

Participant 1:   Or control by neglect.

The participants consider the age of the baby.

Participant 1:   Again it's about small babies, isn't it? Because you can't do that when they are older.

Participant 2:   Unless they continue to be really passive or withdrawn.

Participant 3:   Could we say the baby's depressed?

Participant 4:   Do you know when he was asleep like that, I thought if I didn't know that baby was still alive I would have thought he wasn't even breathing.

The participants agree that for an infant of six weeks, the issue of whether the mother can help the infant to regulate his affect is paramount. The mother is described as adversely controlling the infant's environment by her failure to respond to his needs. He appears to the observers to be depressed in the sense of not being stimulated sufficiently by the mother. In fact one of the partici-pants responds by seeing the antithesis of liveliness in the infant as his not seeming to be breathing. Elsewhere the participants consider the infant's passivity and sleeping as possibly defensive against a potentially dysregulating maternal presence.

Participant 1:   I just got a sense that he is so passive.

Participant 2:   You know I mean the falling asleep was like a switch being turned on.

Participant 1:   I mean I was thinking it was extremely passive. Babies usually resist or give you some indication . . .

Participant 3:   Well they want to do something. They want to play a bit.

Participant 2:   But it was like a switch turned on.

Absorption and dissociation

Mother's demeanour is confusing to the observers. They note that she does not express pleasure in her baby and that she appears very still and unsmiling. One participant thinks that she saw her smile once fleetingly. The others are unsure and wonder what to make of her behaviour.

Participant 1:   I think . . . there was this fleeting smile but I didn't see any other pleasure.

Participant 2:   . . . we didn't actually see the front of her face when she was feeding.

Participant 3:   She was gazing.

Participant 4:   We saw a profile but she was gazing. Maybe she's one of those people that don't smile very much, I don't know.

Participant 3:   But then I thought she was gazing at the baby's face at the bottle level – that was the other thing I wasn't sure about.

Participant 1:   And her face was transformed when she was smiling . . . and I thought she looks a lovely looking person but it was such a contrast – before her whole face was so . . .

Participant 4:   Is she normally serious because she was . . . nothing was happening.

The participants seem to be observing a high degree of absorption in mother's demeanour. As Turton et al. (2004) point out, absorption can be a component of dissociation (Bernstein & Putnam, 1986) but is a broader concept than dissociation (Roche & McConkey, 1990). It was unclear from the videotaped material if there was evidence of dissociation in mother or infant. Nevertheless, mother had been subjected to a traumatising experience, and she is seen face to face with the product of that trauma. We could envisage different possible responses to such a dilemma. Mother could be pulled into thinking about aspects of her experience, absorbed in the past, but aware at a conscious level of both the ideation and feelings about what happened and her experience and feelings in the present. A different view would be that mother is avoiding activation of the potentially distressing traumatic associations by a process of defensive exclusion (Erdelyi, 1993; Whittlesey et al., 1999). In the second case, the process is unconscious and can be thought of in terms of inhibitory control mechanisms or psychodynamically as repression, a defence mechanism against intolerable mental contents and affect.

Using the PIRAT category of dissociation, the participants were unsure whether they could identify dissociation in the mother. Elsewhere in the transcript, the participants noted the following behaviours in mother and infant during a sudden noisy interchange elsewhere in the room:

Participant 1:   . . . there was all the noise going on in the room and I just felt like putting myself in his [baby's] position then, that he'd want to lock into something . . . and he didn't . . . but you would expect a six-week old baby to expect a little help from his mum.

Participant 2:   And if you looked at mum she didn't even flinch, did she? Or even look him in the eye.

Mother's disconnection from her external surroundings mirrors the disconnection between herself and her infant. Baby already has no expectation, it seems, of finding comfort or reassurance in his mother, although he still looks for engagement with other people, as the participants' comments in relation to his interest and attention towards the health visitor, Emily, testify:

Participant 1:   . . . then I remembered the infant with Emily and he certainly wasn't passive then.

Participant 2:   I also feel that when he started to wriggle and cry in Emily's arms, there was almost a sense of 'you will put this right for me'. You know it seemed as if he had confidence in you and that part of the reason he was able to cry was that somehow he must have felt that . . . you would make things right.

But what is the infant's experience of his mother's seemingly unfathomable state? Again we can return to the question posed earlier in relation to the PIRAT category of infant–parent: frightened/wary. In their paper on frightened, threatening and dissociative parental behaviour, Hesse and Main (2006: 321) describe a behaviour indicative of dissociation as follows: 'the parent appears to have become unresponsive to, or completely unaware of, the external surround, including the physical and verbal behaviour of their infant'. They argue that such behaviour is 'likely to be intrinsically alarming to the infant'. The studies that support Main and Hesse's work on the dysregulating and disorganising effects on the infant of frightened/frightening parental behaviours use the Adult Attachment Interview and the Strange Situation to examine the interrelationship of attachment patterns between parent and infant. Such studies therefore mainly apply to infants of 12 months or more (e.g. Abrams et al., 2006; Schuengel et al., 1999), and suggest that in certain circumstances dissociative behaviour in the parent can be so alarming that the infant is left without a coherent attachment strategy so that his behaviour and emotional and attentional capacities become disorganised. In the case of the six-week-old baby that we have been observing through the eyes of the participants and the lens of PIRAT, we are perhaps seeing the early disruption of attachment behaviours between mother and infant. Referring to parental dissociation, Hesse and Main (2006: 321) state: 'because the parent is visibly "not there," the infant is left with "nowhere to go" '. In this conceptualisation dissociation is seen as violating the safety-seeking and spatial nature of attachment in which there is negotiation of optimum levels of proximity and distance. In parallel, of course, there is a psychological space that cannot be fulfilled by the absent parent and the dispossessed infant. It is intriguing to note how the language used by the participants echoes the words chosen by Hesse and Main to describe what seems to be the same phenomenon. The participant is considering the baby's experience of the health visitor compared to his experience of his mother:

Participant 1:   I mean the truth is that you was present for that little boy and that was the only point in the whole . . . you know there was no sense anywhere else that anyone was there. You were so present and that was so sad.

In relation to the PIRAT category of infant–parent: dissociative, the participants thought that there were moments where the infant appeared to be dissociated:

Participant 1:   The bit where I thought he had dissociated was where at the end just before she went to put him to sleep I thought I saw mum turn him and he had closed his eyes and that's the way he stayed.
Participant 2:   Yeah, he uses that mechanism.

Conferencing the PIRAT category of avoidant, the participants again wonder about dissociation in the infant:

Participant 1:   Was he asleep?
Participant 2:   Yeah, was he sleeping?
Participant 3:   That was what I was thinking. This arm looked quite good but this arm was like this and his jaw was very . . . and he wasn't a peaceful sleeping baby, was he?
Participant 4:   I thought that was dissociative behaviour actually because that's a very extreme behaviour, isn't it?
Participant 5:   . . . he didn't move, not even a tiny bit. It was extraordinary, especially for a little baby.
Participant 4:   So could you not describe that as an emotional withdrawal into a state of self-stilling, because I'm trying to get my head around dissociative?

It is difficult for the participants both to see clearly what is happening on the videotape and to think in terms of dissociation in a six-week-old baby. In the psychoanalytic literature, infants suffering extremes of relational stress have been described as exhibiting 'freezing' behaviour, a primitive psychobiological response to danger, thought of as a precursor to later developing more organised defence mechanisms available to the developing ego (Fraiberg, 1987).

Schore (2003) sees dissociation in the infant as a response to extreme failure in the caregiver's affect regulatory function. Instead of modulating the infant's arousal levels, the caregiver is inaccessible and fails to respond to her infant's expressions of emotion and stress contingently, offering minimal or unpredictable caregiving. Schore describes two separate response patterns in the infant to trauma induced by the caregiver: hyperarousal and dissociation (Perry et al., 1995; Schore, 1997). In the initial stage of hyperarousal the infant cries, screams and is highly aroused. If the caregiver does not initiate repair and calm the infant, hyperarousal is quickly followed by hypoarousal as the parasympathetic arm of the nervous system comes into play. Schore points out that in the very young infant it is the primitive, early-developing system in the dorsal motor nucleus of the vagus that comes into play rather than the late-developing ventral vagal system. While the latter enables rapid regulation of social interactions, the earlier system is described as contributing to 'severe emotional states and may be related to states of "immobilisation" such as extreme terror' (Porges, 1997: 75). Porges talks about the 'metabolically conservative immobilised state mimicking death associated with the dorsal vagal complex'. One of the participants, it may be recalled, commented that if she had not known the baby was alive she would have thought he had stopped breathing. The participants did not see distressed behaviours on the part of the baby, so the participants consider whether his emotional withdrawal or putative dissociation is already a response to chronic exposure to a withdrawn and dysregulating mother, resulting in what Tronick and Weinberg (1997: 68) describe as a 'disengaged and self-directed regulatory style characterised by self-comforting, self-regulatory behaviours (e.g. looking away, sucking on their thumb), passivity, and withdrawal as a way of coping with their state'. Tronick and Weinberg are describing infant responses to depressed mothers, and suggest that the coping style of such babies becomes generalised so that they are less engaged and exhibit more negativity with a friendly stranger than infants whose mothers are not depressed (Field et al., 1988). As the participants observed, the infant in the PIRAT study was active in eliciting the attention of the health visitor, a complete stranger to him. They noted how he made 'lots of noises' and 'locked into' her and, paradoxically, the sense that he was still hopeful of finding a lively relationship to meet his dependency needs made his situation resonate even more poignantly with the observers.

Observers' responses

Inevitably, watching the videotapes of the mother and infant aroused power-ful feelings in the participants. As we have seen, there was hope that the baby would find the contingent responses that he was primed to expect and that would give him the warmth and companionship that he needed. Participants identified with the helplessness and hopelessness of the infant who cannot reach out to his mother. They struggled with their countertransference feel-ings of sadness, anger, confusion. The realisation of mother's circumstances – that she was so much younger than they had thought and the enormity of what had happened to her and what was being expected of her – challenged and modified their perceptions:

Participant 1:   It's very interesting actually because that slight feeling of, you know, erm anger with this mother, not responding to her baby, sort of disappears . . .

The circumstances of the baby's birth were not revealed until the end of the coding sessions so that it was not possible to discuss the implications of possible ongoing trauma, retraumatisation, dissociation or depression in the mother and the experience of the baby in the presence of his mother. Since we do not have further material relating to the case, such discussion would rest on conjecture. Nevertheless, it is known that mother did not disclose the rape and concealed her pregnancy until 24 weeks. The months that the baby is inside the mother are a time for a rich fantasy to develop around the baby and, if all goes well mother and infant already have a sense of each other before the moment of birth. Sometimes the fantasy takes a darker turn, and attributions to the baby are already negatively toned. A lively, kicking baby can be construed as hostile or aggressive, for example. Sometimes mother is in a state of denial about the pregnancy. There is no investment of fantasy and hope for the forthcoming baby. When the baby arrives, he feels unreal as if he does not belong to her. Sadly, this would be the experi-ence of both mother and baby. In the case of a baby conceived through rape, the physical process of birth might be experienced as a repetition of the trauma and in fantasy the baby becomes the rapist – responsible for mother's pain, humiliation, exposure and devastating helplessness. Negative feelings towards her baby might induce guilt and distress in the mother, mak-ing her feel that it is safer for him if she maintains a barrier between them. Raphael-Leff (2003) has schematised such a relationship in terms of mother's fantasy as bad mother with bad baby so that a protective barrier is needed between them.

PIRAT and the identification of risk

The usefulness of PIRAT in clarifying thinking about a parent–infant dyad and in specifying the nature of concern in the relationship is borne out by the discourse of the participants in relation to the codings and the codings themselves. Certain categories were found to be more problematic than others, especially as applied to a baby under two months old. A category such as dissociation is difficult to identify, especially in an infant where withdrawal may be due to lack of stimulation rather than stilling as a primitive response to threat. Nevertheless, without prior knowledge of the case history of the dyad, the participants in the study were able to apply the category definitions to their observations in order to pinpoint the locus of difficulty in the relationship and to form a compelling account of the painful dilemma faced by mother and infant.

Acknowledgement

I would like to thank the participants in the PIRAT training and reliability study for their stimulating and thoughtful responses to the material described in this chapter.

References

Abrams, K.Y., Rifkin, A. & Hesse, E. (2006) Examining the role of parental frightened/frightening subcategories in predicting disorganized attachment within a brief observational procedure. *Development and Psychopathology*, 18: 345–361.

Baradon, T., Broughton, C., Gibbs, I., James, J., Joyce, A. & Woodhead, J. (2005) *The practice of psychoanalytic psychotherapy: Claiming the baby*. London: Routledge.

Beebe, B. (2006) Co-constructing mother–infant distress in face to face interactions: Contributions from microanalysis. *Infant Observation*, 9: 151–164.

Bernstein, E.M. & Putnam, F.W. (1986) Development, reliability and validation of a dissociation scale. *Journal of Nervous and Mental Disease*, 174: 727–735.

Broughton, C. (2008) *Measuring parent–infant interaction: The Parent–Infant Relational Assessment Tool (PIRAT)*. Unpublished doctoral thesis, The Anna Freud Centre and University College London, UK.

Erdelyi, M.H. (1993) Repression, the mechanism and the defense. In D.M. Wegner & J.W. Pennebaker (Eds.), *Handbook of mental control*. Englewood Cliffs, NJ: Prentice Hall.

Field, T., Healy, B., Goldstein, S., Perry, S., Bendell, D., Schanberg, S., et al. (1988) Infants of depressed mothers show 'depressed' behaviour even with nondepressed adults. *Child Development*, 59: 1569–1579.

Fraiberg, S. (1987) Pathological defences in infancy. *The selected works of S. Fraiberg*. Columbus, OH: Ohio State University.

Hesse, E. & Main, M. (2006) Frightened, threatening, and dissociative parental behaviour in low-risk samples: description, discussion, and interpretations. *Development and Psychopathology*, 18: 309–343.

Muir, E. (1992) Watching, waiting and wondering: Applying psychoanalytic principles to mother–infant intervention. *Infant Mental Health Journal*, 13: 310–328.

Panksepp, J. (2001) The long-term psychobiological consequences of infant emotions: Prescriptions for the twenty-first century. *Infant Mental Health Journal*, 22: 132–173.

Perry, B.D., Pollard, R.A., Blakely, T.L., Baker, W.L. & Vigilante, D. (1995) Childhood trauma, the neurobiology of adaptation, and use-dependent development of the brain: How states become traits. *Infant Mental Health Journal*, 16: 271–291.

Porges, S.W. (1997) Emotion: An evolutionary by-product of the neural regulation of the autonomic nervous system. *Annals of the New York Academy of Sciences*, 807: 62–77.

Raphael-Leff, J. (Ed.) (2003) *Parent–infant psychodynamics: Wild things, mirrors and ghosts.* London: Whurr.

Roche, S. & McConkey, K.M. (1990) Absorption: Nature, assessment and correlates. *Journal of Personality and Social Psychology*, 59: 91–101.

Schore, A.N. (1994) *Affect regulation and the origin of the self: The neurobiology of emotional development.* Hillsdale, NJ: Lawrence Erlbaum Associates, Inc.

Schore, A.N. (1997) Early organization of the nonlinear right brain and the development of a predisposition to psychiatric disorders. *Development and Psychopathology*, 9: 595–631.

Schore, A.N. (2003) *Affect dysregulation and disorder of the self.* New York: W.W. Norton.

Schore, A.N. (2005) Back to basics: Attachment, affect regulation and the developing right brain: Linking developmental neuroscience to paediatrics. *Paediatric Review*, 26: 204–217.

Schuengel, C., Bakermans-Kranenburg, M.J. & van IJzendoorn, M.H. (1999) Attachment and loss: Frightening maternal behaviour linking unresolved loss and disorganised infant attachment. *Journal of Consulting and Clinical Psychology*, 67: 54–63.

Stern, D.N. (1985) *The interpersonal world of the infant.* New York: Basic Books.

Trevarthen, C. (2001) Intrinsic motives for companionship in understanding: Their origin, development, and significance for infant mental health. *Infant Mental Health Journal*, 22: 95–131.

Tronick, E.Z. & Weinberg, M.K. (1997) Depressed mothers and infants: Failure to form dyadic states of consciousness. In L. Murray & P.J. Cooper (Eds.), *Postpartum depression and child development.* New York: Guilford Press.

Turton, P., Hughes P., Fonagy, P. & Fainman, D. (2004) An investigation into the possible overlap between PTSD and unresolved responses following stillbirth: An absence of linkage with only unresolved status predicting infant disorganization. *Attachment and Human Development*, 6: 241–253.

Whittlesey, S.W., Allen, J.R., Bell, B.D., Lindsey, E.D., Ethan, D., Speed, L.F., et al. (1999) Avoidance in trauma: Conscious and unconscious defence, pathology and health. *Psychiatry*, 62: 303–312.

Winnicott, D.W. (1965) The theory of the parent–infant relationship. *Maturational processes and the facilitating environment.* London: Hogarth Press.

Chapter 13

Epilogue – 'Ghosts and angels in the nursery'

Windows of opportunity and remaining vulnerability

Tessa Baradon

This chapter examines some of the elements that underpin movement and stagnation in the therapeutic endeavour for change. It also looks at the building blocks for transformations of the relational system, as they occur in small, mutually constructed sequences and over periods of time.

The metaphors of 'ghosts' (Fraiberg et al., 1975) and 'angels' (Lieberman et al., 2005) 'in the nursery' belong in the domain of environmental influences in the epigenetic story. They describe how earliest experiences with primary love objects are embodied in the individual's transactions with the next generation. The 'ghosts' are the mental and affective residues of the parent's own infantile and childhood trauma that underpin re-enacted damage in the relationship with this particular baby. The psychological power of the ghosts to repeat damage over generations lies in the affects that are unconsciously carried over. Pain, helplessness, terror that overwhelmed the suffering baby became dissociated from memory (Fraiberg, 1980), and the passive experience of victimisation is often turned into active identification with the aggressor (Freud, 1936). By contrast, 'angels' in the nursery are those early benevolent emotional experiences with primary love objects that bestow on the baby a sense of having been protected and cared for, and are passed on to the next generation through the parent's capacity to be a 'good enough' (Winnicott, 1960, 1965) parent to their own children. It is Lieberman's and her colleagues' contention that, in cases where relational trauma threatens supremacy of the ghosts, a parent's access to memory of the angels of care in her past may protect her infant from impingements of her damaged internal world and defensive projections. Access to internal angels can be redeeming not only in transgenerational but also in recently inflicted trauma, such as illustrated by Woodhead and Joyce (Chapters 3 and 4, this volume). Furthermore, as the therapy unfolds, the relationship with the therapist may constitute an emergent procedural angel, as will be discussed below.

In any individual a measure of ambivalence is expectable. 'Ghosts and angels coexist in dynamic tension with each other, at times actively struggling for supremacy and at other times reverting to a quiescent state that temporarily allows the person to inhabit a "conflict-free sphere" (Hartman, 1939)'

(Lieberman et al., 2005: 506). In my view, the parent's capacity to receive her baby as vulnerable and dependent, and yet separate, lies at the core of the parent's good enough parenting. It is during conflict-free times that the baby can be related to in his own right and not as a transference object. Thus, the relative strength of the ghosts and the angels in the parent's representational world shapes the quality of her infant's experiences in his earliest love relationship at any given moment, and aggregated over time. The call upon parent infant psychotherapy is to work with the unconscious processes and representations as they are expressed in the here-and-now of parental care to support loving and benevolent, and contain malign and hating, affective repetitions.

Much clinical experience has accumulated demonstrating that in working through painful or conflictual psychic material that has been excluded from consciousness, the 'baby is liberated, as it were, from the distortions and displaced affects which have engulfed him in the parental neurosis' (Fraiberg, 1980: 70). As the parent moves from inchoate affect states to representation, we are also increasingly sensitive to the forms of intimate relational knowing that are embedded and expressed implicitly throughout life (Stern et al., 1998; Stern, 2004; Lyons-Ruth, 1998; Clyman, 1991; Davis, 2001). Smell, touch, gaze, gesture, verbal prosody are primary elements of the bidirectional language of the baby and mother. Through the affective and action sequences co-constructed (Beebe, 2000; Beebe et al., 2005) between them, patterns of the unique 'dance' of a parent and infant dyad are created.

It is in this dynamic process of transformation of old and creation of new relational procedures that the therapist participates. Crucially, and in contrast to focusing overly on negative transference processes, consideration of the transference to the therapist needs to be extended to the embodiment of angels through the new relational experiences. The therapeutic attention moves between representing symbolically past repetitions in order to facilitate affective working through, and the current laying down of non symbolic emotional–behavioural procedures for being with the other. The therapist's interest, compassion, reflectiveness towards the traumatised infant in the parent alongside the adult parental endeavours, and her receptivity and pleasure towards the baby, provide new experiences of safety. These may counteract the malignant but familiar background of safety that draws out the traumatising repetitions (Sandler, 1987). Thereby, the therapist herself may become an 'angel' in the present experience. Sometimes, through the experience with the therapist, the parent may get into contact with angels in her own internal world.

> Stacey's initial representation of her father was (see Chapter 10) of an unhearing object: kind but neglectful, he was 'blind to what went on in the house when he wasn't there . . . or he wouldn't accept it'. As she worked in the therapy, Stacey's fury with her father emerged: 'demands

demands . . . I have to look after him but he will do nothing for me'. 'Doing nothing' resonated with her feeling that he failed to rescue her from her abusive mother when she was a child. Her anger then moved on to disappointment in her father's past and present frailties. But a few months later I began to hear snippets of appreciation: 'We went out for a meal, my dad and Chas [baby] and me, like a family. It was nice', and 'My dad, Chas loves him, he takes Chas out when I need to rest', and 'His OCD and shouting drive me mad, but he's my dad, we are close, I love him'.

The journey Stacey made in relation to her father was facilitated by her relationship with the therapist, whom she saw as 'trying to help', 'someone who listens', 'like the mother I never had'. She also took increasing pleasure in 'sharing Chas'. A video clip from the fifth month of therapy shows Stacey and therapist simultaneously gasping with delight as Chas accomplishes a new move, and then smiling to each in recognition of their mutual pleasure. Finding a benevolent object in the therapist may well have been made more readily possible through unconscious residues of father's care in her childhood, as much as there was a re/finding of a good father through the therapist. In this, there may also have been repair of the infant within her that enabled Chas to get the love and protection that she did not have as a child.

For the adult, the advent of parenthood is a developmental stage wherein a representational reorganisation of dyadic and oedipal relationships with her own parents takes place (Bradley, 2000; Birksted-Breen, 1986; Stern, 1995). Pregnancy and childbirth locate (the) woman 'midway between two generations – a child of her own procreative parents and parent to her (future) child' (Raphael-Leff, 2000: 8). The baby acts as a mnemonic to mother's intimate experiences with her own parents. For an adult who carries the scarring memories of emotional pain, fear, abandonment, having a baby/ becoming a parent can hold a promise of healing, of working through anger and revenge, as in the case of Stacey above. The shift from grievance to understanding in relation to their own parent is critical in releasing a parent from the grip of scathing self-criticism in relation to their own parenting. 'I'm a rubbish parent' is frequently the other side of the coin for a parent who is damning of her own parent.

The following example is taken from a session early in the parent–infant psychotherapy of Anthony, age nine months, and Therese, whose post-puerperal breakdown and consequent hospitalisation led to separation from Anthony when he was one week old.

Therese refers to a comment of the therapist that sometimes the way things felt for her as a child may have bearing on how she is feeling now with Anthony. Therese says that she does not have many memories of the past but most of the memories concern her mother's derogatory comments. She says she does not want to repeat this pattern, nor for Anthony to be anxious and highly strung like she was as a child.

TB: It sounds as though there are lots of ghosts along the way that you want not to be like . . . as though you could be in a situation of constantly monitoring yourself, worrying whether you're doing it right.

Therese: Yes. Well, I don't know if that's just a symptom of being depressed. I don't know why it is I need constant reassurance all the time. I mean it's pretty exhausting really.

In this brief exchange Therese is preoccupied with her fear about damaging her baby, which she links to the damage caused to her as a child. She talks about needing reassurance all the time, but it would appear that the reassurance she receives is relentlessly undone by her harsh superego.

In a session towards the end of the therapy Therese was retelling the events leading to her post-puerperal psychosis and hospitalisation. She referred to her mother:

Therese: She was the one who understood the situation most clearly. You know, if she hadn't . . . I don't know where I would have gone. I mean I would have been sectioned anyway. And she's really proved herself to be an incredible grandmother. I think she understood how I was, without even admitting or saying, because maybe she recognised those feelings in herself from when we [brother and Therese] were young, but of course . . .

TB: She didn't get the help.

Therese: (*sadly*) No, she didn't get the help. No. I think my Dad said, you know, 'You've got two beautiful children, get on with it'. So that was her way of, kind of . . . (*Therese becomes tearful*)

TB: It is very moving, as you describe it, for both of you – you and your Mum.

Therese: As time has passed I've definitely got less hard on myself about what happened.

TB: As well as less hard about your mother . . .

Therese: Yes.

In this session Therese moves away from recriminations to a more positive identification with her mother. She makes the intergenerational link that her psychosis mirrored her mother's unacknowledged breakdown. Her mother, she says, had drawn upon her own postnatal experiences to understand her daughter's condition, and had found her daughter the help that she had been denied. Therese, in turn, shows empathy for her mother's unhappiness when a young mother and is surprised by her growing forgiveness of herself.

For most parents, their emotional link to their baby taps into residues of infantile sexuality in themselves. Where this has been filled with suffering and become conflictual, the mother may experience the bodily relationship between herself and her baby as frightening or repulsive. Yet, the oral sexuality of the baby – grasping, exploring, devouring with the mouth, may reach into the joyful sexuality of taking in and creating in the parent's own sexuality. Alongside this is the sensorial pleasure of producing–expelling of breast feeding in the mother and defecation in the infant (notice how frequently parents identify with the visceral relief of their infant's poo-ing). The revisiting of the oedipal organisation of the mother and father is done with them now being the powerful procreator. The therapist also ensures the triangulation of both baby and parent's experience, in providing the 'third' (often paternal, reflective) and in joining with the parent in 'co-parenting' (observing, understanding, taking pleasure in) the baby.

The conscious wish for their baby to have a better experience than their own is a strong motivation for change in many parents. Moreover, the therapy capitalises on, and is strengthened by, the developmental pull in both infant and parent in the earliest period while relationships are being formed. The urgency imposed by timetables of development (Schore, 1994, 2003) is supported by the tenacity of the developmental pull in infancy. Winnicott wrote: 'By and large analysis is for those who want it, need it, and can take it' (1962: 169). When an infant is trapped in a derailed attachment with his parent, he will want, need and hungrily/passionately take the therapy for himself with his parent. In this way, babies make such good patients. The therapist offers herself as a live attachment object (Alvarez, 1992; Baradon, 2005) to the baby in order to keep his developmental pathway open, while the parent cannot do this. Lieberman and Harris (2007) emphasise the active role of the therapist in cases of trauma and the onus to relate to the trauma directly. The therapeutic work with the infant embedded in the AFC–PIP model addresses the deficits in adult provision for the baby's psychological needs. In affording the baby experiences of being reflected on and contingently responded to, the baby's agency in procuring the quality of presence in the adult he needs as 'the material for constructing an image of [him]self' (Chapter 9, this volume). In time, he transfers to his parent his experiences with the therapist – laying his claim on her, rewarding his parent with the overt expressions of his love and confirming her tenuous hopes.

Thus, a confluence of developmental elements in the baby and in the parent can come together in the therapeutic work as the baby moves along his developmental course and the parent psychically becomes a parent. Alongside the real baby's forward pull, visceral memories in the parent of being a cared-for infant, benign identifications with their own parents and/or the therapist, and the confirmation that comes with fertility and procreation can be discovered through the relationship with the therapist. Moreover, once pleasure enters a faltering relationship, progressive movement is powerfully reinforced through joy, mutuality and affirmation.

Even where parental disturbance is a critical concern, we may find that psychotherapeutic work during this early window of opportunity can make long-term contribution to the wellbeing of the baby and go some way towards helping the parent think about their baby's emotional states. For example:

> A year after parent infant therapy with her and Chas had ended, Stacey (Chapter 10 and above) phoned and asked for an appointment (Chas now aged 3.6 years). She said she was having her 'symptoms' again, and the medication was not helping (diagnosed as BPD, Stacey suffered panic attacks, feelings of derealisation, rages). In parallel to the emergency psychiatric intervention she received, Stacey asked to see me regularly. We used the sessions also to monitor how Chas was responding to this episode of illness. Initially he was able to verbalise 'I don't like it when you shout, mummy' as well as anxiously expressing his love for her. As time went on, he became more tearful and angry. But, with my support, Stacey was able to think about Chas's fears and upset and to talk to him in an appropriate manner about their predicament. Eventually Stacey was hospitalised again, and Chas showed his grandfather he was missing his mummy. When she came out of hospital, he returned to her care.

Stacey and Chas's experience illustrates a number of important themes.

First, the importance of the early input in guiding their later interactions. At referral – when Chas was an infant – their affective dialogue was characterised by lack of integration of loving and hating feelings. With the therapeutic work the potential fixedness of split representations and ways-of-being-with mother/other in Chas was circumvented. In their later presentation, in the emotionally charged circumstances around her relapse, Chas had sufficient experiences of being loved and protected to access benevolent memories/images of mother and himself-with-mummy that helped him through his frightening loss of her to illness and separation. We see here an example, perhaps, of angels in the nursery, and consequent resilience, *in situ*.

For some families, parent–infant psychotherapy cannot be a one-off/once and forever intervention. This may be due to a cyclical pattern of parental disturbance, as above, or particular change of circumstances that places exceptional pressure on the parent–infant relationship and, through this, on the baby. Moreover, each developmental stage of the child throws up new challenges that require parent and child to reach a different relational organisation, for example toddlerhood poses particular problems around aggression and separation–individuation (Mahler et al., 1975). Particularly vulnerable parents and infants may need to receive further professional input around these nodal phases, as a form of developmental help (Freud, 1965, 1974; Edgcumbe, 2000) accompanying the trajectory of early childhood.

While some traumatised mothers and fathers seem to be endowed with a capacity to take in and make good with very little, as was the case with Stacey, there remain a minority of cases where there seems a predisposition to psychotic breakdowns, borderline traits, addictive tendencies, severe depression, and obsessive symptoms (see Chapter 5, this volume).

In the case below, there was a history of mental illness in the maternal grandparents' family (mother's father) and neglect of Ellen and her siblings, as small children, on the part of her high-flying mother. One may question, therefore, a possible genetic environment with an overlay of severe emotional deprivation. In the limited parent–infant psychotherapy sessions that Ellen attended, the carapace of her defensive organisation seemed to relieve her from guilt and shame, provide a sense of self continuity in the face of fragmentation, and protect her from breakdown.

Ellen, first-time mother to baby Joe, was struggling with deep envy of her child receiving what she did not.

TB: . . . and Joe has a father who lives with him and loves him, you may envy him for that . . .
Ellen: I do (*crying*) and I resent having to share David [husband/father] with him.
TB: Mm.
Ellen: Why is that wrong? I have to look after myself; I don't have it within me to look after Joe! Life is not easy, better he learn that early on.

Ellen appeared to be experiencing a state of 'primary maternal persecution' wherein the baby is felt as dangerous to the mother's psychic organisation by 'revealing her disavowed baby self or infantile neediness' (Raphael-Leff, 1996: 386). Her grievance with her mother formed an obsessive rumination, fixing her in an ongoing mental state of the bereft and frightened child, woven with envy of her son that placed her as a rivalrous sibling with him. Above all, Ellen seemed not able to experience the therapist and therapy (as other attempts at therapy before this) as sufficiently benign to achieve a measure of integration of the good and bad mother/good and bad baby. Thus, while the need for an actual, present 'angel' in the form of the therapist seemed absolutely crucial, it was out of reach for this mother and, through her withdrawal from therapy, also denied to her infant (see also illustration in Chapter 5).

The case of Ellen illustrates a commonality to many of the cases in which, in my experience, parent–infant psychotherapy fails to mitigate the suffering of the dyad. In hard-to-treat parents a central characteristic often appears to be unresolved ambivalence, with an unyielding split between the 'good' and 'bad', 'loving' and 'hating', 'safe' and 'dangerous'. 'Primary persecutory anxiety' dominates the parent's representations and experiences of their baby.

In addition, the therapist becomes part of the malign system in the internal world of the parent. This may lie in an immediate negative transference or through inevitable disappointment. It may be fed by intense envy of the therapist, who is seen as possessing all the good and unable to share the patient's suffering. In such a case, there can be no place for experiences of a 'new object' who can offer the good enough mothering so craved for, but also negated.

It is not surprising, therefore, that research findings conclude that 'deep disturbance can't be treated short-term' (Moran et al., 2008). The nature of disorders rooted in earliest relations is such that change – through the experience of another kind of relationship – is often hesitant and slow. Moreover, some aspects of the therapy itself can be extremely painful and evoke resistance. Addressing the trauma in the parent and in the relationship can bring relief, but also mobilises fears of, and defences against, re-traumatisation.

In addition there is the therapist's relationship with the baby. Attending to the baby patient in the room may, at least in the early stages of the work, evoke pain, envy, rage and other persecutory emotions and consequent defences in the parent. Such responses are part and parcel of the therapeutic work and often can helpfully be worked through, opening also a space for other constellations of a 'third'. However, as seen in the case of Ellen and Joe, for example, there was an immediate hostility to the therapist who was seen to create dependency and yet not meet need, coupled with a conscious wish not to share the therapist with her son.

Finally, a word about the therapist's experience of the therapeutic endeavour.

This type of work presents challenges at many levels. With a real baby in the room there is no escape from the immediacy of primitive feelings and somatic expressions of trauma. These penetrate the therapist in all modalities – the visceral absorbance of smell, sound, sight, the emotional waves of pain, rage, joy, awe, envy, taken in bodily as well as symbolically through the spoken word. Inevitably the material from infant and parent resonates with both the infantile and mothering (and fathering) self of the therapist.

In terms of working with traumatised babies, it is very hard to witness cruelty, in any form, to a baby. As Pally (2005, 2007) has pointed out, the therapist's own attachment system kicks in response to an infant's need for safety and solace. Thus she may struggle with strong counter-responses (Sandler, 1993) as well as countertransference, as the affective correlates of trauma permeate and bring forth phantasies of rescue, or feelings of rage, helplessness, shock. A particular risk in this work is that one may get emotionally caught up in the trauma, often through identification with the infant. If the therapist can bear in mind, and remain moved by, the frightened child within the parent and her feelings of helplessness in relation to her baby, she may remain empathic to the adult when observing baby's suffering in her care. At other times, however, she may become over-identified with the parent's internal narrative as, for example, when – in an 'analytic enactment' (McLaughlin, 1991) – one finds oneself resonating the parent's dislike for the baby (Baradon, 2002). Thus, relational trauma can strain capacities of the therapist to maintain a mentalising stance (Fonagy, 1999) towards *all* the patients present.

When the therapy does not take root – either the parent does engage or the process is cut short, as with Ellen and Joe above – the therapist is left with holding the concern for the baby. There are also cases where child protection issues force the therapist to change her stance whereby 'the client is the relationship' and prioritise the best interest of the child over that of the parent. 'When a clinical choice must be made because the best interests of the child collide with the parents' wishes or psychological needs, the child's well-being must always come first' (Lieberman & Harris, 2007: 214). Where legal responsibility for child protection requires action on the part of the therapist, very powerful feelings of helplessness and failure, often mirroring those in parent and infant, may need processing.

Despite the enormous challenge of working with at least two very needy patients at the same time, parent–infant psychotherapy can be extremely rewarding work. It touches the attachment core of the therapist and acts as a mnemonic to her own experiences of safety, love and restitution. It can fire her identifications with the parents' procreativity (what Raphael-Leff, 1996, terms the mother's 'generative crucible'), and put her richly in touch with her bodily and symbolic capacities to create and to nurture which, hopefully, become new angels in the baby's and his mother's nurseries.

References

Alvarez, A. (1992) *Live company*. London: Tavistock/Routledge.

Baradon, T.J. (2002) Psychotherapeutic work with parents and infants – Psychoanalytic and attachment perspectives. *Journal of Attachment and Human Development*, 4(1): 25–38.

Baradon, T.J. (2005) 'What is genuine maternal love?': Clinical considerations and technique in psychoanalytic parent infant psychotherapy. *Psychoanalytic Study of the Child*, 60: 47–73.

Beebe, B. (2000) Co-constructing mother–infant distress: The microsynchrony of maternal impingement and infant avoidance in the face-to-face encounter. *Psychoanalytic Enquiry*, 20(3): 421–440.

Beebe, B, Knoblauch, S., Rustin, J. & Sorter, D. (2005) *Forms of intersubjectivity in infant research and adult treatment*. New York: Other Press.

Birksted-Breen, D. (1986) The experience of having a baby: A developmental view. In J. Raphael-Leff (Ed.), *Spilt milk: Perinatal loss and breakdown* (pp. 17–27). London: Institute of Psychoanalysis.

Bradley, E. (2000) Pregnancy and the internal world. In J. Raphael-Leff (Ed.), *Spilt milk: Perinatal loss and breakdown* (pp. 28–38). London: Institute of Psychoanalysis.

Clyman, R.B. (1991) The procedural organisation of emotions: A contribution from cognitive science to the psychoanalytic theory of therapeutic action. *Journal of the American Psychoanalytic Association*, 39 (supplement): 349–382.

Davis, T.J. (2001) Revising psychoanalytic interpretations of the past: An examination of declarative and non-declarative memory processes. *International Journal of Psychoanalysis*, 82: 449–462.

Edgcumbe, R. (2000) *Anna Freud: A view of development, disturbances and therapeutic techniques*. London: Routledge.

Fonagy, P. (1999) *The process of change and the change of process: What can change in a good analysis?* Keynote address to the Spring meeting of Division 39 of the American Psychological Association, New York.

Fraiberg, S. (1980) *Clinical studies in infant mental health: The first year of life*. New York: Basic Books.

Fraiberg, S., Adelson, E. & Shapiro, V. (1975) Ghosts in the nursery: A psychoanalytic approach to the problems of impaired infant–mother relationships. *Journal of the American Academy of Psychiatry*, 14: 387–421.

Freud, A. (1936) *The ego and mechanisms of defence*. London: Hogarth Press.

Freud, A. (1965) *Normality and pathology in childhood*. London: Hogarth Press.

Freud, A. (1974) A psychoanalytic view of developmental psychopathology. In *The writings of Anna Freud* (Vol. 8, pp. 57–74). New York: International Universities Press, 1981.

Lieberman, A.F. & Harris, W.W. (2007) Still searching for the best interests of the child: Trauma treatment in infancy and early childhood. *Psychoanalytic Study of the Child*, 62: 211–238.

Lieberman, A.F., Padron, E., Van Horn, P. & Harris, W.W. (2005) Angels in the nursery: Intergenerational transmission of benevolent parental influences. *Infant Mental Health Journal*, 26(6): 504–520.

Lyons-Ruth, K. (1998) Implicit relational knowing: Its role in development and psychoanalytic treatment. *Infant Mental Health Journal*, 19(3): 282–289.

Mahler, M.S., Pine, F. & Bergman, A. (1975) *The psychological birth of the human infant*. London: Hutchinson.

McLaughlin, J.T. (1991) Clinical and theoretical aspects of enactment. *Journal of the American Psychoanalytic Association*, 39: 595–614.

Moran, G., Nuefeld Bailey, H., Gleason, K., DeOliveira, C.S. & Pederson, D. (2008) Exploring the mind behind unresolved attachments: Lessons from and for attachment-based interventions with infants and their traumatized mothers. In H. Steele & M. Steele (Eds.), *Clinical applications of the Adult Attachment Interview* (pp. 371–398). New York: Guilford Press.

Pally, R. (2005) A neuroscience perspective on forms of intersubjectivity in infant research and adult treatment. In B. Beebe, S. Knoblauch, J. Rustin & D. Sorter (Eds.), *Forms of intersubjectivity in infant research and adult treatment* (pp. 191–242). New York: Other Press.

Pally, R (2007) The predicting brain: Unconscious repetition, conscious reflection and therapeutic change. *International Journal of Psychoanalysis*, 88: 861–881.

Raphael-Leff, J. (1996) Procreative process, placental paradigm and perinatal psychotherapy. *Journal of the American Psychoanalytic Association*, 44: 373–399.

Raphael-Leff, J. (2000) Introduction: Technical issues in perinatal therapy. In

J. Raphael-Leff (Ed.), *Spilt milk: Perinatal loss and breakdown*. London: Institute of Psychoanalysis.

Sandler, J. (1987) *From safety to superego*. London: Karnac.

Sandler, J. (1993) On communication from patient to analyst: not everything is projective identification. *International Journal of Psychoanalysis*, 74: 1097–1107.

Schore, A.N. (1994) *Affect regulation and the origins of the self*. Hillsdale, NJ: Lawrence Erlbaum Associates, Inc.

Schore, A.N. (2003) *Affect disregulation and disorders of the self*. New York: W.W. Norton.

Stern, D.N. (1995) *The motherhood constellation*. New York: Basic Books.

Stern, D.N. (2004) *The present moment in psychotherapy and everyday life*. New York: W.W. Norton.

Stern, D., Sander, L., Nahum, J., Harrison, A., Lyons-Ruth, K., Morgan, A. et al. (1998) Non-interpretive mechanisms in psychoanalytic therapy: The 'something more' than interpretation. *International Journal of Psychoanalysis*, 79: 903–921.

Winnicott, D.W. (1960) The theory of the parent infant relationship. *The maturational process and facilitating environment*. London: Hogarth Press and the Institute of Psycho-Analysis, 1965.

Winnicott, D.W. (1962) The aims of psycho-analytical treatment. *The maturational process and facilitating environment*. London: Hogarth Press and the Institute of Psycho-Analysis, 1965.

Winnicott, D.W. (1965) The relationship of the mother to her baby at the beginning. *The family and individual development*. London: Tavistock.

Index

Made in the USA
San Bernardino, CA
25 January 2017